DATE DUE

JUN 1 0 2005	FEB 1 0 2008
	FEB 1 0 2008
MAR 2 5 2005	MAY 1 6 2008
	MAY 1 3 2009
MAY 0 9 2005	SEP 1 0 2010
	WIDENER
FEB 1 0 2006	MAY 2 6 2011
FEB 1 0 2006	
JUN 0 5 2006	
AUG 1 5 2006	
DEC 1 8 2006	
FEB 1 0 2007	
MAR 2 0 2009	

Despite the Odds

Despite the Odds

THE CONTENTIOUS POLITICS
OF EDUCATION REFORM

Merilee S. Grindle

PRINCETON UNIVERSITY PRESS
PRINCETON AND OXFORD

Copyright © 2004 by Princeton University Press
Published by Princeton University Press, 41 William Street,
Princeton, New Jersey 08540
In the United Kingdom: Princeton University Press,
3 Market Place, Woodstock, Oxfordshire OX20 1SY
All Rights Reserved

LIBRARY OF CONGRESS CATALOGING-IN-PUBLICATION DATA

Grindle, Merilee Serrill
Despite the odds : the contentious politics of
education reform / Merilee S. Grindle
Includes bibliographical references (p.) and index.
ISBN 0-691-11799-3 (cl. : alk. paper) —
ISBN 0-691-11800-0 (pbk. : alk. paper)
1. Politics and education—Latin America.
2. Educational change—Latin America. 3. Education
and state—Latin America. I. Title.
LC92.A2G75 2004
379.8 2003064944—dc22   2003064803

British Cataloging-in-Publication Data is available

This book has been composed in Galliard

Printed on acid-free paper. ∞

www.pupress.princeton.edu

Printed in the United States of America

1   3   5   7   9   10   8   6   4   2

For Alexandra and Stefanie

CONTENTS

TABLES AND FIGURES

TABLES

FIGURES

ACKNOWLEDGMENTS

This book, like others, is a collective enterprise. Its contents were shaped by numerous discussions with public officials, politicians, union leaders, teachers, national and international education experts, academics, and others. I am deeply grateful to the more than one hundred people who generously shared their expertise, time, and perspectives with me and with Madeleine Taylor, who carried out the research in Minas Gerais. The world of policy reform is fraught with complexity and risk, and these individuals provided real-world insight into the interplay of forces that shaped, constrained, and promoted new education systems in several Latin American countries. I hope, in reconstructing the stories they told us, that I have been able to reflect their insights, concerns, and commitments. I promised confidentiality to many of those I interviewed, but have tried, when quoting them, to indicate the vantage point from which they were observing the process of reform.

I was ably assisted in preparing this book. Madeleine Taylor, an anthropologist by training, undertook interviews and documentary research in Minas Gerais, Brazil, with superb skill and insight. On her return, she worked tirelessly to help me understand the nuances of the case and the actions of its protagonists. At Harvard, Andrea Broda, Carolina Gutiérrez de Taliercio, Aaron Jette, Rebeca Sánchez de Tagle, Bertha Angulo Curiel, and Helen Hawkins provided valued input; they collected and analyzed data, developed tables and graphs, and provided excellent editorial support. Mansueto Almeida of MIT translated important work from Portuguese to English with efficiency and timeliness. I hope these individuals will recognize how important their skills were to the final product and accept my thanks for their efforts.

In each country, many people helped smooth the way for my research. In Mexico, Gustavo Merino, José Angel Pescador Osuna, Teresa Bracho, and Laura Certucha Llano were exemplary and helpful hosts to this project. In Ecuador, I am grateful to Carlos Crespo, Benjamin Ortiz, and Jamil Mahuad, among others, for taking an interest in the research and facilitating it. Research in Bolivia was a pleasure, due in part to the helpfulness of Amalia Anaya, Manuel Contreras, Gonzalo Chavez, Sonia Araníbar, and George Gray Molina. In Nicaragua, Vanessa Castro, Miguel Gomez, and Humberto Belli took a real interest in the project and helped make my stay there both productive and enjoyable. In Minas Gerais, Madeleine Taylor was able to count on the insights and advice of Carlos Alberto da Vasconcelos Rocha and Luiza Pinhiero Machado, among others.

We could not have gone far in reconstructing the events of the 1990s without these generous and committed people.

Early in the research process, Barbara Nunberg and Barbara Bruns of the World Bank showed an interest in it and encouraged me to pursue it; Eduardo Doryan and Donald Winkler also indicated the importance of pursuing it. I am particularly grateful to the Inter-American Development Bank, and to Nohra Rey de Marulanda and Armando Loera for facilitating a grant that allowed me to pursue research in Ecuador and Bolivia. Juan Carlos Navarro of the IDB understood that I was not an expert on education and nevertheless encouraged me to undertake the activity. Manuel Contreras, also of the IDB, provided insightful instruction along the way and raised important issues for me to consider.

My colleagues in curiosity, Joan Nelson, Judith Tendler, Javier Corrales, and Victoria Murillo probed and questioned and encouraged. At Harvard, Fernando Reimers never hesitated to take time from his busy schedule to provide sources of data, contacts, information, and advice. To all of these friends I say, thank you! I am grateful to the Kennedy School of Government for supporting parts of the field research, summer writing time, and research assistance. In particular, Fred Schauer seemed willing to trust that some product of my efforts would eventually appear. Colleagues at the David Rockefeller Center for Latin American Studies at Harvard provided an energetic place to test out my ideas and acquire new ones. Chuck Myers of Princeton University Press set a very high standard for professionalism among editors and was consistently supportive of this book.

Steven, Alexandra, and Stefanie provided just the right mix of support and good humor to keep me plugging away, putting the pieces of research together. I wonder if they know how much they contributed to the everyday life of this researcher? They should know of my gratitude.

ABBREVIATIONS

ADEOMG	Associação dos Diretores das Escolas Oficiais de Minas Gerais (Association of Public School Directors of Minas Gerais), Brazil
AMIE	Associação Mineira de Inspectores Escolares (Association of Minas School Inspectors), Minas Gerais, Brazil
AMISP	Associação Mineira de Supervisores Pedagogicas (Association of Minas Teaching Supervisors), Minas Gerais, Brazil
ANDECOP	Asociación Nacional de Colegios Particulares (National Private School Association), Bolivia
ANDEN	Asociación Nacional de Educadores Nicaragüenses (National Association of Nicaraguan Educators)
APPMG	Associação de Professores Publicos de Minas Gerais (Association of Public Teachers of Minas Gerais), Brazil
CEBIAE	Centro Boliviano de Investigación y Acción Educativas (Bolivian Center for Educational Research and Action)
CEPAL	Comisión Económica para América Latina (Economic Commission for Latin America)
CEUB	Comité de Educadores Universitarios Bolivianos (Committee of Bolivian University Educators)
CGT	Confederación General del Trabajo (General Confederation of Workers), Argentina
CIDE	Centro de Investigación y Desarrollo de la Educación (Center for Education Research and Development), Chile
CNMN	Confederación Nacional de Maestros de Nicaragua (National Confederation of Teachers of Nicaragua)
CNOP	Confederación Nacional de Organizaciones Populares (National Confederation of Popular Organizations), Mexico
CNTE	Coordinadora Nacional de Trabajadores de la Educación (National Coordinating Council of Education Workers), Mexico
COB	Central Obrera Boliviana (Bolivian Workers Organization)
CONED	Congreso Nacional de Educación (National Education Congress), Bolivia

CONFETEC Confederación de Trabajadores de la Educación y la Cultura (Confederation of Education and Cultural Workers), Nicaragua

CONIAE Confederación de Nacionalidades Indígenas del Ecuador (Confederation of Indigenous Nations of Ecuador)

CONMERB Confederación Nacional de Maestros Rurales de Bolivia (Confederation of Rural Teachers of Bolivia)

CSUTCB Confederación Sindical Unica de Trabajadores Campesinos de Bolivia (Single Union Confederation of Rural Workers of Bolivia)

CTERA Confederación de Trabajadores de la Educación de la República Argentina (Confederation of Education Workers of the Argentine Republic)

CTEUB Confederación de Trabajadores de la Educación Urbana de Bolivia (National Confederation of Education Workers of Bolivia)

CUT Central das União dos Trabalhadores (Central Union of Workers), Brazil

EB/ Educación Básica/Proyecto de Desarrollo, Eficiencia, y
PRODEC Calidad (Basic Education/Development, Efficiency, and Quality Project), Ecuador

ETARE Equipo Técnico de Apoyo a la Reforma Educativa (Technical Support Team for Education Reform), Bolivia

FAMBH Federação dos Associaçãos de Moradores de Belo Horizonte (Federation of Neighborhood Associations of Belo Horizonte), Brazil

FAPAEPMG Federação dos Associaçãos de Pais e Alunos das Escolas Publicas de Minas Gerais (Federation of Public School Parents, and Students, Associations of Minas Gerais), Brazil

FECODE Federación Colombiana de Educadores (Colombian Federation of Educators)

FREPASO Frente de País Solidario (Country Solidarity Front), Argentina

FSLN Frente Sandinista de Liberación Nacional (National Sandinista Liberation Front), Nicaragua

GDP Gross Domestic Product

GNI Gross National Income

GNP Gross National Product

IDB Inter-American Development Bank

ILO International Labour Organization

IMF Inter-national Monetary Fund

LAN *Latin American Newsletters*

MBL	Movimiento Bolivia Libre (Free Bolivia Movement)
MIR	Movimiento de Izquierda Revolutionaria (Revolutionary Left Movement), Bolivia
MNR	Movimiento Nacionalista Revolucionaria (Nationalist Revolutionary Movement), Bolivia
MPD	Movimiento Popular Democrático (Popular Democratic Movement), Ecuador
MRTKL	Movimiento Revolucionario Tupac Katari de Liberación (Revolutionary Tupac Katari Liberation Movement), Bolivia
NGO	Nongovernmental organization
NPE	Nueva Política Económica (New Economic Policy), Bolivia
OECD	Organisation for Economic Co-operation and Development
OREALC	Oficina Regional de Educación para América Latina y el Caribe (Regional Office for Latin American and Caribbean Education), UNESCO
PAN	Partido Acción Nacional (National Action Party), Mexico
PRD	Partido Revolucionario Democrático (Revolutionary Democratic Party), Mexico
PREAL	Programa de Promoción de la Reforma Educativa en América Latina y el Caribe (Partnership for Educational Revitalization in the Americas)
PRI	Partido Revolucionario Institutional (Institutional Revolutionary Party), Mexico
PROMECEB	Programa de Mejoramiento de la Calidad de la Educación Básica (Quality Improvement Program for Basic Education), Ecuador
PRONASOL	Programa Nacional de Solidaridad (National Solidarity Program), Mexico
PRS	Partido da Reforma Social (Social Reform Party), Brazil
PT	Partido dos Trabalhadores (Workers' Party), Brazil
SINDUTE	Sindicato Unico dos Trabalhadores em Educação (Single Union of Education Workers), Brazil
SNTE	Sindicato Nacional de Trabajadores de la Educación (National Education Workers' Union), Mexico
SUTEP	Sindicato Unico de Trabajadores de la Educación Peruana (Single Union of Peruvian Education Workers)
TIMSS	Third International Math and Science Study
UDA	Unión de Docentes Argentinos (Union of Argentine Teachers)

UNAS   Unidad de Apoyo y Seguimiento a la Reforma (Educa-
            tion Reform Support and Follow-up Unit), Bolivia
UNDP   United Nations Development Programme
UNE   Unión Nacional de Educadores (National Teachers'
            Union), Ecuador
UNESCO   United Nations Educational, Scientific and Cultural
            Organization
UNICEF   United Nations Children's Fund
USAID   United States Agency for International Development
UTE   União de Trabalhadores em Educação (Union of Educa-
            tion Workers), Brazil

A NOTE ON TERMINOLOGY

For simplicity, throughout this book I use the terms *ministry* and *minister* to refer to organizations and roles that are in some places (Mexico and Minas Gerais) known as secretariats and secretaries. In addition, I use the term *union* to refer to national organizations that in some countries are structured as federations or confederations. Further, I use the term *school director* to refer to a role that is referred to in some countries as principal.

Despite the Odds

Chapter One

A CONUNDRUM: REFORM DESPITE THE ODDS

THIS BOOK POSES a conundrum for political analysis: How can we account for successful reform initiatives when the political cards are stacked against change? Education reform, which was high on political agendas throughout Latin America in the 1990s, is an intriguing case for posing this question. Definition of objectives and means, the interests of winners and losers, and shifting burdens of responsibility and accountability were among the many factors that brought reformers, politicians, teachers' unions, education administrators, governors, mayors, and others into conflict over the nature and scope of education policy during the decade. In these conflicts, the lineup of antireform forces was almost always imposing; support for change was, at best, lukewarm; and political institutions were usually unfriendly to initiatives that would alter the status quo.

Despite these political odds, at least twelve countries in Latin America introduced important changes in national education policies during the 1990s.[1] Defying predictions that they would shy away from contentious issues, politicians supported many of these changes, even in the face of mobilized opposition, acrimonious debates, and resistant bureaucracies. Although the reforms were not always as thoroughgoing as their proponents hoped, introduction and at least partial implementation of new education policies was a notable characteristic of the decade. How did this happen?

The mobilization of interests and the distribution of institutional power are important factors in understanding the origin and nature of conflicts over policy. But neither interests nor institutions fully account for policy reforms that occur despite the political odds. In such cases, it matters a great deal how policy changes are introduced, approved, and implemented and how reformers manage this process as it unfolds over time. Often, the policy process introduces opportunities to alter the political equations and institutional biases that impede change. This is what made it possible for Latin America's reform proponents in the 1990s to create conditions under which new education policies could be introduced and sustained in political and bureaucratic environments rife with opposition. This book focuses on explaining these unexpected outcomes.

Most analysts of education policy seek to assess efforts to improve conditions in the sector—increasing the efficiency with which services are delivered, reducing illiteracy and repetition rates, boosting student learning through new curricula and pedagogy, measuring the impact of standards-based testing, evaluating the results of school autonomy, and so forth. Research to assess the efficacy of various policy alternatives for improving education is a centrally important undertaking. But this kind of analysis usually takes the process of reform for granted—how improved education becomes part of a political agenda, how reform initiatives are developed, what interactions and negotiations shape or alter their contents, how important actors and interests respond to change proposals, how initiatives are implemented and sustained once they are introduced.

These are the issues I seek to address; my objective is to understand the political dynamics that make alternative policy choices possible. Thus, when I refer to reform, I am not making a normative judgment about the appropriateness or goodness of specific change proposals, but simply signaling deliberate efforts to make changes in policies about education. The reforms undertaken may or may not improve the quality of services; I leave this determination to education specialists. My focus is instead on the politics surrounding initiatives for bringing about change.

Centrally, I am interested in how reformers find room for maneuver in introducing new policies, particularly when new policies are politically contentious. But I am also interested in the limitations reformers face when they are not sufficiently sensitive to important sources of resistance or where the forces of opposition overwhelm change initiatives. Indeed, my findings indicate some ambiguity about the future of education reform where the support of teachers has been ignored, where hostile unions continue to oppose change, and where incentives for politicians, administrators, teachers, and parents work against new initiatives. In detailing some cases of relatively successful reform, I hope the following chapters represent a challenge to those who doubt the possibility of change; in detailing some failures, the book can also be a basis for considering how the politics of reform might be approached differently the next time around. At the most general level, it should provide insight into the tension between the interests and structures that inhibit change and the ability of reform agents to promote it.

ADVOCATING FOR CHANGE

Throughout Latin America in the 1990s, advocates of change argued persuasively that better education was critical if countries were to wage effective battles against endemic poverty and inequality, if they were to gain advantages from rapid globalization, and if they were to build and sustain democratic citizenship and institutions.[2] They routinely urged politicians to commit more resources to education. Research centers, universities, and think tanks produced numerous studies of the problems of current systems and the imperatives for change. Similarly, international discussions during the 1990s emphasized the importance of education to political, social, and economic development.

These advocates had good reason to stress the importance of attending to problems of public education. While most Latin American countries had achieved respectable literacy rates and widespread access to primary schooling by 1990, the region faced old and new education challenges. Increasing the supply of education was an ongoing problem. Some countries—Argentina, Bolivia, Chile, Panama, and Uruguay—had managed to achieve an average of eight years or more of schooling by the 1990s, but this average was five years or less in Brazil, El Salvador, and Nicaragua.[3] Secondary school completion rates were below 20 percent in Honduras and Nicaragua, under 40 percent in Costa Rica, Paraguay, Brazil, Ecuador, El Salvador, Mexico, and Venezuela, and did not reach 60 percent in Argentina, Chile, and Peru.[4] Because education is a critical factor explaining the persistence of inequality and poverty, the failure of the region to provide this service more effectively indicated a more general failure to address divisive social ills.

A second problem was that of investment in education. In many countries, the social sectors had borne the brunt of austerity budgeting during the economic crises of the 1980s; by the early 1990s, mounting evidence of the deterioration of services and coverage could not be ignored. Regionally, between 1980 and 1985, public expenditures on education declined by 18 percent, and while some countries began to reverse the trend in the latter half of the 1980s, other countries did not.[5] Expenditures declined as a portion of GNP between 1980 and 1991 in Costa Rica, the Dominican Republic, Ecuador, El Salvador, Mexico, Paraguay, and Uruguay.[6] Teacher pay fell throughout the region and absenteeism increased as teachers, like many of their students, abandoned the classroom to find means to contribute to fragile household incomes. Textbooks and educational materials, school breakfasts, teacher training, and other critically important inputs suffered significant cutbacks.

Thus, by the early 1990s, many ministries of education had made no substantial investments in expanded or improved facilities for a decade and were spending almost all of their budgets on salaries for personnel. In practice, this meant schools fallen into decay, no restocking of textbooks, no equipment replacement or repairs, and demoralized employees working two or even three jobs in order to make ends meet. In addition, a variety of perverse incentives for teachers and administrators undermined performance in the classroom and in organizations responsible for education services.[7] Access to education was unequally distributed between urban and rural areas and, during the decade, many families with the resources to do so exchanged publicly provided services for private ones.

But the concerns of most reformers went beyond issues of improved access to education and greater investment in the sector to a third problem. Increasingly, they were worried by evidence that the quality of education was low and, at times, abysmal. Many children attended school but learned little, an alarming number of them repeated grades, and dropping out of school with only a few years of education was the most frequent response to classroom failure and household economic need. Latin America's children did poorly on assessments of their accomplishments in mathematics and language, and scores systematically revealed differences between rural and urban schools and public and private ones. Increasingly, education experts asked if these children were going to have anything but dismal futures in an increasingly competitive global labor market.

Advocacy for responding to such concerns was advanced when innovative ideas for new programs and policies were communicated more frequently and rapidly by the internet and when their circulation coincided with extensive international dialogues about human development. Comparisons of country achievements using a variety of social welfare indicators increased government sensitivity to their international reputations. To add further to the interest in change, international development agencies increased their loan portfolios in education and became important advocates of reform and of particular approaches to improved teaching, learning, efficiency, and effectiveness. More generally, rapid globalization encouraged new concerns about the probable destinies of countries with low skilled labor forces but with wage structures that made them internationally uncompetitive.[8]

In addition, the political context in many Latin American countries was ripe for increased advocacy of reform. Democratic institutions were in place in almost all countries in the region by 1990, and the adoption of a variety of neoliberal economic reforms had increased citizen concern that governments were seeking market solutions to public problems regardless of their implications for equity, welfare, or national integration.[9] The number of NGOs and community organizations interested in social conditions mushroomed during this period.[10] Moreover, in some countries, powerful economic ministries were becoming more concerned about the efficiency of public sector investments and more aware of the importance of political and social conditions to international competitiveness. Considering only these factors, the situation seemed propitious for promoting education policy change. But new policies would also unleash contentious political realities.

New Policies, New Politics

By the 1990s, advocates for education policy change believed that reformed systems should increase the amount of learning in the classroom and that they should provide citizens with appropriate skills to lead productive lives in the twenty-first century. They argued that educational management had to become more efficient and should be the responsibility of those best able to oversee the day-to-day delivery of services. They were adamant that education be delivered by those with the knowledge and incentives to do it well.[11] Within this broad consensus, many models for how to achieve these objectives vied for the attention of reform advocates.

To turn the vision into reality, multiple reform proposals of the 1990s centered primarily on improving educational quality. Quality enhancement meant addressing the problem of poor management and inefficient use of resources by increasing accountability and reallocating responsibilities for performance. In the most ambitious reforms, states, municipalities, school directors, or local school boards were to be given responsibilities for hiring, promoting, disciplining, and firing teachers; national ministries were to be restructured, their jobs newly defined as setting national standards, monitoring outcomes, and financing rather than day-to-day tasks of classroom instruction. New initiatives would include efforts to reduce repetition and dropout rates by altering curricula and changing pedagogy. Multiculturalism and bilingual education were often part of such proposals. More attention to teacher training and monitoring often went hand in hand with proposals to tie salaries to performance and to greater accountability to supervisors or local communities. National standards were an important ingredient of reform ideas in several countries, and reform advocates supported regular examinations of student and teacher performance.

These kinds of reform proposals introduced new political dynamics into the process of policy making and implementation. In earlier periods, many Latin American countries promoted policies to increase access to education and, during the 1950s, 1960s, and 1970s, schooling was expanded to many rural areas and to poor children in mushrooming urban squatter settlements. At the center of these access policies were efforts to increase education budgets, train and hire more teachers, build more schools, distribute more textbooks, and administer more programs.

In general, these reforms were politically popular. Although they cost money and required some administrative capacity, access reforms provided citizens with increased benefits and politicians with tangible resources to distribute to their constituencies. They created more jobs for teachers, administrators, service personnel, construction workers, and textbook and

TABLE 1.1
The Politics of Access and Quality Reforms: A Comparison

	Access Reforms	Quality-Enhancing Reforms
Typical actions to carry out such reforms	• Build infrastructure • Expand bureaucracies • Increase budgets • Hire administrators • Hire service providers • Buy equipment	• Improve management • Increase efficiency • Alter rules/behavior of personnel • Improve accountability • Improve performance • Strengthen local control
Typical political implications of such reforms	Creation of benefits: • Jobs • Construction and provisioning contracts • Increased budgets • Increased power for ministries and managers	Imposition of costs: • Loss of jobs • Loss of decision-making power for some • New demands, expectations, responsibilities for others
Typical political response to such reforms	• Unions of providers welcome reforms and collaborate with them • Politicians welcome tangible benefits to distribute to constituencies • Communities are pleased to receive benefits • Voters support changes	• Unions of providers resist reforms • Administrators seek to ignore or sabotage change • Many politicians wish to avoid promoting reforms • Many voters are unaware of changes (at least in the short term)

school equipment manufacturers. They increased the size and power of teachers' unions and central bureaucracies. In fact, unions were often among the principal advocates for broader access to public education. Given these characteristics, it is not too much to argue that these reforms were "easy" from a political economy perspective.

This could not be said of most of the 1990s initiatives in education. As indicated in table 1.1, quality-enhancing reforms generally involved the potential for lost jobs, and lost control over budgets, people, and decisions. They exposed students, teachers, and supervisors to new pressures and expectations. Teachers' unions charged that they destroyed long-existing rights and career tracks. Bureaucrats charged that they gave authority to those who "know nothing about education." Governors and mayors frequently did not want the new responsibilities they were to be given. Parents usually did not participate in designing the reforms, often did not understand them, and generally deferred to professionals in making judgments about educational quality. Although public opinion singled out education as a critically important problem, and reform advocates were frequently eloquent in promoting new initiatives, the politics of putting them in place and implementing them were contentious and difficult, a far cry from the situation faced by promoters of access-type reforms. Indeed, when reformers failed in efforts to introduce significant quality-enhancing reforms, politicians were pleased to fill the gap by reverting to more popular activities like building schools and improving infrastructure.

Moreover, when compared to some of the economic policy reforms that were introduced in the 1980s and 1990s to deal with high levels of debt, spiraling inflation, and severe fiscal and trade imbalances, quality-enhancing education reforms shared a number of characteristics that made their adoption and implementation significantly different and, in some ways, more difficult. Many of the first generation economic reforms, for example, required that governments give up or scale back on functions involved in regulating markets, managing complex tariff regimes, or licensing a variety of economic activities.[12] These changes had political costs in terms of public sector job losses and administrative reorganizations, and they were often conflictful. Nevertheless, their primary purpose was for government to do less rather than more.

In contrast, education reforms meant that central government ministries of education would have to take on new roles and pursue old ones more effectively and efficiently. Often, regional and local governments were expected to take on responsibilities they had never carried out before. These education reforms required that governments do more rather than less.

Similarly, some of the first generation economic reforms could be put in motion with little more than the stroke of a pen—devaluation and deregulation are good examples. Although difficult to decide upon, they were relatively easy to implement. Second generation reforms like those in education, however, required long chains of implementation activities and decisions. Ultimately, education changes had to be adopted at the classroom level if they were to improve the extent to which children learned critical skills and abilities; this meant that multiple layers of implementers needed to be on board for new initiatives to succeed. At any point in a long chain of decision-making responsibilities, reform activities could fall victim to sloth, political contention, mistaken judgment, organizational jealousies, and logistical tangles.

Moreover, these changes meant that governors, mayors, bureaucrats, teachers, students, parents, and communities needed to adopt new ways of thinking and behaving and learn to be more accountable in multiple ways. And, to add to the complexity, the benefits of these reforms would become evident only over the long term when students began to demonstrate that their lives were more productive and that they had expanded choices about their economic and social destinies. Generating and sustaining interest in them was therefore an additional challenge.

In comparing the political difficulty of social sector reforms to earlier macroeconomic policy changes, Joan Nelson has written that they are "a different ball game, with far more actors, less leverage, different fields of play, a much longer playing period (with unpredictable time-outs), and uncertain scoring."[13] In fact, the education reforms of the 1990s were so complex and politically contentious that it was reasonable to assume they would fail to be adopted, implemented, and sustained. That reform proponents might ever succeed was, according to many analysts, a long shot.

The Odds against Reform

In Latin America in the 1990s, quality-enhancing education reforms presented a classic case in which those opposed to reform were highly organized, very vocal, and politically important. In contrast, those who might benefit from change were generally unorganized, dispersed, and politically quiescent. Moreover, political institutions tended to be biased against changes in policies about education. Yet, in country after country, reform happened, as indicated in table 1.2.

The table challenges important approaches to political economy—how do they explain the incidence of considerable reform progress in political landscapes seeded with the potential for failure? Many of those who study the politics of reform identify sources of conflict, dissent, and resistance to change. They do so by asking probing questions about who will be hurt by reform and who benefits from the status quo. They are concerned to explain the factors that underlie the maintenance of inefficiency, inefficacy, and inequality and the kinds of conflicts that will surround efforts to introduce change. They often assess the ways in which institutions privilege powerful interests and place obstacles in the path of reformers. These are critically important factors in the politics of reform. By focusing on sources of conflict, resistance, and constraints, however, political economy models that focus on winners and losers or on institutional constraints tend to overdetermine failure and underexplain the potential for change.

Winners and Losers in Conflict Equations

A dominant theme in formal political economy is the way in which proposed policy changes create material winners and losers.[14] In the generic analytic case of the politics surrounding reform initiatives, losers are

TABLE 1.2
Education Reform Initiatives in Latin America*

Country	Date	Substance of Reform	Extent of Implementation**
Argentina	1977	Transfer of primary schools to provinces	High
	1991	Transfer of secondary and remaining primary and vocational schools to provinces	High
	1993	National education law: responsibilities of national and provincial governments; curriculum reform; national testing of students	Moderate
Bolivia	1994	Institutional development of ministry of education	Moderate
		Curriculum reform, bilingual education	Moderate
		Teacher training and professionalization, new standards for hiring, promotion	Moderate
		Girls' and rural education emphasis, school councils	Moderate
		National testing of students	Moderate
		Decentralization and school councils	Moderate
Brazil	1980s–1990s	Financial autonomy of schools	High
(dates vary	1990s	Democratization of selection of school principals	Moderate
by states)	1983–1993	School councils	Moderate
	1988	National testing for students	High
	1991	Autonomy to municipal education systems	High
	1993	National ten-year plan for education	Moderate
Chile	1981	Devolution of administrative responsibility to municipalities	High
		Voucher system	High
	1990	Poverty reduction program	High
	1991	Recentralization of labor relations	High
	1993	Improved pedagogy	Moderate
	1995	Greater school autonomy	Moderate
	1997	Financial incentives for school performance	Moderate
Colombia	1989–1993	Decentralization to municipalities and school autonomy	Moderate
	1994	National education law strengthens departmental (state) role in education	Moderate
	1996	Incentive pay to teachers	Moderate
Costa Rica	1996	Commitment of 6 percent of GDP to education	Moderate
		More days of schooling	High
		Teacher pay linked to performance	Moderate

Table 1.2 (*cont'd*)

Country	Date	Substance of Reform	Extent of Implementation**
Dominican Republic	1997	National education law: decentralization/ community participation; curriculum reform; teacher/school director training; national testing of students	Moderate
Ecuador	1996	New structure for basic education	Moderate
		New pedagogical model	Low
	1998	Decentralization	Low
		Parent councils	Low
		Teacher evaluation	Low
	1999	Family subsidies	Suspended
El Salvador	1991	Decentralization of rural schools, community councils, school autonomy	Moderate
	1996	National education law	Moderate
		Teacher career	Low
Guatemala	1991	National education law	Low
	1993	National education development program	Moderate
		Infrastructure and textbooks, parent councils	Moderate
	1994	Decentralization	?
Honduras	1995	Decentralization	?
	1996	National education law	Low
		National education improvement plan	Low
Mexico	1992	Decentralization to state level	High
		Parent councils	Low
		Career ladder for teachers	Moderate/low
		Curriculum reform	Moderate
Nicaragua	1991	Parent councils	Moderate
		Curriculum reform (textbooks)	High
	1993	School autonomy	Moderate
Panama	1997	Regional and local school councils	Moderate
Peru	1992	Decentralization to municipal councils	Suspended
		Municipal council manages labor relations	Suspended
		Voucher system	Suspended
		National testing of students	Suspended
Uruguay	1995	Expansion of schooling	Moderate
		Teacher training	Moderate
		Curriculum reform	Moderate
Venezuela	1989	Decentralization to states	Low
	1990	Teachers' career	Moderate
		Public funds for private education	High

* The table includes "meaningful" reforms—those whose purpose was to introduce significant changes in the education system—as well as those that were more symbolic than real. Inclusion in the table does not imply successful implementation of the initiative.

** Extent of implementation is an estimate of the degree to which a reform had been put in practice by the end of the decade. It does not refer to the degree to which the changes have actually improved the quality of education delivered.

clearly aware of their potential losses and quick to oppose change, while winners are much less likely to benefit in the short term or be aware of long-term gains. Losers have incentives to organize to protect the status quo; winners lack clear incentives to organize for change and therefore face difficult problems of collective action.[15] Further, reform is politically difficult because electorally sensitive politicians have incentives to postpone it, given imbalances between the power of winners and losers. In such situations, political economists find that incentives for winners, losers, and politicians conspire against many reform initiatives.

In the case of the 1990s education reforms in Latin America, this model has strong empirical referents. Almost all reforms imposed at least short-term burdens on politically important groups that readily defined themselves as losers. Most prominent among them were teachers' unions, which resisted the loss of benefits, jobs, and security. These unions were often the largest and most powerful organized groups in a country. Indeed, Mexican teachers belonged to the largest union in all of Latin America. Many of these organizations had colonized ministries and achieved privileged positions in personnel decisions. Annual job actions for improved salaries frequently shut down schools and ministries and paralyzed government decision making. If reform initiatives were to succeed, union leaders faced significant losses of power and prestige. As a consequence, nearly everywhere, the announcement of new-style education sector reforms was met by protests, strikes, and vociferous opposition from the teachers' unions.[16]

Bureaucrats in education ministries also frequently defined themselves as losers in proposed reforms, fearing they would lose their jobs or responsibilities or be forced to abide by new performance standards.[17] And, where the provision of jobs for supporters was a fundamental characteristic of party systems, as it is throughout much of Latin America, party leaders stood to lose extensive patronage opportunities if new standards and systems were put in place. In addition, opposition political parties were often outspoken critics of social sector policy changes for both ideological and electoral reasons; the charge that national governments were abandoning their responsibilities by introducing initiatives that would first decentralize and then inevitably privatize education resonated effectively in political debates in many countries.[18]

Winners—parents with school-age children, citizens who benefit from living in a well-educated society, employers who need skilled workers in order to compete effectively in domestic and international markets, new entrants into the labor market—were also created by education reforms. Characteristically, however, they were not well-informed of the benefits that would accrue to them, they were unorganized, they lacked access to policy-making circles, or the benefits they would receive were too distant to be taken seriously.[19] Even employers—often well organized and influential—usually focused their political energies on other issues or sought to remedy education deficits by supporting private school initiatives, developing firm-level training for workers, or making charitable contributions to individual schools.[20] No doubt many winners also distrusted government enough to be wary of promises for improvement of services in the future; by the early 1990s, they had heard many such promises and yet had lived through a decade or more of disappointment with economic conditions and sluggish responses to state policies.

Thus, considerable empirical evidence supports the analytic perspective provided by formal political economy: education reforms produce winners and losers who differ significantly in the incentives to organize and influence public policy. The model provides a powerful and intuitive explanation for the existence of opposition to changes that might be socially beneficial. But reform outcomes are not a simple matter of weighing the interests that support and oppose change. Effective in identifying winners and losers, formal political economy is less able to provide insight into the factors that enhance or weaken the power of these interests, nor does it anticipate how outcomes are altered by the strategic choices of reform advocates. Significantly, it does not provide a way to understand the behavior of reformers, those "policy entrepreneurs" who commit themselves to the pursuit of change despite the odds.

Institutions That Empower Losers

Other political economists have taken the analysis of interests further by exploring the extent to which political institutions explain success and failure in reform initiatives.[21] For example, they demonstrate how differences in power between the executive and legislative branches or differences created by the distribution of power in presidential and parliamentary systems can affect the destiny of reform initiatives.[22] According to other analyses, the number of political parties, the degree of party discipline, or the extent of centralized control that party leaders have over their memberships can determine reform outcomes.[23] In reforms that pass through legislative institutions, the function of congressional committees and rules can create more or fewer barriers to change. Informal institutions such as patronage rights and clientelist networks also affect opposition and support for change. These factors, it is claimed, influence the access that winners and losers have to decision-making arenas and determine the value of their political resources.[24]

In the generic case of reform explained by institutionalists, interests defending the status quo tend to be more powerful than those that seek change. This is because antireformers are usually winners of prior contests over policy and, as a consequence, they have colonized institutions of power in the society and government. They use these institutions to ensure that policy favors their interests. In cases in which reform is promoted, these same institutions help them defend their interests. Moreover, institutionalists stress the extent to which reform proponents are constrained by the institutions that structure and channel their actions. As in rational choice political economy, then, institutional analyses present a general perspective in which the cards are stacked against change.

Empirically, this approach finds ready support. In Latin America in the 1990s, it was common to find ministries of education that were weak compared to teachers' unions or to observe that (reformist) ministers would come and go while (resistant) bureaucracies were entrenched. Many ministries were colonized by teachers' unions, and the close alliance between ministry and union was a frequent source of frustration to reform-minded ministers. The reliance of party systems on clientelist payoffs for supporters often worked hand in hand with the interest of unions in taking over control of the ministries. In initiatives involving various forms of decentralization, relationships among different levels of government and among different roles in the education bureaucracy were significant factors in slowing or limiting change initiatives.

To their credit, institutional analyses provide for more complex scenarios about change than do purely interest-based approaches. They acknowledge that institutions have histories that shape values and behavior and that create ongoing incentives for conflict and cooperation over time. Political institutions at times legitimate formal and informal mechanisms for overcoming resistance to change, such as opportunities for legislative vote trading and pact making to provide majority approval for reformist measures. Institutional traditions of executive dominance in policy making can also shift power relations among institutions, giving presidents greater technical capacity than legislatures to design solutions to major national problems or providing them with decree powers to avoid legislative resistance or gridlock. In fact, institutional analyses sometimes indicate how strategies for coalition building, communication, and legislative relations open up or shut off opportunities for maneuvering around constraints in introducing politically difficult reforms.[25]

Yet, practitioners of this approach more frequently find actors constrained by institutions than situations in which agents of change alter or maneuver around institutional roadblocks.[26] In comparative policy research that focuses on the experiences of developed countries, in particular, researchers have frequently used differences in institutions to explain differences in policies because institutions constrain and shape the options available in particular political contexts.[27] In many developing countries, however, where institutions are less strong and durable, there may be more opportunities for maneuvering around the constraints they impose on reform initiatives.

Modifying Analytical Biases

Current political economy models provide insights into the incentives that motivate winners and losers and suggest how institutions shape the political fortunes of reform initiatives. Clearly, interests and institutions are important factors in the politics of reform. Yet, even in the presence of empirical evidence of strong losers and weak winners, and of institutions that privilege the status quo and constrain reformers, the interests and incentives that affect winners and losers and the biases of institutions are not always enough to understand the politics of reform.

For example, a simple arithmetic of winners and losers fails to capture the factors that affect the ability of losers to obstruct change. In the 1990s education reforms in Latin America, and in the cases to be explored in this book, unions varied considerably in the extent to which they were compromised by ties to particular political parties and the extent to which they were able to engage in actions that effectively obstructed reform. In some cases, union-party alliances strengthened the position of the unions; in other cases, such ties made it more likely that reformers could marginalize the unions. In addition, unions that represented all teachers were in a more powerful position to affect the process of change than those representing only a portion of those who worked in the sector.

Moreover, the power of losers in some countries was weakened when the teachers' unions were not widely respected by the public, their image soiled by perceptions of low levels of professionalism, the bossism of their decision-making structures, and public dismay over the dismal state of public services.[28] In addition, although the structure of education bureaucracies and the incentive systems that motivated public sector workers usually put them at odds with reform initiatives, my cases indicate that reformers were able to take advantage of patronage and appointment powers to salt their organizations with supporters of change.

Changes were also possible because reforms of the 1990s did not necessarily pose a simple binary choice. In fact, some reform initiatives were negotiated agreements that allowed change to occur in the context of greater tolerance by the opposition. In the case of new policies involving decentralization, for example, opposition of teachers' unions was initially very strong. They viewed these initiatives as poorly disguised efforts to break the unions by forcing them to negotiate separately with numerous regional or local governments or local school boards over salaries, appointments, and conditions of employment. But in some cases, decentralization reforms were negotiated to maintain salary and benefit decisions at central levels, thus undermining some of the opposition of the unions. Such compromises may not have been optimal in the eyes of the reformers, but they did allow other important changes to go forward.

Strategic choices about timing also affected the outcome of many reform initiatives. My cases indicate that reformers were able to select opportune moments for pushing ahead with change proposals, and they made strategic retreats when the timing was inauspicious for change. Even more impressively, reformers in some cases were able to delay reforms until they had successfully altered the political landscape to support their initiatives. The cases presented here demonstrate numerous ways in which the strategic choices of reform proponents fundamentally altered union and bureaucratic tolerance for change. Reformers also took the lead in altering incentives in ways that were more supportive of reform. Similarly, they sought to create networks for promoting reform initiatives in environments that were hostile to change.

Thus, the cases suggest that reform initiatives need to be viewed as dynamic political processes that unfold over time, as complex chains of decisions subject to the interaction of reform advocates and opponents in particular institutional contexts that are sometimes subject to alteration. In the following chapters, I adopt a strategic choice approach to argue that the process through which the 1990s education reforms became part of national agendas, and were designed, adopted, implemented, and sustained had significant implications for reform outcomes. In this process, protagonists had different opportunities to influence conflicts and decisions. In many cases, for every action or decision that was taken, there was some possibility for altering the conflict equation and the institutional biases that surrounded a proposed change.[29]

I also indicate that reform proponents had the widest scope for undermining opposition and promoting change while they were engaged in ensuring that education was an important issue on national political agendas and while new policies were being designed. At these moments, they were most able to seize the initiative and affect the capacity of interests and institutions to resist change. Moreover, strategic actions at these moments in the policy process shaped the subsequent political dynamics surrounding their proposals, at times facilitating change and at times making it more difficult. Once new initiatives were announced, however, reformers typically lost some capacity to manage the political destinies of their proposals. Thus, their room for maneuver varied over time and was both a result of their own actions and a condition shaped by the power of interests and institutions opposed to change.

REFORM CHOICES AND PROCESS

This book analyzes a series of education reform episodes. It focuses primarily on initiatives in Bolivia, Ecuador, Mexico, Nicaragua, and the state of Minas Gerais in Brazil.[30] The comparative analysis indicates how, in the case of contentious policies, process can shape outcome through the strategic choices of reform advocates and opponents.[31] The cases focus on efforts to improve the quality of the content and structure of basic education services.[32] When these are deemed successful, I mean the extent to which a reform initiative survived approval and implementation and the extent to which it was sustained over time without sacrificing its original objectives. This allows for the fact that the dynamics of approval and implementation can alter the content of policies through negotiation, improved technical analysis, and variable management capacity, but rules out experiences in which reforms are so watered down by such interactions that they cease to embody significant change.

Each reform episode incorporates several phases across time—agenda setting, design, adoption, implementation, and sustainability. In practice, these phases are interrelated, as when the anticipation of implementation problems affects how policies are designed or when actions taken (or not taken) during implementation alter the meaning and content of policy. Thus, it is useful to explore these episodes in ways that seek to identify and understand such interrelationships in specific phases. Indeed, each of these phases can be understood as an arena in which political and bureaucratic interactions take place and affect what happens in subsequent arenas. This process orientation reveals that actors differ in the extent to which they participate in different arenas.[33] As an example, the case studies indicate that teachers' unions were usually not important in setting a national agenda for education reform, and often did not participate in policy design, but became critically active participants in arenas in which policies were approved, implemented, and sustained. Thus, the engagement of interests in opposing or supporting change varied across distinct arenas.

Of course, all the reform episodes unfolded in larger economic, political, and social contexts that were characterized by politically relevant individuals, interests, and institutions—presidents, ministers, parties, interest groups, legislatures, executive bureaucracies, courts, media and public opinion, other levels of government, and so forth. At each phase in a reform process, institutions shaped the incentives faced by actors, including winners and losers, and affected their ability to influence the outcome of conflict. Similarly, reform scenarios were influenced by historical legacies of state-society relationships, political cleavages, prior policy initiatives, and other social and political conflicts. Moreover, many reform episodes

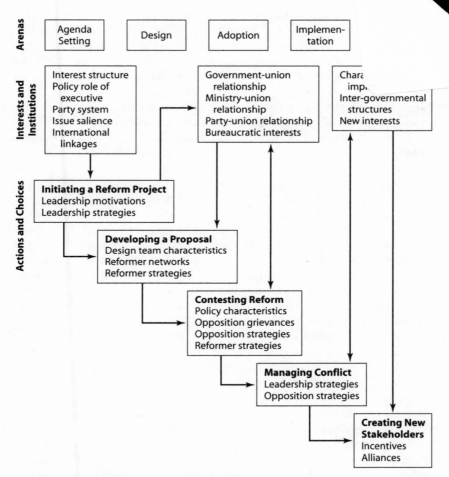

Figure 1.1 The Process of Education Policy Reform

were preceded by earlier initiatives that ended in success or failure, and these colored the way in which new initiatives were assessed, designed, and implemented. These factors created the interests and set the broad rules of the game within which new initiatives were played out. Reform episodes did not get written on a tabula rasa.

Figure 1.1 presents a stylized model of the education policy reform process in which interests, institutions, and reformers interact. In brief, it indicates the arenas in which political and bureaucratic action shape policy proposals and their potential for success. It signals a series of interests and institutions that may be important in affecting the activities of reform proponents and opponents in the different arenas. It also indicates that such factors do not determine reform, but rather affect the characteristics, motivations, strategies, and actions of actors in the reform process. Thus, for example, the role of unions in national politics, traditions of executive leadership in policy development, and the political salience of education may influence why, when, and how an issue gets on a national political agenda by affecting why leaders might take up the education reform flag and what kinds of strategies they might adopt in carrying it forward.

Early in education reform processes, reform leaders—usually presidents and ministers but also other important executives—appoint or empower design teams to put together proposals for change. An important aspect of how these design teams pursue their activities is their composition and style of work. In addition, the placement of design teams within government can be important in the bureaucratic politics that encourage or impede reform. Similarly, the work of design teams is influenced by the international and domestic networks they mobilize. They generate strategies about the range of interests that participate in their activities, and they cultivate political allies to help them pursue reform projects. All of these activities are affected by institutional factors such as the legacy of government, ministry, and party relationships to the principal opponents of education reforms in the 1990s, the teachers' unions.

When reform proposals are announced, a new arena for contestation is created. Certainly the contents of the policies—what interests they affect and what kinds of incentives and sanctions they include—set the basis for conflict. The grievances of affected parties—be they unions, bureaucracies, or politicians at various levels of government—and their strategies are important in determining the fortunes of the proposals, as are the characteristics and strategies of the reformers. Institutional factors such as the union-party and union-ministry alliances and the legacy of union-government relations affect the relative power of actors and significantly influence whether reformers decide to negotiate with or confront the opposition. In turn, the dynamics of how the reform is contested affect the extent to which conflict characterizes the implementation and sustainability of new education policies. Executives are called on to reinforce their leadership roles at this point, and their strategies for managing conflict respond to the kinds and location of contestation.

Just as critically, however, characteristics of the implementing agencies and intergovernmental structures of power help determine whether what has been approved is effectively put in place and sustained over time. The sustainability of the reform is determined by the characteristics of implementing agencies and the relationships among levels of government as well as by the extent to which reform initiatives have been successful in mobilizing new interests. These interests in turn are strengthened or weakened by the incentives they have to sustain reform and by the alliances they are able to develop with reformers.

In the following chapters, I focus in turn on the five arenas in which institutions, interests, and reformers interact. In the cases I studied, the initiation of new reform proposals and the activities involved in designing reforms were arenas characterized primarily by the strategic actions of reform proponents. These activities gave way to new and often more public arenas where reforms were contested and efforts to manage conflict introduced. In these arenas, opponents of reform often had more capacity to stymie change than at the outset of the reform process. Nevertheless, because reformers were able to seize the initiative and in many ways set the terms of reform at the outset, the power of opponents was at times circumscribed, even when they were more directly engaged in resisting change. In addition, when policies were approved and put into practice, new stakeholders at times emerged and new alliances were sometimes formed to help sustain new initiatives. These five arenas were the sites of important strategic actions that significantly affected the outcome of reform initiatives, and are analyzed in greater detail in subsequent chapters.

Finding Reasons for Reform

Before focusing on these policy arenas, however, it is important to situate the reforms in the context of the conditions that characterized national education systems in the early 1990s. This is the task taken up in chapter 2, in which I use empirical data to outline the problems that beset basic education in Latin America at that time. Conditions in that sector were dire indeed. The data indicate that large numbers of children were being very badly educated in the region's public schools. Moreover, low quality combined with inequitable access to reinforce existing class and ethnic barriers and to intensify the difficulty of finding solutions to widespread conditions of poverty and inequality. The management of education systems was overcentralized and stifling. Low standards of achievement among students were reflected in poorly trained and motivated teachers and administrators. By the early 1990s, there was certainly plenty of evidence that something was very wrong with national education systems in the vast majority of Latin American countries.

But policy reforms do not occur simply because evidence accumulates about the severity of a problem or even about the positive benefits of change for welfare and national development. In the same chapter, I also assess a series of hypotheses about the emergence and timing of education reforms. Some have argued that reforms tend to occur when policy makers are faced with economic crises; others that reforms requiring considerable investment are more likely to occur in the context of rapid economic growth; still others link reforms to the electoral cycles faced by politicians; and so forth.

The chapter includes a foray into assessing these and other claims about agenda setting. Interestingly, however, statistical and historical analyses suggest that there are few contextual similarities across countries that can account for the emergence of education reform initiatives. Episodes of reform were not systematically associated with particular economic conditions or with particular characteristics of party systems, governing coalitions, or electoral cycles. Rather, the emergence of reform initiatives is almost universally traced to the interests and actions of political executives or those closely associated with them; their concern to improve education was generally part of broader political and policy agendas they espoused and was significantly influenced by international dialogues about social policy and development.

Leadership for Change

In chapter 3, I explore the issue of leadership choices more fully by delving into the particulars of five case studies of reform. In all of these cases, "reform mongering" by presidents and ministers was important in increasing the salience of education as a policy issue. The chapter demonstrates that these leaders faced significant political and institutional obstacles in their efforts to champion change in the sector. To overcome these barriers, they drew on institutional sources of power to undermine the institutional resources of reform opponents. They sought to control the timing of reform initiatives, to use their powers of appointment to bolster the capacity to lead policy change, and to set the terms under which reform would be discussed in the political arena. They sought to weaken the position of the opposition and at times to garner broad public support for what they wanted to accomplish. In the early phases of reform initiation, then, leadership strategies were critically important to the survival of proposals for change.

Designing Policy

Similarly, seizing the initiative was important in the design phase of the policy process. In chapter 4, I consider the activities of the design teams that put reform proposals together. Design teams play an important role in defining the contents of a reformist initiative and, in the case of education policy reforms, such teams hammered out the specific ingredients of new initiatives in their countries. But in this chapter, I also ask to what extent design team activities were politically important.

The cases of Bolivia, Minas Gerais, Ecuador, and Mexico indicate that design teams were strategic actors in education policy change. Their power was affected by structural and political conditions such as how well placed they were in ministerial and bureaucratic hierarchies and was constrained by their dependence on political patrons interested (or not interested) in supporting change. At the same time, reforms were affected by the strategic decisions of these design teams. How they designed the policies defined who would be the winners and losers in reform and how much they would win or lose. Moreover, their credibility, their interactions with more traditional bureaucrats in public sector ministries, their role as gatekeepers for participation in reform discussions, and their efforts to enlist domestic and international supporters were critical to subsequent conflicts and reform destinies.

Contesting Policy

In chapters 5 and 6, I turn to the issue of how conflict with teachers' unions affected the approval, redesign, or rejection of reform initiatives. Unions were often targeted as the enemy of progress and modernization and were those most frequently criticized for what was seen as a cynical preference for a broken status quo over the promise of change. In response to this charge, the unions frequently decried a hidden agenda that they believed was about saving money, cutting jobs, and replacing public services with market-driven solutions that would only benefit the better off. This discourse between reformers and unions was often shrill and almost always confrontational.

Chapter 5 discusses the issues that created the "us versus them" nature of conflict over reform in Latin America. Almost universally, the unions were enmeshed in complex political relationships with governments, ministries, and parties. These relationships had been built on earlier initiatives to expand and centralize education and on the history of union interactions with particular political parties. Union structures differed from country to country, but most were highly centralized organizations that had the capacity to exert considerable influence in the sector. Across countries, their grievances were similar—they argued that they were paid little, that their demands were not respected, that they did not participate in the design of new policies, and that the reformers were attempting to undermine national political commitments to free public education for all children. Material interests divided reformers from the unions, but their conflicts were also about participation in the process of reform and differences in the values they held.

Chapter 6 moves from a general assessment of the teachers' unions to the dynamics of contestation over reform in the five case studies. While

in earlier chapters I argued that reformers had considerable room to put
education reform on national political agendas and to manage their design, when new initiatives were announced, reform proponents were met
with considerable opposition that constrained how they moved forward
with their initiatives. The unions were central actors in attacking the new
initiatives and, across the five cases, there is considerable evidence that
they used similar tactics.

In the face of this opposition, some governments negotiated over the
contents of reform while others confronted the unions or sought ways
to promote reform by maneuvering around them. The reasons for these
different approaches are complex, but among them is the role of the alliances between particular unions and particular political parties. In some
cases, union-party alliances gave reformers relatively little choice in terms
of how to proceed. In other cases, such alliances provided them with
greater scope to decide how to manage opposition. Moreover, the strategies to engage or exclude unions had significant implications for the extent
of conflict that met reformers when they set about implementing their
new projects.

Implementing and Sustaining Reform

Chapter 7 picks up the story of reform after new policies were agreed to
in four of the case studies. Focusing on the politics of implementing and
sustaining these policies as they were put in practice, I argue that contention over reform moved to new sites and new voices were heard in
debates over the costs and benefits of change. Prior to implementation,
the most active proponents of education policy were found in capital cities,
where they were deeply engaged in convincing national executives and
legislatures of the value and feasibility of reform, managing bureaucratic
resistance to change, and confronting nationally organized unions. Similarly, international assistance agencies were actively engaged in studying,
proposing, and assisting reform program development in alliances with
national reform entrepreneurs.

As soon as efforts were made to put the reforms into practice, however,
alternative sites for conflict emerged. State and local governments, schools,
school councils, and local communities became important places where
much of the fate of reform was decided. As this happened, governors, mayors, school directors, teachers, and local union organizations became the
principal protagonists of ongoing struggles among those who favored reform and those who opposed it; at times, parents and local communities
were brought into the fray.

In some cases, new groups of reformers emerged within state or municipal education departments or at the school level and sought to increase

the extent of change. While many teachers' unions continued to press for increased benefits and to resist the reforms at national levels, they also were active in subnational arenas. School directors often found themselves empowered by reform initiatives, but teachers frequently had a very different perception of the costs and benefits of change. Parents at times backed reform, but at other times were suspicious of it. Given this patchwork, central perceptions about what was happening could be at odds with more local realities.

Finding Room for Maneuver

In the concluding chapter, I assess the research findings for insights into the tensions between structure and agency in policy change scenarios. It is clear from the cases that room for maneuver in introducing change expanded and contracted over time as the policy process introduced new arenas of contestation. The choices the reformers of the 1990s made in distinct arenas during this ongoing process mattered for the outcome of the initiatives they sponsored, sometimes enhancing the degree of success they enjoyed, in some cases undermining it. Moreover, the politics of education reform in the 1990s created a legacy of interests and institutions that would define a political starting point for a future generation of reformers. Among the challenges left for them was that of finding ways to connect more effectively with teachers and parents in the sponsorship and promotion of new reform initiatives.

FIVE CASES OF REFORM

After the broad comparative analysis found in the subsequent chapter, I use detailed analysis of five cases of reform to explore distinct aspects of the politics of educational reform. At first blush, these cases do not seem to have much in common, other than serious educational deficits and equally serious efforts to resolve them. Mexico is one of the largest countries in Latin America, and the state of Minas Gerais in Brazil is larger than most countries in the region; Nicaragua is one of the smallest countries. Bolivia and Nicaragua are among those with the lowest GNP per capita, Mexico and Brazil among those with the highest. Nicaragua's reform is internationally recognized as having been a radical departure from past practice and a pioneer in the pursuit of school autonomy; Mexico's reform is sometimes dismissed as having been tepid; Ecuador has trouble demonstrating any significant reformist advances during the decade of the 1990s. Reforms in Mexico and Minas Gerais were introduced rapidly; those in Bolivia and Nicaragua were put in place over the course of several years.

TABLE 1.3
Five Cases of Education Reform in the 1990s

Case	Year	Most Important Aspects
Minas Gerais	1991	• Decentralization (school autonomy) • Teacher/director professionalization • Local councils • Testing
Mexico	1992	• Decentralization (states) • Teacher professionalization • Curriculum/pedagogy
Nicaragua	1993	• Decentralization (school autonomy) • Local councils/parental fees • Curriculum/pedagogy
Bolivia	1994	• Decentralization (municipalities) • Teacher professionalization • Curriculum/pedagogy/ bilingual education • Testing
Ecuador	1999	• Decentralization • Teacher professionalization • Social protection

Nevertheless, the reforms that were proposed shared central elements that are characteristic of quality-enhancing education reforms (see table 1.3). All of them sought to decentralize administration and decision making about education. In Mexico, this meant decentralization to state-level governments, in Bolivia, it meant that provincial and municipal governments would become more active in education decision making. Reforms in Minas Gerais, Nicaragua, and Ecuador sought to decentralize important decisions to the level of the school or clusters of schools and sought to develop parent or community boards to monitor student and teacher performance and make decisions related to the use of school resources. In addition, and with the exception of Nicaragua, the reforms envisioned the professionalization of teachers through increased training, performance evaluation, new career ladders, and new incentive systems. Curricula and pedagogical changes were anticipated in Mexico, Nicaragua, and Bolivia, while testing of students was an important aspect of reforms in Minas Gerais and Bolivia.

Moreover, the cases share important political and institutional characteristics. In the 1990s, all had systems that encouraged executive leadership in the policy process. All but Nicaragua had developed some technical capacity in policy planning, a factor that increased the role of policy designers in the politics of change. These countries all had strong union organizations with a history of activism vis-à-vis government, making it possible to consider how these important actors responded to reform proposals. The unions were also closely allied to particular political parties, a factor that added to their political relevance. Further, they were closely entwined with the education bureaucracy. These characteristics facilitate exploration of the constraints and opportunities for reform created by the mobilization of interests and by particular institutional arrangements, formal and informal.

Each of the cases is also useful for providing insight into particular types of reform. The cases of Minas Gerais, Mexico, and Nicaragua, for example, are widely regarded has having been structural changes that presented major threats to interests and institutional sources of power. After these reforms were put in place, the dynamics of decision making about education—who was engaged in making decisions and at what level these decisions were made—were fundamentally altered. These reforms thus offered possibilities not only for studying opposition to reform but also for exploring the role of new actors in implementing and sustaining the initiatives. The case of Bolivia was chosen as an example of a very comprehensive reform that both restructured decision making and focused seriously on issues of pedagogy and learning in the classroom. In particular, the Bolivian reform emphasized the introduction of bilingual education, a radical departure from previous policy. This case offered an opportunity to explore the considerable challenge of making reform a reality in the classroom, especially in the context of extensive opposition. These cases represent experiences of relative success, even acknowledging that the changes made—at least by the end of the 1990s—were less robust than reformers would have wished.

The case of Ecuador represents a failure to make change. As will become evident, there were numerous reasons that this happened, from the level of the ministry of education to the level of national economic and political crises. Although there were many features unique to the Ecuador case, I believe it also represents characteristics of "politics as usual" in the education sector, where a variety of interests and institutional factors militate against change initiatives. The case is therefore useful as a counterpoint to the other cases in demonstrating some of the pathologies that inhibit education reform and in suggesting how reformers sometimes make strategic errors as they attempt to advance their visions of change.

Other cases, of course, might have been selected. Certainly education reform in Chile is often cited as a new model for the delivery of services and for having been quite thoroughgoing. I did not pursue this case, however, primarily because the major changes were put in place in the early 1980s, under the military dictatorship of Augusto Pinochet.[34] I wished to focus on reforms of the 1990s in contexts in which it was not possible simply to steamroll reform from above. Other cases—Argentina, Colombia, and El Salvador come to mind—would have provided useful sites for analysis. That I chose not to explore these cases owes something to issues of access, convenience, and prior work in some countries that shortened my learning curve. I hope that by providing a general framework for understanding the politics of reform, others might be encouraged to test it using alternative experiences such as these.

In the chapters to follow, I draw on these cases in some detail to explore different aspects of the process of policy reform. The cases are presented in different order in each chapter, depending on the characteristics of the arenas of political contention I wish to highlight and the richness of individual cases in demonstrating them. Throughout, what I seek to understand is how the interaction of winners and losers, the institutional context, and the strategies of reform proponents open up or close off room for maneuver in efforts to improve the quality of education provided for the children of Latin America.

Chapter Two

FROM PUBLIC PROBLEMS TO

POLITICAL AGENDAS

"ALL AGREE THAT the single most important key to development and to poverty alleviation is education." So argued James Wolfensohn, president of the World Bank, in early 1999.[1] And, indeed, the case for investing in education is a very strong one.[2] Worker productivity, technological innovation, and global competitiveness are all increased through advances in education. Educated parents have fewer children, promote improved health among them, and are more likely to find jobs and earn incomes sufficient to maintain themselves and their families. Educated citizens participate more frequently in politics at local and national levels, and educated societies are likely to have political institutions conducive to peaceful conflict resolution. These development benefits are among numerous reasons why Latin American governments might have wanted to pay attention to education in the 1990s.

Equally important, through education, Latin American governments could deal with one of the most intractable problems of the region. In the early 1990s, 156 million Latin Americans lived in poverty, and about 70 million of them lived in extreme poverty.[3] Lack of education was systematically associated with these conditions.[4] The poor were disproportionately illiterate, disproportionately among school-leavers at a young age, and disproportionately among those whose children received little schooling and performed poorly when they did. Lacking education, poor people were disproportionately among those who could not find productive sources of employment, who could not move beyond the lowest level occupations, and who increasingly crowded the informal sector in urban and rural areas. If national education systems could be made more effective and equitable, Latin American countries might do much to deal with the devastating conditions of poverty and inequality that trapped so many of their citizens in unproductive and unfulfilling lives.

In addition to these general arguments, by the early 1990s, evidence clearly indicated that existing systems were failing to provide decent learning opportunities to the region's young. As the profile of achievements and deficits presented in this chapter demonstrates, repetition and dropout rates, deficits in student learning, lack of internal efficiency, and poor standing in international comparisons made an eloquent case for the importance of improving education.

Further, governments in the 1990s could count on a wealth of ideas about how to restructure their national systems, improve the capacity for learning and teaching, and address issues of inequitable access to education. The period was one of intellectual ferment and experimentation in education circles, and policy makers had ample opportunities to become informed about what other countries or localities were doing. School autonomy, decentralization to state and municipal governments, student-centered learning, improved information and control systems, standardized testing, teacher professionalization, vouchers, family assistance grants, and compensatory programs were among the ideas discussed by those concerned about the reach and quality of education systems in the region.

Rarely, however, do major policy reforms get on national political agendas simply because a good case can be made for their importance, because evidence accumulates about the deficiencies of the existing system, or because new ideas stimulate interest in alternative ways of structuring and managing public responsibilities. Instead, almost always, problems become priorities on public agendas through political action. Given that so many governments paid so much attention to education during the 1990s, what stimulated the political activities that resulted in new policy proposals?

In addition to describing the empirical condition of education early in the decade and the range of ideas about how to solve education deficits, this chapter also explores the circumstances under which education found a place on national political agendas. I find that economic conditions, electoral cycles, and interest group mobilization—often thought to be sources of policy change—are not consistently associated with education reform initiatives. Instead, I find a clear pattern of policy entrepreneurship by political executives whose interest in education was often tied to larger political and economic objectives. These leadership choices are critical to the birth of education policy initiatives.

EDUCATION ACHIEVEMENTS AND DEFICITS

At first glance, Latin America's educational performance by the early 1990s might be viewed in very favorable terms. All of the region's constitutions guaranteed education as a right of citizenship, and most parents registered their children in school when they reached the appropriate age. By some of the principal outcomes that specialists look for in assessing the accomplishments of an educational system—the adult literacy rate, enroll-

TABLE 2.1
Educational Achievements and Deficits in Latin America, 1990

	Adult Literacy Rates*			Gross Enrollment in Primary Education			Number of Teachers per Thousand Population**	Public Expenditure onEducation	
								% of GNP	$US Per Pupil
	Total	M	F	Total	M	F			
Latin America/ Caribbean	84.8	86.4	83.3	105.0	106.2	103.7	22	4.0	$369
Sub-Saharan Africa	50.3	60.1	40.9	74.8	81.9	67.6	10	4.6	231
Arab States	51.2	64.8	36.7	81.4	90.0	72.4	19	4.9	416
Eastern Asia/ Oceania	79.5	87.7	71.0	118.5	122.0	114.8	14	3.0	103
Southern Asia	47.6	59.9	34.5	90.3	102.6	77.1	9	3.7	80
More developed regions	98.0	98.7	97.3	102.8	103.1	102.5	22	5.0	4391

Source: UNESCO (2000:114, 115, 117, 119).
* Percentage of literate adults in the population aged fifteen years and over.
** Includes all levels of education: preprimary, primary, secondary, and tertiary.

ments, and gender disparities—the region had made significant progress. In 1950, 42 percent of Latin Americans were illiterate; by 1990, this figure had declined to 15 percent, and by 2000, to 12 percent.[5] By 1990, there were 75.5 million children enrolled in primary school in the region, approximately 85 percent of the total primary school age group.[6] Literacy rates and enrollment figures for females trailed those of males, but not by much. In 1990, 83.3 percent of Latin America's female population was literate, compared to 86.4 percent of its male population, and girls composed 49 percent of primary school enrollments.[7]

Moreover, Latin America's achievements compared favorably to those of other regions of the world. Table 2.1 compares its educational attainments in 1990 with those of other regions. Latin American countries were ahead of other developing regions on a number of dimensions of education. Levels of illiteracy were relatively low, the primary gross enrollment rate was relatively high, and the population-teacher ratio was as high as that of more developed regions. Public support for education was also greater than in some other parts of the world. In addition, Latin America stood out in providing better access for girls to basic education. Girls continued to suffer from a wide range of discriminatory practices and attended school less than boys, but compared to other regions, Latin America's record for gender equity was good.[8]

TABLE 2.2
Percentage of Illiterates,* 1950 and 1990

	1950	1990
Argentina	14	4
Bolivia	68	20
Brazil	51	20
Chile	20	6
Ecuador	44	12
El Salvador	61	26
Guatemala	71	36
Mexico	43	12
Paraguay	34	10
Venezuela	48	10

Source: UNESCO (2000:30).
*Population aged fifteen years and over.

There were, of course, major differences in achievements by country within the region. All countries made major gains in combating illiteracy between 1950 and 1990, but table 2.2 indicates that illiteracy continued to be a significant problem for Bolivia, Brazil, El Salvador, and Guatemala. In mid-decade, net enrollments were low in Colombia and Nicaragua; Brazil, Chile, Costa Rica, Honduras, and Venezuela continued to exclude 10–15 percent of eligible children (see table 2.3). Despite these failures, Latin America's national education systems had done a creditable job of improving access to basic education by the 1990s for the vast majority of children. Much of this expansion in education occurred between 1950 and 1980, when the number of children enrolled in primary school more than quadrupled and the number in secondary school expanded more than eightfold.[9]

The region's record in providing quality education, however, was much less impressive. Repetition rates were high in a number of countries, as indicated in table 2.4, and dropout rates in Colombia, El Salvador, Guatemala, Nicaragua, and Paraguay suggested real problems relating to system effectiveness. According to a UNESCO/UNICEF study, in 1989, only 38 percent of Dominican children graduated from the sixth grade, of Brazilians, only 35 percent, and of Nicaraguans, only 19 percent.[10] In the early 1990s, on average, children in Latin America remained in school for seven years, but the average level of education achieved was only through fourth grade.[11] These data suggest that internal efficiency was extremely low.

TABLE 2.3
Primary Education in Latin America, 1990

	Compulsory Education (Years)	Primary Education (Years)	School-Age Population (000)*	Gross Enrollment Ratio (%)**	Net Enrollment Ratio (%) +
Argentina	10	7	4,673	106	..
Bolivia	8	8	1,350	95	91
Brazil	8	8	27,239	106	86
Chile	8	8	1,993	100	89
Colombia	5	5	4,155	102	69
Costa Rica	10	6	432	101	86
Cuba	9	6	909	98	92
Dominican Republic	10	8	..	97	..
Ecuador	10	6	1,585	116	..
El Salvador	9	9	1,245	81	..
Guatemala	6	6	1,539	81	..
Honduras	6	6	845	108	89
Mexico	6	6	12,643	114	100
Nicaragua	6	6	677	94	72
Panama	6	6	330	106	91
Paraguay	6	6	652	105	93
Peru	6	6	3,280	118	..
Uruguay	6	6	319	109	91
Venezuela	10	9	4,235	96	88

Source: UNESCO (2000:141).
* Population of the age group which officially corresponds to primary schooling.
** Total enrollment in primary education, regardless of age, divided by the population of the age group which officially corresponds to primary schooling.
+ Enrollment for the age group corresponding to the official school age of primary education.
.. Data not available.

Other information, although incomplete, also suggests problems in achieving good quality education in many countries. Tests of language and mathematics skills in the third and fourth grades indicate that, with the exception of Cuba, average scores were low on a test described as "much more simple and less sophisticated than the tests administered in industrialized countries."[12] The average student in the region answered only 50 percent of the questions correctly and, except for Cuba, there were not large differences in results among countries (see table 2.5).[13] Colombia, one of two Latin American countries included in the 1995

TABLE 2.4
Internal Efficiency of Primary Education

	Percentage of Repeaters		Percentage of 1995 Cohort Reaching	
	1990	1996	Grade 2	Grade 5
Argentina	..	5	..	..
Bolivia	3	..	..	..
Brazil	..	18	..	..
Chile	..	5	100	100
Colombia	11	7	76	73
Costa Rica	11	11	96	88
Cuba	3	3	100	100
Ecuador	..	3	89	85
El Salvador	8	4	89	77
Guatemala	..	15	78	50
Honduras	12	12	..	..
Mexico	9	7	93	86
Nicaragua	17	15	76	47
Panama	10	..	..	..
Paraguay	9	9	92	78
Peru	..	15	..	..
Uruguay	9	9	99	98
Venezuela	11	10	96	89

Source: UNESCO (2000:145).
.. Data not available.

Third International Math and Science Study (TIMSS), ranked far below other countries (see table 2.6).[14]

Moreover, while spending for public education as a percentage of GNP was respectable overall, several countries were committing very little to the sector; in El Salvador, Guatemala, and Paraguay, it was 2 percent of GNP or less (see table 2.7). In addition, public budgets for education were almost entirely committed to current expenditures, most of which was earmarked for salaries of teachers and administrators. Political priorities for primary, secondary, and tertiary education were also clear in 1990. While the current expenditure per pupil was $266 for preprimary and primary school, it was $407 for secondary school and $922 for tertiary education. This added up to a low $369 per pupil overall.[15] Understand-

TABLE 2.5
Student Achievement in Language and Mathematics, 1997

	Language		Mathematics	
	Third Grade	*Fourth Grade*	*Third Grade*	*Fourth Grade*
Argentina	263	282	251	269
Bolivia	232	233	240	245
Brazil	256	277	247	269
Chile	259	286	242	265
Colombia	238	265	240	258
Cuba	343	349	351	353
Dominican Republic	220	232	225	234
Honduras	216	238	218	231
Mexico	224	252	236	256
Paraguay	229	251	232	248
Venezuela	242	249	220	226

Source: Laboratorio Latinoamericano de Evaluación de la Calidad de la Educación (1998:50–51).
Note: The regional average is set at 250 for language and mathematics; standard deviation is set at 50. Students' scores ranged from 65 (lowest) to 397 (highest) in language and from 53 (lowest) to 461 (highest) in mathematics.

ably, in light of this set of problems, many parents with the resources to do so chose to send their children to private schools (see table 2.8). More generally, most countries in the region fit the terms used in a Colombian government study to characterize primary education in that country: "the quality is low, the rate of school failure and dropout is high, there is insufficient class time, and the curriculum is of little relevance for students."[16]

The quality of education was not only low, it was also inequitably provided. Data for individual countries indicate that the poor were less likely than the rich to finish primary school and much less likely to finish secondary education.[17] In El Salvador, for example, 1995 data on twenty- to twenty-five-year-olds indicate that only 20 percent of the bottom four deciles of the income scale graduated from primary school, while 85 percent of the top income decile finished. Even in relatively equitable Costa Rica, only 72 percent of the poorest 40 percent completed primary education, while 99 percent of richest 10 percent did. In Mexico, 63 percent of the poorest and 92 percent of the richest completed primary school. In Brazil, the rates were 30 percent and 95 percent. In Argentina, 41.3 percent of the poorest quintile dropped out of secondary school between

TABLE 2.6
Results of the Third International Math and Science Study, 1995

| | Mean score, Eighth Grade | |
	Mathematics	Sciences
Singapore	643	607
Korea	607	565
Japan	605	571
Hong Kong	588	522
Belgium	565	550
Czech Republic	564	574
Slovak Republic	547	544
Switzerland	545	522
France	538	598
Hungary	537	554
Russian Federation	535	538
Ireland	527	538
Canada	527	531
Sweden	519	535
New Zealand	508	525
England	506	552
Norway	503	527
United States	500	534
Latvia	493	485
Spain	487	517
Iceland	487	494
Lithuania	477	476
Cyprus	474	463
Portugal	454	480
Iran, Islamic Rep.	428	470
Kuwait	392	430
Colombia	**385**	**411**
South Africa	354	326
International average	513	516

Source: International Association for the Evaluation of Educational Achievement (1996a:22) and (1996b:22).

TABLE 2.7
Public Expenditure on Education, 1990

	As Percentage of GNP	As Percentage of Government Expenditure	Average Annual Growth Rate (%) 1990–1996	Current Expenditure as Percentage of Total
Argentina	3.4	..	6.1	..
Bolivia	..	..	..	..
Brazil	4.5	..	6.8	..
Chile	2.7	10.0	12.4	96.8
Colombia*	2.5	16.0	13.5	89.8
Costa Rica	4.6	20.8	7.1	96.9
Ecuador	3.1	17.2	7.5	92.4
El Salvador	2.0	16.6	9.7	..
Guatemala*	1.4	11.8	8.5	..
Honduras	4.1	..	0.9	97.7
Mexico	3.7	12.8	7.8	..
Nicaragua	..	..	..	..
Panama	3.2	..	5.4	97.3
Paraguay*	1.1	9.1	23.0	97.4
Peru	2.3	2.3	13.6	..
Uruguay	3.1	3.1	4.1	91.8
Venezuela	3.1	3.1	7.5	..

Source: UNESCO (2000:165).
* Expenditure of ministry of education only.
.. Data not available.

1992 and 1997, while only 3.7 percent of the richest quintile failed to complete this level of schooling.[18] Mid-decade estimates of repetition rates also indicate significant differences between urban and rural students and among income quartiles (see table 2.9). Because indigenous peoples tend to be among the poorest in the population, they were disproportionately represented among school-leavers. In the late 1990s, nonindigenous adult Guatemalans had received, on average, five years of education; their indigenous counterparts, two years; in Peru, the gap was about three years and in Bolivia, it was five years.[19]

In addition to the low quality and inequitable distribution of education, its administration was highly inefficient at the outset of the 1990s. Although of course there were extensive unmet needs for resources in all

TABLE 2.8
Private School Enrollment in Latin America, 1990

	Private Enrollment as Percentage of Total Enrollment		
	Preprimary	Primary	Secondary General
Argentina	..	..	..
Bolivia	10	10	..
Brazil	26	14	..
Chile	48	39	42
Colombia	52	15	39
Costa Rica	11	5	10
Ecuador	..	..	..
El Salvador	37	15	61
Guatemala	31	16	..
Honduras	18	5	82
Mexico	9	6	12
Nicaragua	24	13	19
Panama	27	8	13
Paraguay	55	15	22
Peru	18	13	15
Uruguay	30	16	17
Venezuela	15	14	29

Source: UNESCO (2000:165).
.. Data not available.

countries, much of the problem was not primarily one of resources, but one of the inefficient use of resources.[20] Management of public education was almost everywhere at fault. Central ministries of education in most countries determined curricula, contracted teachers and supervisors, established standards for teacher training and classroom learning, administered salaries, managed budgets for school construction and repair, commissioned and selected textbooks, and promoted and disciplined teachers and their supervisors. Even minor issues—a dispute over salary, lack of chalk in the schoolroom, a missing shipment of textbooks, a conflict between a teacher and a supervisor—might have to be carried to ministry offices in distant capital cities, increasing inefficiency and lowering morale. Resolving such issues might take months or might never be dealt with. Indeed, dirigiste national ministries of education were accused of being

TABLE 2.9
Estimates of Grade Repetition*

		Rates by Urban and Rural Areas		Rates by Quartile of Income in Urban Areas			
	Year	Urban	Rural	Q1	Q2	Q3	Q4
Brazil	1996	25.6	52.9	43.5	20.5	9.4	4.7
Chile	1996	10.1	19.5	13.8	8.7	9.7	4.2
Colombia	1997	14.3	40.5	21.2	14.1	4.1	6.8
Costa Rica	1997	20.1	20.6	29.6	19.8	12.2	3.0
Ecuador	1997	7.2	..	12.7	4.9	4.1	0.3
Honduras	1997	10.9	24.8	19.0	8.3	6.9	3.4
Panama	1997	6.9	18.3	11.5	3.2	2.4	1.3
Paraguay	1995	10.2	16.9	17.1	7.5	7.4	3.1
Uruguay	1997	8.4	..	14.8	5.5	0.7	0.0
Venezuela	1995	11.0	20.9	15.9	8.3	9.1	2.2

Source: Reimers (2000a:73), based on CEPAL data.
* Children enrolled in school at age nine or ten who have not completed at least two grades.
.. Data not available.

"better at repressing change . . . than operating a system for steady improvement."[21]

Centralization meant that administrators were very removed from what was occurring in the school or the classroom and that monitoring capacities were extremely low. In many countries, ministries even lacked basic information about how many schools and teachers were in the national systems, where schools were located, how many classrooms they contained, what their physical conditions were, and how many students attended them. In periodic discussions of the need for reform prior to 1990, deconcentration of the central ministry to the provincial or state level was at times attempted, and more extensive devolution was tried in Chile and Brazil, but often the results were disappointing. Local control of school systems and school-based management was scarcely on public agendas prior to the 1990s.

Centralization was cemented in place by national control over school financing. As late as 1996, of fifteen Latin American primary education systems, all but one were financed 65–100 percent by national governments; nine countries had no provision for state or municipal financing of education.[22] Only in Brazil, in which major financing came from the state level, did the national government contribute less. Teacher salaries had long been set at national levels in all countries except Argentina, Brazil, and Chile.[23]

The inefficiencies caused by centralization were generally exacerbated by the poor quality of officials who worked in the ministries of education. Characteristically, ministry appointments were made on the basis of patronage. In many countries, national teachers' unions virtually controlled the ministries, determining appointments to administrative and teaching positions, teacher assignments, and promotions. A recurrent problem in many ministries was that of "ghost" workers, to whom salaries were regularly paid but who never appeared for work. In some countries, those trained as teachers occupied all posts, even those for which specialized knowledge was required—accountancy, information technology, personnel management, and so forth. Patronage in some countries virtually ensured security of tenure regardless of performance; in others, it meant frequent changes and great insecurity.[24] Either way, incentives for education bureaucrats and teachers to be productive were undermined. Equally problematic was the short tenure of ministers of education in the 1980s and early 1990s.[25] In Peru, for example, nine ministers were in office between 1988 and 1993; in Brazil, six ministers held office during that period; there were five in Colombia and Venezuela, four in Chile, and three in Argentina and Mexico for those same years.

Mirroring the distribution of power in the national system, teachers' unions were also highly centralized.[26] Because teachers composed such a large portion of public sector workers, their unions were large and usually powerful; at times, they were the largest worker organizations in a country. These unions often adopted rhetoric and demands that identified teachers as workers; they protected the teachers in negotiations over salary and benefits or delivered them over to national political machines, but did little to promote their professional identities or skills. In many countries,[27] strikes were frequent and contributed to shortfalls in classroom teaching. In 1995, strikes cost Bolivia forty classroom days, Costa Rica twenty-one, and Colombia twelve. In 1996, Venezuelan students lost forty-three classroom days to strikes.[28]

While academics debated whether teachers are disadvantaged relative to other professional groups or whether their pay was above or below average for the time commitments they make, teachers universally believed they were underpaid and under-recognized for the important work they were expected to carry out.[29] The principal focus of any organized demands their unions made on political systems in the region was for increases in salaries, benefits, and job security. These perceptions and actions in turn acted as a disincentive in upgrading the quality of teacher preparation and increased teacher resistance to new standards of performance and greater commitment to their work.

To add to the difficulties of the sector in providing quality education, teachers were almost universally poorly trained.[30] Especially at the primary school level, they were usually educated in normal schools, where quality was generally lower than in universities. Particularly among older teachers, university education was not widespread and, particularly in rural areas and in poorer countries, teachers at times had only eighth or ninth grade educations. Moreover, the economic crisis of the 1980s caused serious income losses for teachers in countries such as Argentina, Chile, Costa Rica, El Salvador, Mexico, and Nicaragua.[31] Most teachers had few incentives for professional development, and most had no expectations of improving their conditions through promotions or demonstrations of their capacity as educators.[32] According to some experts:

> [B]y paying teachers poorly, offering them no career ladder, and subjecting new entrants and old timers alike to the pressures and demands of local politicians, many countries have ended up with teachers who are not the best and brightest of every generation. Additionally, the working conditions of teaching place high demands on teachers for which they are poorly prepared and hence decreases their sense of efficacy and self-esteem. This, of course, affects teachers' levels of motivation, their desire to continue with in-service education, with their mentoring role, and their willingness to cope with difficult situations in their teaching career, ultimately abandoning the field.[33]

The highly centralized nature of education planning and administration, as well as the poverty of many areas served by public education, created another characteristic of the system that encouraged low quality—the lack of involvement of parents and communities in local school affairs. Centralization of decision making meant that there were few activities that parents or local communities—teacher attendance and performance, for example—could influence. Poverty, paternalism, and tradition often conspired to convince them that they had no place in education decisions or activities. Many countries, of course, had systems of parent-teacher associations, but most often these were decreed by central policies and ineffective at local levels.[34] In some countries and in some communities, there were traditions of "cooperation" with local schools, through which parents were called upon to provide funds for maintenance, special programs, and special events. But as one education expert in Mexico noted, "'cooperation' is very different from participation."[35]

By the early 1990s, then, it was clear that Latin America's education systems were broken. This is the inescapable conclusion of the data on the quality, equity, administration, incentives, and community participation in the old system. The reforms that emerged in many countries sought to redress these quality-constraining problems.

QUALITY-ENHANCING REMEDIES

By the early 1990s, education specialists in Latin America were engaged in numerous discussions about how systems should be structured, how schooling should be carried out, how parents and communities could contribute to enhancing the quality of education, and how the accomplishments of schooling could be assessed. The publication of the UNDP's first *Human Development Report* in 1990 helped raise political consciousness throughout the region about the importance of education in human development, and it caught specialists' attention by comparing country achievements and shortfalls. International meetings of educators also contributed to wider domestic discussions. The Education for All meeting at Jomtien, Thailand, organized by UNESCO, UNDP, UNICEF, and the World Bank in March 1990, served as a stimulus to many would-be reformers in the region.[36] A host of world and regional conferences drove home the importance of education in national development.[37] Attendance at such meetings also helped form and cement cross-national networks among education specialists and improve knowledge about reform initiatives.

Further, the advocacy of bilateral and multilateral agencies was difficult to escape during these years, as were the numerous international publications that emphasized investment in the social sectors and promoted particular kinds of changes that were widely adopted. Education specialists traveled frequently through the region, carrying with them modes of analysis and frameworks for resolving problems; the wider availability of the Internet also helped promulgate knowledge about innovation. Specific reform ideas moved extensively across borders—Chile's model of reform, for example, was closely studied in Nicaragua and Peru, while Mexico looked to Spain for ideas, reformers in Ecuador sought experiences from Brazil, Nicaragua, and the United States, and Venezuelan reformers found models in Brazil and El Salvador. Out of this ferment, a series of remedies for the region's educational deficiencies emerged.

Decentralization and School Autonomy

Most of the reforms promoted during the 1990s included some form of decentralization.[38] In Argentina, Bolivia, Chile, Colombia, Mexico, and Venezuela, decentralization took the form of giving responsibility for the administration of primary education to state and municipal governments. In Brazil, El Salvador, Guatemala, and Nicaragua, the emphasis was on the promotion of school autonomy, at times bypassing regional and local levels of government. At times, school or community councils were invested with powers to hire and fire teachers and school directors. Where

they were created, considerable thought and discussion went into the composition and function of these councils—how many teachers, parents, representatives of the community; what role for the school director, students,
the mayor; what decisions over funding and expenditures, teacher attendance, school maintenance; and so forth.

Carefully balancing power and interests, new structures of authority
and responsibility were expected to increase the capacity of parents, communities, local officials, and others to hold teachers, directors, and schools
accountable for their performance. They were also expected to increase
director and teacher interest in teaching and give them a bigger stake in
what was occurring in the classroom. Because most countries had long
traditions of centralized decision making and administration, opening
doors for regional, local, or community control over education was "something to be invented" during the decade.[39]

Efficiency and Management

Central to most reforms were efforts to increase the efficiency of education
systems by restructuring central ministries of education, redefining their
activities, and devolving administrative duties to more local levels of government or to the schools. Some ministries of education were downsized.
Chile, having introduced major educational changes far in advance of
other countries, reduced the ministry of education from some 20,000
people in 1980 to 3,000 in the late 1980s by turning personnel and infrastructure management over to municipalities.[40] In Nicaragua, central staff
was reduced from about 900 people in 1990 to under 400 in 1992.[41] In
Peru, the ministry of education was reduced from 2,100 people in the
mid-1980s to 450 employees in 1993.[42]

Management reforms also introduced computer-based systems of information and control. These involved, often for the first time, acquiring
data on how many schools, teachers, and students a country had, where
they were located, and what resources they were receiving. These efforts
also provided information on ghost workers and allowed for closer financial management. They were expected to provide the data for evaluating
the performance of schools and teachers. International agencies were
prominent funders of these information technology innovations. They
often helped promote data collection as a first step toward other, more
difficult kinds of changes. Although costly, information technology infrastructure could be put in place with greater speed than more contentious
and difficult changes, and relatively steady progress could be expected in
training administrators to use it.

In Bolivia, a census allowed reformers to create an education map that
provided much more accurate information than had been available in the

past.[43] In 1992, Colombian reformers had, for the first time, useful figures on teachers and payrolls.[44] Nicaraguan officials had information on the progress of school autonomy available to them by the late 1990s.[45] At about the same time, national data on education, poverty, and health in Ecuador helped administrators design targeted compensatory programs for those who lived in poor regions. In most countries, new educational information programs allowed for tracking of student performance, and at times, school and classroom performance. By the late 1990s, most ministries of education had launched websites that offered basic demographic information on education. While this information was not always used in decision making, central administrators achieved greater capacity to understand what was happening in education than had been the case in the past.

As part of decentralization initiatives, central education ministries acquired redefined responsibilities, giving them greater capacity to set national norms and standards, and to monitor student, teacher, and school performance. With better information, they would be in a better position to hold teachers and supervisors accountable for carrying out their responsibilities. In some countries, decisions about textbooks, pedagogical methods, hiring and firing teachers and supervisors, and some resource allocations were taken over by lower levels of government or by the school, even while most national governments continued to set teacher salaries.[46] These reforms could be expected to eliminate some of the bottlenecks and headaches that went with administering a national system through centralized decision making and labor relations. In these initiatives, Mexico stood out for the extent to which central officials retained decision-making power over content and pedagogy, while Nicaragua, El Salvador, and some states in Brazil were remarkable for the extent to which they promoted school-based management.[47]

Teaching and Learning

The learning deficit in Latin America's schools, so clearly revealed in the results of standardized tests, encouraged emphasis on new approaches to learning and teaching.[48] *Constructivismo*, a pedagogical movement that encouraged student-centered learning and an activist role for the teacher in creating appropriate learning activities and materials—directly challenging the style of rote memorization practiced by most teachers in the region—became a rallying cry for many reformers.[49] Education specialists emphasized the cognitive development of students, their mastery of problem-solving skills, and the variability of individual skills and development. Because new approaches to learning implied radically different pedagogies, normal schools and university teacher development programs became sites for reformist initiatives; they also became sites for ideological battles over how best to carry out learning in the classroom.[50] Many reforms considered how incentives for improved teaching could be introduced.[51]

Increased concern over learning encouraged education specialists to champion diagnostic tools such as standardized tests for students and school and teacher evaluations. In some countries, national examinations had long been used to determine if students should be promoted to the next grade or graduated. The new emphasis, at least in theory, was to be on the use of tests for diagnostic purposes and to assess overall school performance. Cuba initiated testing of students in 1975 and Chile followed suit in the early 1980s, pioneering a system for rewarding schools for improvements in performance.[52] By the end of the 1990s, this country had almost two decades of standardized test scores that could be used to assess the achievements of the education system and track changes at the classroom level.[53] Costa Rica introduced testing in the 1980s, and Argentina, Brazil, Colombia, the Dominican Republic, and Mexico did the same in the early 1990s.[54] By 1998, at least fifteen countries were using national performance tests.[55] In a few countries, tests for teachers were promoted as a way of calibrating salaries and managing promotions and incentives.[56]

A variety of nongovernmental organizations developed local level education programs, particularly in poor and rural communities, and these added to the intellectual ferment about how education systems could be improved. Experiments in alternative approaches to learning and teaching, such as the *escuela nueva* in Colombia, the *escuelas integrales* in Venezuela, and the Fe y Alegría movement in many countries, provided concrete examples of new models of instruction and learning.[57] Similarly, when international agencies became involved in funding innovations, reformers were encouraged to become conversant with new approaches to education as practiced in such places as Memphis, Tennessee, or Chicago, Illinois.

Compensatory Programs

Along with ideas and experiments expected to improve the overall quality of education, reformers were also concerned about the inequities in the systems that discriminated against rural, indigenous, and other poor children.[58] As we have seen, by the early 1990s, a wide range of studies and discussions pointed to the inequitable distribution of access to and quality of education in countries of the region. The many ways that poverty and inequality could be linked to education deficits encouraged specialists to consider ways to provide additional resources for schools in poor areas, to compensate poor parents for the opportunity costs of sending their children to school rather than to work, to encourage better trained teachers to take posts in poor and remote areas, and to expand secondary education opportunities in underserved rural areas.

Compensatory programs included the P900 program in Chile—additional resources to the lowest performing 10 percent of schools—Mexico's Telesecundaria program—distance learning for rural secondary school education—and Brasilia's *bolsa escola* program—subsidies to poor households for school attendance. Each of these programs was widely studied and at times emulated.[59] While often very innovative, they were targeted for particular schools, regions, or populations; some of those most concerned about the link between education and inequality argued that equity should be a principal focus of overall educational planning and programming, not left as an afterthought for action at the programmatic level.[60]

From Problems and Remedies to Politics

Evidence about the deficiencies of the existing system and the availability of new ideas and new models about how things could be done better provided excellent rationales for altering education systems throughout the region. However, it does not follow that reforms are put in place because of the failures of the past or because there are promising models for the future. Certainly, education reformers were often strongly motivated to improve conditions in their countries, but the task of moving from a recognition of problems and solutions to a situation in which political decision makers are willing to consider taking action to resolve them is not simply a matter of demonstrating the nature of the problem. For reform to get on national political agendas for action, it must have political salience as an issue and influential voices to promote it.

GETTING ON THE POLITICAL AGENDA

Because many countries introduced education reforms in the 1990s, it is possible that a similar set of economic or political conditions encouraged an increase in the political salience of this issue. Indeed, the association of reform and particular contextual conditions has been of considerable interest in research about the widespread introduction of economic policy reforms during the 1980s and 1990s. Analysts have been interested to learn if economic crises, for example, could be a generalized condition that encourages policy reform, if politicians are likely to introduce difficult policy changes during their "honeymoons" soon after taking office, if reforms are introduced when international financial institutions force the issue, and so forth.[61] Given that education reforms are often as politically contentious and difficult as economic policy reforms, can their emergence on national political agendas be associated with particular economic or political conditions?

Of course, it is difficult to specify the moment when education policy reforms appeared on national agendas. Many of the reforms of the 1990s were being considered, debated, and designed long before they were announced or promulgated into law. In Bolivia, for example, education reformers began to consider how to alter the national education system in the second half of the 1980s, but it was not until 1994 that an education law was passed by congress. In Mexico, the political context was being readied for reform from 1989 until 1992, when a national political agreement was hammered out with the teachers' union. In contrast, Peru's reform came together quickly in 1992. Moreover, most initiatives were built on some prior experience of reform or at least discussion of it. Indeed, there were few countries in which more and better education was not being discussed at some level in the political system.

Thus, the analysis of conditions that might be associated with reformist agenda setting in education must necessarily be approximate rather than definitive. In the following discussion, I focus on specific reform episodes, as explained in the previous chapter. I have selected these episodes from table 1.1, and the dates I use correspond to the announcement or legislation of a significant change in education. In the analysis of economic factors that might influence agenda setting, I explore conditions in the four years that led up to that date; in the case of political factors, I use information about the most proximate elections prior to and after the reform date. As a third step, I used a broad range of specific cases to assess more specific factors that might help explain the origin of efforts to put education on national political agendas. Because this assessment seeks to understand why reforms got on these agendas, the analysis focuses on the timing of the reform initiative, not on whether it was successfully adopted and implemented or not.

Economic Conditions and the Reform Agenda

Perhaps the most well-researched hypothesis about the politics of economic adjustment is the extent to which economic crises are associated with reformist initiatives. Negative GDP growth, high rates of inflation, large fiscal deficits—these were ingredients of economic crises that played a role in the introduction of many market-oriented reforms in the 1980s and 1990s. Despite their ubiquity, however, findings of a wide variety of studies suggest that these crisis conditions were neither a necessary nor sufficient condition for reform initiatives, although they frequently facilitated policy change.[62] Borrowing from this political economy literature, a plausible hypothesis about education is that economic crises stimulate reform initiatives because policy makers wish to increase the efficiency of public services and reduce fiscal pressures on government. Similarly, if economic crises mean that governments turn to international financial institutions for relief, social sector reforms might figure in conditionalities for assistance.

Just as plausibly, however, education reforms might be associated with economic growth. Because social sector reforms often imply increased spending by government, it is possible that policy makers take advantage of periods of growth to promote these reforms. During such times, they may feel more comfortable embarking on difficult reforms that are likely to put increased pressure on the public budget. This may even be true of some decentralization reforms that seek to reduce fiscal burdens on central governments, as well-designed decentralization initiatives often require additional money up front if they are to be effective over the longer term.

To assess the extent to which specific economic conditions were associated with initiatives to improve national education systems in the 1990s, data on GDP growth, inflation, fiscal deficits, and government revenues and expenditures in the four years preceding reform for sixteen countries in Latin America were assessed.[63] For those years, the analysis focused on finding consistent patterns and associations among the variables. The findings cast considerable doubt on the ability of economic variables to explain when education policy reforms were likely to get on public agendas. Instead, a wide variety of economic conditions appear to be consistent with the increased political salience of education.

The bulk of countries experienced growth rather than decline in GDP in the years leading up to the reform initiative. However, the extent of growth varied from less than 1 percent for El Salvador and Venezuela to more than 10 percent for Chile and varied by as much as six or seven points within some countries (Chile and Venezuela, for example).[64] Moreover, Argentina, Nicaragua, and Peru had negative GDP growth rates in three out of the four years before the reform, Brazil in two out of four years, and Honduras in one year. Thus, there is little evidence of a consistent pattern of growth in the years preceding reform initiatives.

Inflation rates and the condition of public budgets within and among countries also showed little consistency as explanations for agenda setting. Bolivia, Chile, Guatemala, and Panama experienced inflation rates lower than 20 percent for at least three of the four years prior to the reform, while Brazil, Peru, Nicaragua, and Argentina registered rates higher than 100 percent during the same number of years. Data on budget deficits in thirteen countries indicate that during the four years prior to the reform, Argentina, Bolivia, Brazil, and Peru had fiscal deficits every year, while Chile and Panama consistently produced surpluses. One year prior to the reform, ten of thirteen countries had fiscal deficits; two years prior, eight registered deficits; and three years prior, seven were in deficit. Given the ubiquity of deficits in Latin American public budgets, this condition might be most conducive to reform when coupled with other difficult conditions, such as poor growth and high inflation. Peru met all three of these conditions for all years, but none of the other countries experienced the three crisis conditions for more than two out of the four years.

In addition, average government revenues as a percentage of GDP fail to indicate any consistent pattern during the four years preceding the reform initiatives. Again, countries varied in terms of positive and negative growth. In year three, revenues in five countries went up in relation to the previous year while they declined in six countries; in the second year before the reform, revenues in seven countries increased and decreased in seven others; in the year prior to the reform, eight countries had higher revenues and three lost revenue relative to GDP. Chile declined and Bolivia grew in terms of their revenues in every year prior to the reform. A similar situation characterized total government expenditures as a proportion of GDP. In year three, five countries had higher expenditures than in year four, and six countries spent less. In year two, six countries increased spending while seven decreased it, and in the year prior to the reform, seven countries increased spending and five decreased it. Only Bolivia consistently increased expenditures, while only Chile and Mexico consistently constrained it.

Were countries forced to consider education reform by international financial institutions? A review of IMF stabilization and structural adjustment agreements gives no evidence of conditionalities for education reform.[65] Of course, even if reforms were not imposed through conditionality, availability of funding from international sources might have encouraged reform initiatives.[66] Table 2.10 indicates the growth of bilateral and multilateral assistance for education development from 1980 to the late 1990s. While only partial data are available for Latin America, in the column indicating Inter-American Development Bank and Caribbean Development Bank funding, overall, they indicate increased international willingness to support education reforms. The World Bank loaned about $75 million to Latin American and Caribbean countries for education in 1990; by 1997, the figure was well over $500 million.[67]

Certainly international discussions of the links between education and development were important in encouraging some reformers to take up the education cause. As we will see in later chapters, however, the involvement of international agencies in reform initiatives often came after the reformist initiative had become a priority on the political agenda and a design team was already at work fashioning its contents. In explaining the emergence of reform on national agendas, then, the availability of international fund-

TABLE 2.10
Education Development Cooperation
(Millions of Current US$)

Year	Bilateral*	Multilateral		UN	World GDP Deflator (1990=100)
		International Aid**	IDB and CDB Only+		
1980	3395	668	68	146	21
1985	2301	1394	127	141	42
1990	3642	2083	64	285	100
1992	3465	2852	271	301	135
1993	3740	3222	500	284	160
1994	4419	3315	970	279	191
1995	4550	1737	147	302	210
1996	4226	1886	291	275	223
1997	3553	2789	1041	284	234

Source: UNESCO (2000:120).

* Official Development Assistance by OECD donor countries, members of the Development Assistance Committee.

** Includes expenditure on educational development cooperation by nine multilateral banks and funds: African Development Bank, Arab Multilateral, Asian Development Bank, Caribbean Development Bank, European Development Fund, Inter-American Development Bank, Islamic Development Bank, OPEC Fund, and World Bank.

+ Educational development cooperation expenditure by the Inter-American Development Bank and Caribbean Development Bank only.

ing may not be strongly associated with such initiatives, although it is difficult to ignore the ways in which such funders raise the salience of reform in international discussions of development or the importance of their support in the design and implementation phases of the policy process.

Political Conditions and the Reform Agenda

In cases of economic policy reform that have been studied, several hypotheses about the kinds of political conditions that might stimulate reform initiatives have been proposed.[68] For example, a "mandate hypothesis" holds that politicians proceed with reforms when national elections give them significant margins of victory. Might this offer one explanation of education reforms? Table 2.11 provides data on the outcomes of presidential elections in sixteen Latin American countries prior to reform initiatives in education. The percentage of the vote captured by the winning

TABLE 2.11
Electoral Outcomes and Executive-Legislative Power Balances Prior to Reforms

	Year of the Reform Initiative	Presidential Election Year	Presidential Mandate		Legislative Majority of Presidential Party/Coalition	Reform Legislated?
			% of Total Vote	Winner/ Runner-Up Gap**		
Argentina	1991	1989	47.4%	10.4	Yes	Yes
Bolivia	1994	1993	33.8	13.8	Yes	Yes
Brazil	1993	1989	49.9*	5.7*	No	Yes
Chile	1991	1989	55.2	25.8	Yes	Yes
Colombia	1994	1994	50.6*	2.1*	Yes	Yes
Costa Rica	1996	1994	49.6	1.9	Yes	Yes
Ecuador	1998	1996	47.8*	7.9*	No	No
El Salvador	1991	1989	53.8	19.3	Yes	Yes
Guatemala	1991	1990	64.6*	34.3*	No	Yes
Honduras	1996	1993	51.1	9.7	Yes	Yes
Mexico	1992	1991	50.4	19.3	Yes	Yes
Nicaragua	1993	1990	54.7	13.9	No	No
Panama	1997	1994	32.0	2.4	No	?
Peru	1992	1990	56.5	22.6	No	No
Uruguay	1995	1994	31.4	1.2	Yes	Yes
Venezuela	1989	1988	54.6	14.6	Yes	Yes

* Second round.
** Difference between percentage of votes received by winner and runner-up.

candidate is compared with the difference between his showing and that of his closest competitor. By these data, the size of the mandate extends from a bare 1.2 point difference in Uruguay to 25.8 points in Chile and 34.3 points in a second round election in Guatemala. The size of the mandate does not appear to explain the timing of reform initiatives.

Reforms might also be a function of favorable relationships between the executive and the legislature. To what extent did presidents enjoy legislative party majorities when reform initiatives were announced? Executive dominance in policy initiation has long been a tradition in most Latin American countries, and education reform was no exception. In fact, in some countries, such Nicaragua, Panama, and Peru, reforms were decreed rather than submitted to the legislature for approval. In Nicaragua and Panama, reforms went forward without congressional approval, while in

Peru the reform was suspended. In most countries, however, political executives sought legislative approval; table 2.11 indicates that when they did so, most of them enjoyed legislative majorities. However, even in Guatemala and Ecuador, where executives did not have such a political advantage, the reforms were legislated. Legislative majorities may be important to reform, but apparently some executives found ways to promote new initiatives even in their absence.[69]

To what extent are electoral cycles associated with reform? Because some policy reforms place burdens on important groups or on large sectors of the population, it has been hypothesized that reformers will capitalize on "honeymoon" periods to introduce them. During the period just after they have taken office, their public popularity is generally highest; moreover, the length of time before the next election is longest, so politicians would have a maximum amount of time to recover from negative political consequences of contentious reforms.

Table 2.12, comparing dates of elections with dates of reforms, indicates that only in Colombia was a reform introduced in the same year as the election. Bolivia, Chile, Ecuador, Guatemala, Uruguay, and Venezuela introduced reforms one year after elections. Argentina, Costa Rica, El Salvador, Honduras, and Peru introduced reforms two years after elections and either two or three years before the next election. In Nicaragua and Brazil, reforms were introduced three years into a presidential administration and in Mexico, in the fourth year of an administration. Of course, as indicated, reforms may spend considerable time on the agenda for action before they are announced or approved, so the data do not fully test the hypothesis.

To what extent might reform-sponsoring politicians have been responding to public opinion about education in the 1990s? Public opinion in Latin America consistently placed education near the top of public concerns, as indicated in table 2.13, and this might have encouraged democratically elected politicians to be responsive to this issue.[70] But politicians seeking to formulate policies to tap citizen interest would find little guidance about what to do, given the data in table 2.14, which presents the earliest cross-national data available on attitudes toward education. It indicates that education at primary, secondary, and tertiary levels was more likely to be deemed good or very good than deficient or very deficient. Fifty percent or more of citizens in thirteen countries rated their primary schools as good or very good; only in Argentina, Brazil, Peru, and Venezuela did the majority of those polled rate their primary schools as deficient to very deficient. Thus, while public opinion signaled that education was important, it did not consistently guide politicians to select quality-enhancing reforms as a reasonable response to citizen interest in the sector.

Mobilized interest group pressure, on the other hand, is more difficult to ignore or misread, especially if it comes from particularly influential

TABLE 2.12
Reform and Electoral Cycles

	Presidential Election Years	Presidential Inauguration	Reform Year**	Electoral Cycle in Years	Reform Announced Years After/Before Elections	
					After	Before
Argentina	May 1989/May 1995	July 1989	1991	6	2	4
Brazil	Nov. 1990/Dec. 1995	Jan. 1990	1993	5	3	2
Bolivia	May 1993/June 1997	Aug. 1993	1994	4	1	3
Chile	Dec. 1990/Dec. 1993	Mar. 1990	1991	4	1	3
Colombia	June 1994/June 1998	Aug. 1994	1994	4	--	4
Costa Rica	Feb. 1994/Feb. 1998	May 1994	1996	4	2	2
Ecuador	Feb. 1997/July 1998*	Aug. 1998	1998	4	1	0
El Salvador	Mar. 1989/ Mar. 1994	Apr. 1989	1991	5	2	3
Guatemala	Nov. 1990/June 1993*	Jan. 1990	1991	4	1	2
Honduras	Nov. 1993/Nov. 1997	Jan. 1994	1996	4	2	2
Mexico	July 1988/ Aug. 1994	Dec. 1988	1992	6	4	2
Nicaragua	Feb. 1990/Oct. 1997	Apr. 1990	1993	6	3	3
Panama	May 1994/ May 1999	Sep. 1994	1997	5	3	2
Peru	June 1990/June 1995	July 1990	1992	5	2	3
Uruguay	Nov. 1994/Oct. 1999	Mar. 1995	1995	5	1	4
Venezuela	Dec. 1988/ June 1993*	Feb. 1989	1989	5	1	4

* Elections took place before the electoral cycle concluded.
** Dates of important reforms selected from table 1.2.
-- Legislative process of the reform initiative had already begun when the president took office.

groups in the population—teachers, the Catholic Church, economic elites, or intellectuals, for example. In much political theory, of course, interest groups are thought to be the principal forces responsible for getting issues on political agendas. If important interest groups advocate reform, politicians might seek to respond to them for electoral or ideological reasons.[71] Indeed, there is some evidence to indicate that politically influential groups were concerned about education prior to the reformist initiatives. Universities and think tanks, for example, at times generated critiques of current policies and organized seminars and conferences to raise concerns about the quality of education.[72]

Table 2.13

Concerns of Citizens in Latin America, 1998*

	Education	Labor Market**	Crime and Drugs +	Corruption	Poverty	Inflation/ Price Increases	Terrorism/ Political Violence	Health	Other ++	Don't Know
Argentina	18.8%	47.8%	08.6%	09.8%	03.9%	00.8%	03.7%	01.7%	03.9%	00.4%
Bolivia	27.5	24.4	03.7	09.4	10.2	02.3	00.8	05.7	06.8	05.8
Brazil	06.4	49.9	15.9	05.5	03.9	00.9	04.5	08.9	03.9	00.2
Colombia	09.4	33.9	02.6	06.9	05.8	03.3	32.3	02.7	03.3	00.0
Costa Rica	15.7	20.9	19.5	13.5	06.6	07.7	04.5	00.6	10.1	00.0
Chile	10.4	41.5	12.4	02.1	05.6	05.1	06.0	06.1	10.7	00.0
Ecuador	21.6	29.2	06.6	08.2	08.4	09.8	05.3	02.6	07.2	00.7
El Salvador	24.1	29.2	19.1	04.2	02.7	06.3	02.1	02.1	10.1	00.0
Guatemala	57.2	06.5	13.4	03.8	07.6	02.2	02.1	02.4	04.5	00.0
Honduras	27.4	16.3	21.2	07.1	08.9	07.1	02.6	02.4	06.4	00.4
México	06.3	28.0	11.5	08.7	08.8	21.1	02.7	02.4	10.2	00.3
Nicaragua	17.1	42.4	09.0	08.3	07.8	05.8	01.8	02.0	04.2	00.7
Panama	14.7	44.8	07.2	03.0	09.6	04.8	01.8	07.4	06.0	00.3
Paraguay	33.0	22.5	04.7	06.7	03.8	03.3	02.8	08.2	04.0	09.0
Peru	11.7	58.5	04.4	03.3	10.7	02.5	03.2	01.4	03.3	00.9
Uruguay	07.6	60.3	10.4	02.8	04.0	02.0	02.2	02.5	07.8	00.2
Venezuela	28.1	18.8	08.8	14.3	03.4	09.0	02.5	08.1	04.5	00.5

Source: Latinobarómetro (1998).

* The question asked was: "From the list of problems that I am going to show you, which would you consider to be the most important?"

** Combines four responses: low salaries, conditions in the labor market, unemployment, and opportunities for the young. When these responses are disaggregated, education captures first place among respondent concerns in Bolivia, Costa Rica, Ecuador, El Salvador, Guatemala, Honduras, Nicaragua, Paraguay, and Venezuela.

+ Combines two responses: crime and drugs.

++ Combines three responses: environment, health, and other.

Table 2.14

Public Opinion about Education, 1995*

	Primary				Secondary				University			
	% Very Good	% Good	% Somewhat Deficient	% Very Deficient	% Very Good	% Good	% Somewhat Deficient	% Very Deficient	% Very Good	% Good	% Somewhat Deficient	% Very Deficient
Argentina	03.5	29.1	45.2	19.6	02.8	30.1	47.3	15.3	10.4	35.6	26.6	08.4
Bolivia	18.1	40.7	31.2	07.3	10.8	51.5	29.1	05.4	22.5	44.6	18.9	07.8
Brazil	02.8	38.1	40.0	17.4	03.5	44.4	33.9	25.8	05.8	51.7	25.8	09.5
Colombia	16.3	41.7	31.6	09.6	15.8	42.8	31.6	08.5	21.3	44.9	19.3	07.6
Costa Rica	49.1	34.2	12.6	28.0	45.2	35.8	13.4	03.5	03.9	58.1	31.6	05.4
Chile	14.6	50.7	26.2	06.8	17.0	46.0	29.5	05.3	30.5	45.4	11.3	02.7
Ecuador	10.7	45.7	33.4	08.5	10.1	47.9	32.7	06.7	15.2	44.4	25.3	07.9
El Salvador	28.3	53.6	15.2	02.0	22.4	55.3	17.3	02.1	33.7	46.7	12.1	01.3
Guatemala	24.0	38.3	30.0	05.1	23.7	41.7	27.1	14.8	37.4	41.1	14.8	03.3
Honduras	24.2	43.6	26.2	04.4	22.9	48.3	22.7	36.0	25.7	45.0	19.1	03.4
Mexico	17.9	54.4	34.8	10.5	18.9	51.2	33.1	12.7	22.8	34.8	21.5	12.3
Nicaragua	23.4	48.3	22.7	04.2	22.4	49.3	23.0	04.0	28.4	49.4	14.9	02.9
Panama	12.2	48.2	32.1	06.6	09.6	49.9	33.0	06.6	16.9	51.8	23.3	04.3
Paraguay	08.5	46.3	35.3	06.7	06.0	50.2	34.0	05.5	14.0	48.3	19.8	04.2
Peru	08.3	41.3	35.8	12.1	06.4	40.9	35.1	12.6	09.4	47.0	23.3	05.6
Uruguay	16.4	54.3	24.8	02.8	14.3	49.6	29.2	03.7	17.0	47.3	18.0	04.4
Venezuela	05.3	19.3	44.3	29.9	04.6	19.9	42.9	31.8	08.7	26.6	33.8	27.9

Source: Latinobarómetro (1995).

* The question asked was: "We would like to know your opinion about education in [country]. Taking everything into consideration, would you say that [country's] primary education is very good, good, somewhat deficient, or very deficient? What about secondary education? And what about university education?"

In addition, in several countries, national meetings brought together representatives of important groups to discuss education problems. In Argentina, a National Pedagogical Congress composed of representatives of the Church, academics, bureaucrats, professionals, the unions, and provincial governments debated education issues between 1984 and 1988 and helped raise their salience in that country.[73] In Venezuela, a presidential commission was convened in 1985 to assess conditions in the sector; a national education congress followed in 1989.[74] Ecuador was the site of two similar national education congresses during the 1990s.[75] In 1990, a nonprofit organization of concerned business elites in the Dominican Republic sponsored a broad consultation with the ministry of education, the teachers' union, the Catholic Church, the universities, and a variety of NGOs and subsequently promoted a national education plan.[76] Education decentralization was a focus of concern in the Colombian Constituent Assembly in 1991.[77]

Nevertheless, due to the need to generate consensus among participants with distinct interests, commission and conference results tended to be long on statements about the importance of education to national development and short on concrete ideas about what needed to be changed. With the exception of the Dominican Republic, few such activities could be directly linked to concrete government commitments to alter existing conditions. At most, they signaled that some groups would be receptive to such commitments.

Moreover, many national education commissions were created after reforms had been designed. In El Salvador, such a council was created in 1995 to provide advice and feedback to the ministry on the reform of 1991; a similar advisory group was appointed in Uruguay in the wake of a reform initiative.[78] In Bolivia, a national council composed of reform opponents coalesced after an initiative was announced.[79] Reform evaluation councils were also created in that country and in Paraguay after new policies were in place. In Costa Rica, an activist minister spearheaded a national consultation on education reform as a way of promoting his reform agenda.[80] Presidents in Colombia and Chile appointed education commissions with similar motivations. In Argentina, a national education pact was created two years after a reform was approved, and a council of ministers of education from the provinces was convened by the national ministry. Thus, although there was generalized concern about the sector in many countries, mobilization of support and opposition was frequently a response to an education agenda, not a stimulus to it.

There was also little evidence of nonelite mobilization around the need to alter national education systems. Although a large number of nongovernmental and religious organizations became involved in education activities during the 1980s and 1990s, almost all of them worked at grassroots levels to introduce new approaches to education; very few became actively engaged in lobbying government to overhaul the education system in general. Bolivia and Ecuador provide partial exceptions to this pattern; in both countries, organizations of indigenous groups mobilized to press for the introduction of bilingual education prior to broader reformist initiatives. In Bolivia, teachers' unions and the peak labor organization joined in advocacy of this change. With the possible exception of Uruguay, I found no evidence that groups of parents actively organized to demand changes in the sector.[81]

In most countries, then, education was considered important by many citizens and in a number of countries, there had been national discussions of the issue. At the same time, however, there was little evidence that specific interest group lobbying or mobilized public demand had pressed the issue of education reform on political leaders. Interest group pressure, like other political conditions, did not seem to be consistently associated with Latin America's education reform initiatives.

Politicians, Reformers, and Agendas

Cross-national patterns of economic and political factors that might explain when education reforms got on political agendas appear to be elusive. By examining individual cases of reform, however, it might still be possible to identify some generalizations about agenda-setting dynamics. Indeed, an analysis of twelve cases found that presidents and other high-level officials largely controlled when and how education reform was raised in political circles. They also played a major role in determining why the issue of education was important to pursue. Thus, specific education reform initiatives could largely be understood as elite projects that emerged from centers of decision-making power.

Reform proponents were consistently located in the executive branch, but their specific position varied across countries. In Mexico and Bolivia, presidents gave strong backing to reformist drives. In other countries, the most common pattern was that of ministerial activists raising the reform flag. In Brazil, Minister of Education Paulo Renato undertook a series of activities to encourage state governments to go further in promoting education; his actions were replicated in a number of states by activist ministers of education.[82] Long before the president championed reform in Bolivia, a small group of committed reformers worked on national education in the planning ministry. In Costa Rica, education minister Eduardo Doryan, relying on the political support he had from the president and his own popularity, advocated reform of the system. Similarly, in Nicaragua and Uruguay, ministers of education Humberto Belli and Germán Rama took on this task.[83] In fact, in Uruguay, the reformist initiative was known as the "Rama Reform."[84] Chile's Ricardo Lago raised the issue of education reform when he was minister between 1990 and 1992, and El Salvador's Cecilia Gallardo de Cano stood out as the initiator of that country's education reform.[85] In Peru, ministers of finance, labor, and transport led the education reform initiative.[86]

In general, education was championed because it was part of a larger set of concerns of these political executives. In some cases, education was part of a project about the modernization of the state and the economy. As such, it was an ingredient in more general neoliberal initiatives involving efforts to move to a market economy and restructure the role of the state in society. Chile's education reforms of the 1980s set a model for neoliberal thinking about how the provision of public services could approximate the functioning of markets. In Mexico, modernization of the economy was an explicit purpose of the president, although the education reform was not cast in a market-oriented mold. Costa Rica's minister was clear that education would play a part in promoting the fortunes of the country in a new, more competitive global economy.[87] In Peru, education became widely associated with a broad set of market-oriented reforms sought by President Fujimori.[88] In Bolivia, President Gonzalo Sánchez de Lozada believed that education was centrally important to the modernization of Bolivia's economy and society and a key to poverty alleviation.

Education was also part of a larger reformist initiative in several countries that had experienced or were experiencing deep political conflicts. In these cases, improving the quality of education was expected to strengthen the legitimacy of the national state and help overcome some of the consequences of conflict and violence. In Colombia, years of political and military strife had produced a state that was weak in its capacity to deliver public services and to resolve conflict, a state that was held in low regard by citizens. Reformers believed that decentralizing education and other public services would improve their performance and provide tangible evidence of a more effective—and more democratic—state. It was also expected to give evidence of greater capacity to resolve conflicts and create conditions for civil peace.[89] Strengthening state legitimacy also stood behind presidential commitment to decentralization in Venezuela.[90] In El Salvador, education reform emerged in the context of the peace process and offered reformers an opportunity to incorporate—possibly co-opt—"practical" teachers who had been providing education in regions controlled by guerrilla forces.[91] In Nicaragua, new textbooks and school autonomy provided reform advocates with a way to counteract ten years of revolutionary ideology and organization in the school system.[92]

In some countries, reforms were distant from any concern to improve education. In Argentina in 1991 and in the 1981 reform in Chile, for example, fiscal unburdening was the principal motivator of decentralization of education.[93] Some state-level Brazilian reformers advocated decentralization to municipalities out of similar kinds of efforts to shift the fiscal burden to other levels of government.[94] In some cases, also, reformers were particularly concerned about the strength of the teachers' unions and sought reform as a way of weakening their hold on the administration and delivery of education and their prominence in national politics. In Mexico, President Salinas was convinced that his modernizing project could not go forward without weakening the powerful teachers' union.[95] In Bolivia, education reformers were committed to breaking the education union, and in Colombia, an important objective of reformers was weakening the teachers' organization.[96]

In summary, then, the protagonists who sought to put reform on the agendas of government were activist presidents and ministers. Their motivations were mixed, but included education reform as a feature of broader political projects to modernize the economy, legitimate the state, increase the likelihood of peace or the hegemony of the winners in war-torn countries, shift the fiscal burden of education to others, or weaken the teachers' unions. In subsequent chapters, these agenda-setting dynamics will be revisited in closer examination of reform initiatives in Bolivia, Ecuador, Mexico, Minas Gerais, and Nicaragua.

Chapter Three

SPONSORING REFORM: EXECUTIVE LEADERSHIP, FORMIDABLE CONSTRAINTS

ADVOCATES OF REFORM in Latin America in the 1990s certainly could argue that better education was an important and necessary step toward economic development, more democratic polities, and greater security and equity for their societies. And they could certainly demonstrate national education systems in need of reform. As indicated in the last chapter, the condition of most public school systems was dismal, evidence of the failure to prepare students for productive lives was abundant, and arguments about the benefits of change were persuasive. The reform-minded could consider such factors to be propitious for launching proposals for change.

Important barriers to change warned of the magnitude of the political task they would be taking on, however. Unions would counter proposals for change with demands for better salaries and benefits. They would point to the difficulties teachers faced in the classroom and in their communities; they would protest against the pauperization of the profession. They would question the motivations of the reformers and accuse governments of seeking to privatize public responsibilities for education. Strikes could be anticipated. In addition, reformers would face the opposition of ministries and political parties. Frequently, too, a legacy of failed reform initiatives would lend credence to pessimism about change—similar initiatives had failed in the past, why should they succeed now?

In these contentious environments, presidents in Mexico and Bolivia actively sought to put education reform on national political agendas. In Ecuador, Minas Gerais, and Nicaragua, education ministers took up the reform banner. Studies of the political economy of reform at times refer to the activities of reform mongers, policy entrepreneurs, heroes, or champions who take up a reform initiative and promote it, often in the face of difficult odds such as those described earlier.[1] This characterization certainly fits the main protagonists in education reform initiatives in the case study countries. They were committed, focused, and often astute in the ways they went about trying to introduce new policies. They had strong ideas about how best to improve education in their countries. Some of them were even heroic in the face of resistance.

In this chapter, however, I am less interested in characterizing these protagonists as heroes than in exploring the political factors that surrounded their reformist agendas and assessing the strategies they chose to promote change. What emerges is a description of the role of leadership in seizing the initiative to alter structures of interest and institutional power. In this chapter, case histories from five countries reveal how policy leadership by political executives mattered in creating increased political space for reform projects.

Each of the cases presents a unique history of reform mongering, yet there are important similarities in the strategies adopted by the proponents of change. As indicated in the conclusion to this chapter, in all countries, a tradition of policy leadership by executives provided an opportunity for reformers to get their ideas on the table. Presidents and ministers attempted to time reform initiatives for moments when conditions were ripe for their approval. They used their powers of appointment to bring others committed to change into positions of leadership. They attempted to weaken the power of unions to resist change. In addition, the lack of well-organized public pressure for promoting education, while robbing them of much needed support, also allowed them to take the lead in defining the terms of debate for their change proposals.

CREATING THE RIGHT CONTEXT: MEXICO

In 1992, the president of Mexico, Carlos Salinas, and his minister of education, Ernesto Zedillo, sat down with the leadership of the Sindicato Nacional de Trabajadores de la Educación (SNTE), and governors of the country's thirty-ones states to sign the National Agreement for the Modernization of Basic and Normal Education.[2] This agreement, the culmination of a long-term effort to decentralize to the state level, restructured education decision making and implementation in the country. It gave governors the responsibility for basic (preschool, primary, and secondary) education and for normal school training of teachers. According to the agreement, states would take on the task of managing some 690,000 teachers and administrators. They would also take responsibility for 1.8 million children in preprimary education, 9.2 million in primary schools, and 2.4 million in secondary schools.[3] Henceforth, states would receive annual educational grants from the federal government and could add additional revenue from their own resources if they wished.

The agreement also created a new career system for teachers, giving them opportunities for professional development and promotion not available earlier. Other innovations were a curriculum more focused on conceptual learning and bilingual education for indigenous groups. The career system would be managed by the central government, as would curriculum and the design and distribution of free textbooks. In addition, central administrators would continue to define training programs for teachers and school personnel, manage testing and monitoring of school performance, and set the basic salaries and working conditions for teachers.[4] In addition, the number of years of compulsory education was increased, local school councils were mandated, in-service training of teachers was expanded, and the annual number of days of schooling was extended.

The 1992 agreement between government, the states, and the teachers' union was a significant achievement in the decentralization of Mexican education, even though it maintained a major role for the national government in education. It was expected to open up opportunities to improve the quality of the country's education. Certainly change was needed. For primary education, 9 percent of students were repeating grades, and only 86 percent of those enrolled were reaching fifth grade.[5] Third grade students scored significantly below the Latin American average on tests of language and mathematics and fourth grade students only slightly above it.[6] Some 15 percent of teachers in the system did not have officially defined qualifications for their jobs.[7] Moreover, as indicated in the previous chapter, rich and poor students had widely different survival rates in school. Indigenous children and those living in poor rural areas were those most afflicted by low achievement.[8] In 1994, 90.1 percent of urban fourteen- and fifteen-year-olds had completed primary school; in rural areas, the rate was 67.5 percent.[9]

To remedy such conditions, decentralization had been sought by several presidents but never effectively achieved. Their failures had all been laid at the door of the teachers' union, SNTE. With over a million members in the early 1990s, it was the only labor organization to represent teachers and educational administrators in the country. SNTE was a highly centralized organization that concentrated enormous power in the hands of its national executive committee. Traditionally, this committee was an instrument wielded by a powerful boss, the secretary-general of the union. In the 1980s, the union was controlled by a self-styled "leader for life and moral guide," Carlos Jonguitud Barrios, whose Revolutionary Vanguard movement had taken control of the national executive committee at gunpoint in 1972. He was widely believed to use gangster-like tactics in managing the organization and expanding his own power and fortune. He was in a good position to do this, given the wealth of SNTE. The union collected 1 percent of teachers' salaries and owned department stores, hospitals, hotels, funeral homes, and other businesses.

Since its founding in 1943, SNTE had been closely linked to Mexico's dominant party, the Partido Revolucionario Institutional (PRI) and was important in maintaining labor peace in the education sector. As part of the National Confederation of Popular Organizations (CNOP), one of the corporatist pillars of the PRI, the union was a powerful player in the country's politics. SNTE controlled a number of political positions in the legislature and the executive branch. In the late 1980s, leader Jonguitud was a national senator, and the union controlled sixteen seats in the chamber of deputies as well as forty-two seats in state-level legislatures; it controlled over one hundred mayors.[10] SNTE had long dominated the national ministry of education through its ability to name people to important posts, including several vice-ministerial positions.[11] Its patronage was important to teachers, as it was able to make a number of perquisites available to them—leaves, loans, and assistance in getting attention from the ministry.[12] Characteristically, school directors, those who headed regional offices of the ministry, and school inspectors were the local arms of the union.

The centralization and power of SNTE mirrored the structure of the education system. While the Constitution of 1917 assigned responsibility for primary education to the municipalities and for secondary and normal schools to the states, and although they began to develop education systems after the Revolution of 1910, the establishment of a national education ministry in 1921 initiated a long process of centralization. The country's most revered educator, José Vasconcelos, who spearheaded this process, was eager to increase access to education throughout the country and acted in the belief that the states and municipalities were not doing enough to achieve this goal.[13] He set a trend. In 1928, 20 percent of students were in the national system; by the early 1990s, 76 percent of public school students and teachers and 79 percent of the public schools were part of the national system.[14] At this time, the federal government contributed some 80 percent of the total educational budget.

Throughout this period, curriculum and teaching materials were determined in Mexico City, as were hiring, promoting, and firing teachers, salaries of all personnel, the distribution of funds to local schools, and school location and construction activities. Teacher training was a centralized task, and a national system of free textbooks, initiated in the late 1950s, helped cement the central government's role in the curriculum. The union gained from this system also; with centralization, its own power increased. The 1960s and 1970s were a period of extensive growth in the educational system and in the 1970s, a half million new teachers were hired, each of them duly registered in the union. Thus, during this extended period, the national ministry and the union shared a strong interest in promoting centralization.

Efforts to reverse this trend emerged in the late 1950s, when a reform-minded minister, Jaime Torres Bodet, sought to decentralize administrative functions of the ministry to the state and municipal level and to diminish the amount of red tape in the system.[15] Union opposition defeated

this effort, as it did another ministerial initiative focused on decentralization in 1969. In 1978, another education minister tried to regain control
by the ministry of its own household by creating offices in every state,
staffing them with officials whose first loyalty was to the ministry, and
giving them responsibility for administration and "non-core" curriculum.[16] It was not long, however, before the union asserted power over
these regional offices and claimed ownership of the directors' positions. A
subsequent effort, meant to transfer these offices to the state governments,
was announced in late 1982 by President Miguel de la Madrid, but union
and ministry opposition was so strong that the change was never approved
by the congress.[17]

    Given the extraordinary presidentialism of Mexico's traditional PRI-
dominated system, these experiences say much about the power of the
union. Moreover, efforts to press forward with change in the 1980s created significant tension with the union's leadership at a time when a severe
economic crisis was cutting into teacher salaries and benefits. Angry primary teachers claimed their wages had declined by 63 percent between
1982 and 1989.[18] Moreover, a significant minority within the union was
calling for increased internal democracy and blamed the PRI government
for its support of Jonguitud Barrios. According to one observer: "The
period between 1978 and 1989 was a period of complete immobility in
the relationship between the government and the union—it was a time
when nothing could be achieved" because of these tensions.[19] Moreover,
by the late 1980s, the ministry of education had become a "gigantic and
impotent bureaucratic apparatus occupying the major part of its time in
tending to internal conflicts and those with the union."[20]

    Thus, on December 1, 1988, when Carlos Salinas became president, he
could anticipate that SNTE, the PRI, and the ministry would all be firmly
opposed to any plan to alter the structure, administration, or standards of
the education system. The president, however, was interested in pursuing
such changes. In no small part, his attention to education was due to
ongoing conflict with the union and his concern with political unrest; at
that point, dissident teachers were creating major public disruptions as
they protested against union leadership and low salaries. Certainly getting the teachers back to the classrooms helps explain his interest in the
issue of education, as does his concern with evidence that dissident teachers were attracted to an opposition party that was threatening the hegemony of the PRI. Nevertheless, these concerns could easily have been
addressed without promoting the kind of changes he thought essential to
the education system.

    In addition to political concerns about SNTE and dissident teachers,
the president was convinced that improved education would have an impact on the distribution of income in the country—with better education

would come better opportunities for poor people to improve their standards of living.[21] In such a perspective, interest in education reform was derivative of the modernization of the country's economy. In his words, the country needed to "reformulate content and methods, maintain a sense of open and modern nationalism, and provide a level of quality that would be competitive worldwide."[22] Moreover, as he admitted some years later, the fact that his mother had been a public school teacher gave him some sympathy for the claims of the teachers.[23] His motivation, then, emerged from political, economic, and personal concerns.

In championing change, however, Salinas faced a significant political dilemma. He was well aware that little could be done to improve the educational system unless the power of SNTE were reduced. His years in government and his prior position as minister of planning and budgeting (1982–1988), where he was involved in annual negotiations with the union over salaries and benefits, had given him a good understanding of the problems created by this organization. But the legacy of prior reform initiatives was also a clear reminder of the importance of SNTE to the management of change. The union was too strong to ignore. And, if the union were somehow destroyed by the government, there would be no structure to control the teachers and their demands, a situation inimical to a basic organizing principle of the PRI regime.

Such an assessment was based not only on the demonstrable power of SNTE and its allies in the ministry, but also on the uncharacteristically weak position of the president after his election in 1988. He garnered a bare 50.7 percent of the vote, the lowest percentage ever received by a PRI candidate until that time, and it was widely claimed that only fraud, coercion, and violence had allowed the PRI to wrest the election from the Partido Revolucionario Democrático (PRD).[24] Although the PRI maintained its majority in the chamber of deputies, with 260 out of 500 seats, it did not have enough votes for passing important legislation and constitutional amendments. Indeed, the authority and legitimacy of the PRI-led government was at its lowest point in decades.[25]

Salinas's situation was not helped by the economic problems that had afflicted the country since 1982. GDP growth in 1988 was 1.2 percent, the public sector deficit was 10.4 percent of GDP, and inflation was running at 114 percent. Real wages were down another 1.3 percent after years of even more significant declines. The external debt reached $100 billion.[26] Added to an increasing crisis of political legitimacy and confidence in the regime, the economic situation further affected support for the PRI government. In 1989, half of respondents in a poll stated that they believed a revolution could be expected within five years.[27] To add to the difficulties, many of the party bosses of the PRI distrusted Salinas and resented the technocratic style he brought into the cabinet and the office of the presidency. Large and important groups of citizens, including the teachers, were deeply angry with the government over declining wages.[28] These were hardly propitious circumstances for undertaking reform.

His first priority, then, was to reassert the traditional power of the Mexican presidency. Accordingly, within weeks of taking office, Salinas ordered the arrest of the powerful and corrupt leader of the petroleum workers' union. The notorious and previously untouchable "La Quina" was jailed in a move that was seen as a clear flexing of presidential muscle. SNTE then offered him another opportunity to achieve a similar win.

The Coordinadora Nacional de Trabajadores de la Educación (CNTE), a movement of teachers based in the country's southern states, had been formed within the union in 1979 to protest against general economic conditions, low teacher salaries, lack of internal union democracy, and the close association of the union with the PRI.[29] In 1980, it engaged in a national march and a sit-in, which, at the time, were new strategies for political protest in the country. Throughout the 1980s, even as SNTE gained increasing control over the ministry, CNTE challenged the government to improve teacher conditions and the union to increase its democratic accountability. Late in the decade, the dissident group claimed a membership of some three hundred thousand teachers. Just as Salinas took office, CNTE vociferously demanded changes in government policy and union practices. In the wake of these demands, SNTE's leadership held a national congress in February 1989 and virtually banished dissident voices within the union. In response, CNTE protested publicly.

In the following months, strikes, mass demonstrations, sit-ins, and marches punctuated the political scene.[30] According to the official record, between February and May, Mexico City experienced "41 marches, 18 meetings, 60 assemblies of union locals, six national assemblies, four forums, two walkouts . . . , six sit-ins . . . and 32 sessions of negotiations."[31] CNTE strikers demanded a doubling of their salaries to make up for the bite that austerity and inflation had taken during the past seven years. In addition, they demanded that the government ensure greater internal democracy in SNTE, that union boss Jonguitud Barrios be deposed, and that the alliance with the PRI be severed. Ending the reign of Jonguitud, who was accused of masterminding the assassination of at least 150 dissident teachers, primarily in the southern states of Oaxaca and Chiapas, was central to CNTE demands.

As the confrontation between the teachers and the government escalated, a half million teachers participated in a twenty-six-day work stoppage in April; schoolchildren throughout the country had an unexpected holiday.[32] In an unusual demonstration of force, parents and university professors joined the teachers in a massive demonstration in Mexico City on April 17. Indeed, the period between February and May was a chaotic one, with CNTE deeply engaged in protest, SNTE leadership trying to control it, and the ministry of education condemning it.[33] For the government, the scope of the protest was alarming—on April 1, Salinas reports having written: "The situation with the teachers is critical. We may go into a state of emergency."[34]

These events raised uncomfortable alternatives for the president. Giving in to the economic demands of the teachers would mean the destruction of the Pact for Economic Growth and Stabilization, his plan for overcoming inflation and introducing an array of economic reforms. Moreover, there was danger in succumbing to the demand to depose Jonguitud. Certainly a large and powerful union without a powerful boss could further threaten the already shaky PRI regime. From this perspective, the fact that CNTE dissidents favored the left-of-center PRD was cause for some alarm. On the other hand, if Jonguitud remained, the SNTE would be a union in disarray, unable to stifle opposition to its boss.

The president's next actions helped resolve this dilemma in a way that was propitious for future reform, however. On April 23, Jonguitud was called to a meeting with the president and given no alternative but to resign. The once-powerful boss of the union did so as he left the meeting, and his second in command soon followed suit. Jonguitud's downfall was widely seen as a successful assertion of presidential power and a message to other unions that might defy Salinas's leadership. Two days later, with presidential blessing, a new secretary-general, Elba Ester Gordillo, was elected to head SNTE.[35] Gordillo had long worked within the leadership group of the union as a close associate of Jonguitud, and, for the newly powerful CNTE, represented the old guard. Moreover, she was emblematic of the kind of imposed leadership characterizing the presidentialist system CNTE activists wanted to see reformed. Despite their preferences, however, and in the face of dissent and competition from other contenders, Salinas was clear in his support for Gordillo; CNTE dissidents were faced with a fait accompli.

Gordillo's task was clear—she had to bring more order and coherence to the union by incorporating the dissidents and weakening the remnants of Jonguitud's machine.[36] She had to work her way into a position of undisputed leadership in the organization. She was largely successful in achieving these objectives. Gradually, her ability to be more flexible than Jonguitud and to respond to some of the demands of the dissidents worked to calm the storms within the union. In addition, in May, the government and the union were able to settle on a 25 percent increase in teacher salaries, which, with the ousting of Jonguitud, was sufficient to send them back to the classroom with some gain, even if it was far short of what they wanted. Then, in October 1989, Salinas announced the plan for the modernization of the education system.

Despite Salinas's gains, the ministry of education was still primarily a creature of SNTE. Manuel Bartlett, the minister of education and a veteran politician, was given the task of wresting control of the organization from the union. He was able to take advantage of a period during which union leaders were focusing on internal conflicts to regain the right to select his own people to head important positions, "doing the dirty work of reclaiming the ministry from the union," as one observer commented.[37] Nevertheless, SNTE was still formidable, its membership intact, and its capacity to corral votes and mobilize labor actions still largely in place. And, with congressional elections looming in 1991, the president was well-advised not to insist on a change that would further annoy the union. Its votes were needed.

The 1991 elections provided a considerable boost to the president. The PRI garnered 61.5 percent of the vote and, with 320 seats in congress, regained the two-thirds majority needed to pass important legislation. To add to this improved environment, the economy had grown by 3.4 percent in 1989 and 4.5 percent in 1990, a very positive experience after the difficult times of the early and mid-1980s; growth continued into 1991.[38] Inflation was reduced to 20 percent in 1989 and capital began to flow back into the country. The president had also instituted a highly popular social fund program, PRONASOL, which garnered him both popular and political support.[39] In addition, teachers received significant wage increases between 1989 and 1991, and these helped defuse union demands for economic justice.[40] Thus, the president was at the peak of his power at the midpoint of his administration. In January 1992, Salinas appointed his minister of planning and budgeting, Ernesto Zedillo, to the post of education minister, with instructions to move the education reform forward.

A POLITICAL ORPHAN AND A PRESIDENTIAL ADOPTION: BOLIVIA

In 1994, the Bolivian congress approved a comprehensive reform that included a wide range of initiatives to improve the quality and relevance of education in the country. The new education law included provisions for institutional strengthening in the ministry of education, decentralization, curricular development and teacher training, professionalization of the teaching career, bilingual education, emphasis on girls' and rural education, community-level parent councils, national testing, and new standards for hiring and promoting teachers and school administrators. Other legislation passed in the same year decentralized responsibilities for educational infrastructure.[41] In 1995, a decentralization law transferred responsibilities for educational personnel to departmental prefectures.

The country's education system was sorely in need of reform in the mid-1990s. By the 1980s, it was serving a growing number of Bolivians increasingly poorly. Geographically, the country was a crazy quilt of high mountains and plateaus, deep valleys, broad plains, and Amazonian jungle, contributing significant problems for communication and policy management. Roads could be impassible during the rainy season, and many villages could be reached only by foot or animal even in good weather. Constructing schools, providing textbooks and teaching materials, and training and monitoring teachers in remote areas was extraordinarily difficult. Until 1993, the ministry of education did not even have accurate records about how many schools, teachers, supervisors, or students there were in the country or where they were located. What figures did exist indicated that rural and indigenous children fell far behind urban children in educational achievement. Over 20 percent of teachers had only a secondary school education, 70 percent were products of the country's normal schools, and less than 2 percent had a university education.[42] Many parents, particularly among the middle classes, were choosing to enroll their children in private or parochial schools because of the low quality of the public system.

Education policies of the past had created difficult problems that needed to be addressed. One of these involved the language of instruction. In the early 1990s, 55 percent of Bolivia's population was made up of indigenous groups whose first language was Aymara, Quechua, Guaraní, or another Amerindian language. Twenty-seven percent of the rural population did not speak Spanish, even as a second language.[43] While the 1952 revolution brought citizenship rights to the nation's rural and indigenous poor, economic, social, and political exclusion continued to relegate this population to second-class status. The last significant education reform, in 1955, had mandated Spanish as the language of instruction and championed the idea of the *escuela única*, a "national classroom" in which all Bolivians would sit together, wearing identical uniforms and studying the same curriculum, regardless of social status, ethnic origin, or geography. Many education specialists, however, had come to believe that early instruction in Spanish was actually encouraging indigenous children to drop out of school or to repeat grades at much higher rates than Spanish-speaking children.

Education had also suffered from dire economic conditions in the 1980s. In the early 1980s, the country experienced a devastating economic crisis just as it was also making a concerted effort to return to democratic rule after a turbulent period of coups, countercoups, and electoral instability. Between 1981 and 1985, per capita annual income fell from an average of $590 to $440, while growth fell precipitously and inflation reached a high of 26,000 percent during 1985. Only the underground economy, fueled by drug production, enabled many Bolivians to survive

this difficult period. In 1985, the government announced a radical stabilization and structural adjustment program, the New Economic Policy
(NPE), which reduced inflation dramatically and set the country on a
course toward economic liberalization. Succeeding governments were
able to maintain the adjustment process, but the cost was high in terms
of political repression of unions and cuts in public expenditures for traditional social services such as education.[44]

But the context for pursuing education changes looked no more promising in Bolivia than it had in Mexico. After the return to democratic government in 1982, and although politicians and elites from time to time
proclaimed that reform was needed, presidents had not given much attention to the sector. In fact, although the reform initiative had a history
dating back to the mid-1980s, it did not find a committed political spon-
sor until 1993. Political leaders had good reason to be skeptical of the
benefits of sponsoring change in the educational system. Teachers' unions
had considerable capacity to disrupt the always-fragile political peace of
the country. Annually, their strikes delayed the start of the school year and
caused paralysis in the ministry of education.

Accommodation between government and unions was common in the
wake of strikes and protests, but the public face of government-union interaction was one of confrontation, distrust, and bitterness. The Confederación de Trabajadores de la Educación Urbana de Bolivia (CTEUB),
along with its constituent federations, were feared by government because
of their capacity to mobilize street protests. The Confederación Nacional
de Maestros Rurales de Bolivia (CONMERB) was equally well known for
its marches in La Paz and other cities and had a reputation for violent
protest. Not surprisingly, education ministry leaders tried hard to keep
relations with the unions on an even keel and to avoid conflict at all costs.
Appointments as minister of education were usually made as part of strategies for creating governing coalitions in congress; in reality, the minister
was generally selected by one of the small parties in exchange for agreeing
to join the government. Tenure was usually brief. Between 1991 and the
middle of 1993, for example, three people held the ministerial post. The
ministry employed some six hundred people and almost all of them owed
their jobs to the unions.

This was the situation that confronted initial efforts to address education. Despite clear indications that the path toward change would be a
very rocky one, some public officials in the mid-1980s began developing
ideas about improving the system. An early proponent of change was the
minister of education during the presidency of Víctor Paz Estenssoro
(1985–1989) who put his staff to work producing a statement about the
urgent need for education reform in the country. The *Libro Blanco,* an
outline of a plan for reform, and the *Libro Rosado,* the subsequent defini-

tion of an actual program that could be presented to congress, helped open the door to the idea of reform. Although the proposal did not result in any action, it was notable for having made the case for education as an urgent necessity and for having "broken with the inertia of the ministers that passed through the ministry of education."[45]

When Jaime Paz Zamora of the Movimiento de Izquierda Revolucionaria (MIR) became president in 1989, he selected Amalia Anaya to be the undersecretary of social policy in the powerful ministry of planning and coordination. A MIR activist, she had been in charge of formulating the party's social policy for the elections. Increasingly, she was convinced of the importance of "building human capital in the country in order to achieve higher levels of economic development" and of education reform "as the best way to improve the quality of life and to correct the inequitable distribution of income."[46] Between 1989 and 1993, Anaya's emerging education reform plan faced formidable opponents at the same time that it lacked strong political backing.

The top-heavy ministry of education was resentful of any initiative sponsored by those outside the organization, including those in the ministry of planning. Early plans for reform were stymied when the education ministry refused to share with Anaya and her team what little information it had about conditions in the sector or the number and location of those who worked for it. In addition, the ideas taking shape in the planning ministry impinged directly on the interests of both union confederations. In particular, the emerging plan opened up the teaching profession to those who were not graduates of the country's normal schools; it provided for evaluating and promoting teachers on the basis of merit, not strictly on seniority; it made union membership voluntary and eliminated automatic subventions from teacher salaries to union dues; it mandated performance standards and testing for teachers; and it said nothing about salaries. The teachers' organizations wanted respect for the principle of seniority, obligatory union membership, salary increases, and the continuation of normal school education and guaranteed employment of their graduates.

The development of the reform plan was also stymied by division within the Paz administration about the wisdom of changing the education system. The minister of planning was a staunch supporter of it, as was the minister of finance. But these important ministers faced the opposition of the minister of education and the concern of the rest of the cabinet that the plan would ignite too much political opposition, particularly from the unions. As the national elections of July 1993 approached, politicians became increasingly cautious about policy proposals that would certainly cause protests in the streets. For the next year, Paz Zamora kept the reform initiative on the shelf, not wishing to face mounting opposition in the context of impending elections.

Gonzalo Sánchez de Lozada, presidential candidate of the Movimiento Nacionalista Revolucionaria (MNR) Party and prominent economic reformer, was much more interested in education reform than Jaime Paz. Sánchez de Lozada emerged on the national political scene in 1985 as the principal architect of the radical economic policy changes that halted hyperinflation and began the introduction of a market-based economy in the country. In 1989, he was selected to head the MNR presidential ticket and won 23.1 percent of the total vote. His closest opponent garnered 22.7 percent. Without an absolute majority of the vote, however, the election would be decided by the congress. In that body, the decision went to third place winner Paz Zamora of the MIR, after intensive bargaining among prospective coalition partners in the legislature.

Sánchez de Lozada, reluctant to engage in the congressional horse trading that was important to put together a governing party coalition, believed he had been cheated of the presidency. In defeat, he and several associates created a think tank, the Fundación Milenio, to study opportunities for political and policy reforms.[47] The young technocrats recruited to work in the foundation were particularly concerned about altering the role of the state in Bolivia by curtailing many of its activities while simultaneously strengthening its efficiency and effectiveness, and opening up the economy to the forces of globalization. The *Plan de Todos*, the electoral platform of the MNR for the 1993 elections, emerged out of the work of this think tank. The plan, widely publicized during Sánchez de Lozada's campaign, gave considerable prominence to reforming the education system to increase quality and reduce poverty, even while it was vague about how these objectives were to be achieved. The idea of education reform was clearly linked to the modernization of the country, a theme that was carried into the campaign.

In the aftermath of the 1993 elections, Sánchez de Lozada demonstrated the capacity to learn from earlier experiences. With 35.6 percent of the popular vote, he turned to congress and actively sought alliances with several parties. This effort assured him the presidency, and he entered office committed to the three strategic pillars of the *Plan de Todos*—"capitalization" of state-owned enterprises, social development and poverty reduction through education and health reform, and popular participation in national development. All of these were brought together in the idea of modernizing the country and the state.

As president, Sánchez de Lozada surprised many by deciding not to start from scratch on a new education reform plan but to take on the orphaned proposal prepared by Anaya and her team.[48] Frequently, he referred to education as the "adopted, but much loved child" of his administration. He asked the vice president, Victor Hugo Cárdenas, an Aymara Indian who had been engaged in education throughout his life, to pay particular attention to the progress of the reform. Then, the president created a super-minister of human resources, giving his appointee responsibility for health, education, and related secretariats. Impressed by the planning ministry team, Sánchez de Lozada decided that it should become part of the ministry of education. Thus, in February 1994, a new reform unit began operation in the ministry, with Anaya as its head.

The detailed redrafting of the project delayed the adoption of what the unions were calling one of the "three damned laws" of the Sánchez de Lozada government.[49] Finally, however, the president submitted the education proposal to congress, marking it as one of three pillars that would contribute to building a new and modern country.[50] On July 7, 1994, Law 1565 was passed with little dissent in the national congress, despite the extensive controversy that had surrounded the emergence of the reformist plan under the previous administration and despite protests in the streets by the unions. The approval of the law was this easy because of the formal coalition between the MNR and several smaller parties in congress.[51] Indeed, the education reform was one of several significant and contentious policy initiatives legislated during the Sánchez de Lozada administration with little debate. Once the president had adopted the reform initiative from the beleaguered design team and given it priority, political approval was relatively easy.

FAST TRACK TO REFORM: MINAS GERAIS

In the Brazilian state of Minas Gerais, education reform happened much more quickly than it did in Mexico or Bolivia. Immediately after a new administration came to power in March 1991, the state minister of education, Walfrido Mares Guia Neto, announced a policy whose purpose was to address the low quality of education in Minas Gerais. Firmly supported by the governor, Helio Garcia, the reform provided for school-based decisions relating to administration, finance, and pedagogy. It addition, it strengthened the role of school directors who would be elected by communities through a competitive process. It also set up a system for community participation in decision making about school management and finance. Increased and improved teacher training was part of the new system, as was a program to test student learning in the third, fifth, and eighth grades. Finally, the reform sought better integration of municipal-level schools in the new system and more collaboration between the state and municipal systems.[52]

At the time of the reform, the state of Minas Gerais was responsible for 2.7 million students, some 12 percent of Brazil's total. The public system—made up of state and municipal schools—provided primary education for 93 percent of those enrolled in school in the state. Of these, 73 percent belonged to the state system. All together, there were 6,500 schools and 204,000 teachers and education employees in the state.[53] The system was not working well, however, either at the state or the municipal level. Only 18 percent of students finished primary school at the appropriate age. In 1991, 27.6 percent of students were repeaters, 50 percent of first graders were repeaters, and the dropout rate was 14 percent; these inefficiencies were estimated to cost the government $200 million a year.[54] Many teachers lacked the qualifications to perform effectively in the classroom, school directors were politically beholden to the politicians who appointed them, and school infrastructure and resources were allocated on the basis of patronage rather than need or planning.[55] These factors suggest that this large state system was providing relatively expensive education of poor quality to its children.

The roots of education reform in Minas Gerais can be traced back to important political changes that occurred at the national level in the 1970s and 1980s. In the late 1970s, widespread political mobilization encouraged the transition from a military dictatorship to a democratic regime. Among important political protests and strikes were those of the teachers of Minas Gerais, who demanded civil rights and a return to democracy and popular elections, along with improved salaries. They organized the União de Trabalhadores em Educação (UTE) in the state and were instrumental in the creation of a national confederation of teachers' unions. The confederation became part of Brazil's peak labor organization, the Central das União dos Trabalhadores (CUT), which in turn became affiliated with the Partido dos Trabalhadores (PT), which teachers and other public sector unions had helped form.

From this period, then, the teachers' union that emerged in Minas Gerais was mobilized around demands for democracy as well as for the rights of workers. In this regard, it differed from other teachers' unions in the extent to which it favored some aspects of school autonomy reform. Throughout the 1980s, the UTE mobilized strikes to demand a minimum salary and periodic adjustments for inflation, and they also called for public service examinations so that teachers could achieve civil service status and tenure, a career system for teachers, and greater autonomy at the school level. These reforms would diminish the extent to which teachers could be hired and fired through patronage and strengthen local control of the education system, opening up opportunities for the PT at this level. In 1986, UTE protested strongly when the state government did not hold firm on its promise to create a minimum salary for teachers and forced the legislature to act.

In 1990, UTE was reconstituted as the Sindicato Unico dos Trabalhadores em Educação (SINDUTE), which organizers hoped would be the only union to represent teachers in the state; in fact, estimates suggested that it represented about a third of the teachers in the state, some thirty to forty thousand of those who had regular teaching appointments.[56] The Associação de Professores Publicos de Minas Gerais (APPMG), which claimed to be apolitical and unaffiliated with any party, continued to draw support from as many as eleven thousand teachers.[57]

In addition to a series of strikes and efforts to mobilize teachers, other events in the 1980s helped raise the profile of public education in the state. In 1983, a statewide congress on education resulted in the Minas Plan for Education. Its recommendations, some of which were adopted, included the creation of local school boards, teacher hiring on the basis of clear and uniform standards, and the election of school directors. The 1988 constitution of Brazil promised that education was to be available to all Brazilians, and it gave responsibility for the provision of this service to the states. As a counterpart to the new federal constitution, the state of Minas Gerais approved a constitution in 1989 that described the system of government as democratic, decentralized, and participatory. It guaranteed the right to eight years of education and promised community participation in the provision of schooling. Further, it promised that poor children would receive economic assistance to attend school.[58]

In 1990, during the gubernatorial campaign of Helio Garcia of the Partido da Reforma Social (PRS), the candidate made a point of stressing the need to improve the state's faltering education system.[59] His main message was that the poor quality of the schools could be counteracted by allowing schools to have more decision-making autonomy and giving teachers, school directors, and parents more capacity to determine how each school operated. He asked campaign officials to begin drawing up plans for a reform, and when he won the election he used the transition period to further plans for new policies in several areas. His campaign coordinator, Walfrido Mares Guia Neto, played a key role in promoting ideas about how to change the education system and in selecting people to be engaged in the planning of it. Not incidentially, Mares Guia Neto had his eyes on the post of education minister in the new administration.

Thus, in January 1991, when Helio Garcia took office, considerable thought had already gone into what could be done to improve schooling in the state. He selected his campaign coordinator and longtime personal friend, Mares Guia Neto, as state minister of education and gave him the green light to proceed with developing the reform plan. The new minister seemed eager to take on this responsibility. He combined political experience with considerable expertise in management and education.[60] He was particularly interested in using the school system of Minas Gerais as an example to the rest of the country of how much change was possible.

As minister, Mares Guia Neto had clear views on what needed to be done. He was convinced that the major problems of the system were its low performance and inefficiencies, the high turnover of teachers, the excessive bureaucratization of all decisions, and the political clientelism that infected the selection of school leadership. He was also clear that decentralization of power to the level of the school was the way to address these problems. While admitting that ideas for having local school councils and elected school principals were not new—other states in Brazil had adopted such changes before 1990 and they had been established in Minas Gerais as a consequence of the 1983 state education congress—he believed that they had not been successfully implemented anywhere. Local autonomy became his mantra. As he expressed it: "The power of decision, until now concentrated in central and regional offices, which were a fertile field for the growth of the bad practices that afflict Brazilian education—clientelism, conservatism, and corporatism—should be transferred to the school."[61]

State ministry officials, UTE, and the state's parents' federation were not pleased with the appointment of Mares Guia Neto and tried to stop it. He had earned their suspicion for having created a network of private schools as a business venture, an activity that raised considerable fears that he would use his position to promote private education.[62] Despite rumblings from the ministry and education interests, however, the governor insisted on this appointment. The new minister immediately asked Ana Luiza Pinheiro to become vice-minister and promised her autonomy in selecting her own team of education reformers. Soon a group of experienced education specialists was in place and the plans for reform took shape rapidly.

The reform adopted the idea of school boards, introduced in 1983, which would have financial and administrative control over the local school. These boards would be elected by a general assembly of teachers, employees, students, and parents. They would oversee the teaching plan of the school, assess the curriculum, approve the school calendar, deal with student problems, manage improvements in infrastructure, determine teacher qualifications, approve the hiring of new teachers and evaluate their performance, and approve the budget and decide on investments and expenditures. The general assembly would elect school directors, after candidates had qualified by taking a test. With so much now to be decided at the school level, the state ministry of education would be in a position to assume a stronger role in allocating resources among schools, setting a basic curriculum, managing the career systems for teachers and other officials, and evaluating the performance of the schools.

Schools would receive regular grants for general operations and, when school councils presented a plan to the ministry, they could receive money from a special education fund for materials, construction, or consultants.

At the same time, schools were encouraged to begin developing teaching methods that responded to the particular needs of the school and their students. In pursuit of this goal, they were expected to develop a five-year teaching plan, which was to be evaluated on an annual basis. There were limits on how far school autonomy could go, however, as the constitution prohibited the hiring and firing of civil servants (teachers) by schools or school councils. Even here, however, schools were granted some rights to hire teachers and consultants who were not civil servants.

Throughout the spring of 1991, the minister continued to speak publicly about the failings of the existing system and the need for school autonomy. As he did so, opposition began to mount to these proposals. At stake was an education reform law that was sent to the legislature in April. As the minister sought to gain legislative approval for the reform, the election of school directors became the most important sticking point. School directors had long been part of the patronage machinery of local politics; and governors, mayors, and legislators had long benefited from the ability to name officials to this position. For example, according to one count, between January and March 1991, just before Helio Garcia took over the governorship, four hundred new directors were selected.[63] The school director's association, ADEOMG (Associação dos Diretores das Escolas Oficiais de Minas Gerais), was very opposed to the idea of leadership election. Seeking to alter the focus of the discussion, the minister referred to the selection of the directors, not their election.

The matter came to a head in late April 1991 in a debate that pitted reformers against the director's association. The minister, members of UTE, ADEOMG, representatives of parents' organizations, and legislators presented arguments. As in the past, when he had spoken of the need to improve education, the minister spoke of the poor performance of the schools in Minas Gerais and of the need to respond with a reform that would be in the best interests of the student, the family, the teachers, and others who served the school. He tried to appeal to the politicians by arguing that if local schools improved, they would get the credit for it. He emphasized the high priority the reform had for the governor and that Helio Garcia was following its progress closely. Debate was important, he argued, but it was also important to understand that the reform had already been carefully designed and subjected to a great deal of scrutiny and that it drew on the experiences of several other Brazilian states.[64]

Although the governor was not present at this debate, he made clear in public events and private meetings that the education reform was a central priority to his administration. According to Mares Guia Neto: "The state governor was convinced that a major reform was needed, knew that there were major political costs involved, but gave full support throughout his tenure. Education was his priority, and everyone, including the state minister of finance and the members of the state legislature, knew it."[65] At the end of June, the reform became law.

REVERSING A REVOLUTION: NICARAGUA

In Nicaragua, ministerial level activism also led to a significant reform. In 1993, education minister Humberto Belli unveiled his plan for altering the structure of educational decision-making and accountability in the country. His autonomous schools program sought to put in place a system of local school management by councils made up of parents, teachers, students, and directors. It was, according to one observer, "one of the most radical decentralization experiments in the Americas, on a par with Chile or the City of Chicago regarding how much responsibility is transferred to the local level."[66]

The program allowed for the voluntary inscription of schools. Once teachers in any school voted to be part of it, they could then make a formal application to the ministry of education. Schools enrolled in the program were to receive funds each month to dispense as teacher salaries and benefits and for routine maintenance tasks. The central government first disbursed the funds to its municipal representative whose responsibility it was to distribute them to the schools on the basis of a formula developed by the center.[67] In addition, autonomous schools were authorized to charge fees. At the secondary level, contributions from parents were to be mandatory; at the primary level, due to a constitutional provision that public education was free, they were to be voluntary.

Funds were to be managed by parent-school councils, which would be responsible for the budget, hiring and firing of personnel—including the school director—and some aspects of the curriculum, planning, and evaluation. This council would share decision-making authority over the school with the director; the capacity of the council to hold teachers and director accountable was ensured by requiring that parents have majority representation. In addition, the council could determine the use to be made of the fees contributed by parents—to add to teacher salaries, to renovate or add to the school, to set up a school library, to purchase computers, and so on. The national ministry of education would remain in charge of supervision of schools, most curricular content, and the allocation of funds to individual schools. The ministry would also continue to be responsible for in-service teacher training and classroom support.[68] Many of these central responsibilities were to be carried out by the municipal level offices of the ministry.

This structure for school administration was a radical change from the existing system. Indeed, the reformist initiative was largely a reaction to the revolutionary government of the Frente Sandinista de Liberación Nacional (FSLN, or Sandinistas) and little can be understood of the motives or actions related to education without reference to a Sandinista/anti-Sandinista divide that characterized policy making throughout much of the 1990s in Nicaragua. Most new policies could be interpreted as counterpoints to what the Sandinista government of 1979–1990 had promoted.[69]

Recognizing the importance of schools to inculcating new values and beliefs, and eager to provide evidence of attention to demands for increased services after a long history of authoritarian rule, the Sandinistas had made education a national priority.[70] Although the earlier Somoza era had provided greater access to schooling for Nicaraguan children, the revolutionary government considered that education had to fulfill a historical role in forming citizens for the new era. The government's approach to education, *"Más, Mejor, y Nueva,"* (more, better, and new) translated into the introduction of government preschools, a massive literacy campaign, and rural schools that combined work and education (more); an improved curriculum and schools organized as integrated learning units (better); and an effort to involve communities and parents in a massive campaign to raise awareness about the objectives of education for the new Nicaragua (new).[71]

When the Sandinista revolution was rejected at the polls in 1990, however, there was little but criticism for its efforts in education. The FSLN government was attacked for having contributed to the creation of a bureaucratized and highly centralized ministry, and it was derided for its command and control orientation to education. Regarded as an effort to impose a "factory model" on the schools, Sandinista efforts to manage activities in the classroom were spurned by education specialists. "The idea was that at a certain time every day, every student in a particular grade would be on page 38 of a specified textbook," according to one critic.[72] In addition, many criticized the explicitly ideological content of the curriculum and its revolutionary messages. Sandinista rhetoric and heroes were promoted through textbooks, and reaction was often particularly harsh about the militarism and violence depicted in teaching materials.[73]

Some of the problems in education could be attributed to the increase in armed opposition to the revolution. By the mid-1980s, the economy of the country was faltering, and funds formerly directed toward education were diverted to the war effort against an antirevolutionary insurgency supported by the U.S. government.[74] In the face of this challenge from the contras, the Sandinistas increased the centralization of decision-making about education and gave greater priority to ideological formation in the classroom. The costs of the war had a significant impact on the quality of education also. Resources for textbooks and educational materials disappeared. Teacher salaries fell to such a low point that many experienced teachers left the classroom, their places taken by "empirical" teachers who often had little education, but who were usually Sandinistas. Thus, for many of its critics, politicization of education was a clear legacy of the FSLN government.

Reaction against the FSLN era was equally political. Violeta Chamorro, supported by a coalition of political parties that campaigned on a platform of reconstruction, reconciliation, and economic development, was elected president in February 1990 with 54.7 percent of the vote, well ahead of the Sandinista candidate. Within Nicaragua's presidentialist system, she enjoyed considerable capacity to pursue new policies and to allow her ministers scope for action. Although early budgets did not indicate an increased priority for education, she was adamant about altering the content of the curriculum away from its promotion of revolutionary goals. In explaining her interest in education, she recalled: "The most important thing when I came into power was to get rid of those [Sandinista] textbooks. Oh, you should have seen them! A scandal!"[75] In fact, funding under the Sandinista government had become so restricted that very few schools even had textbooks or other educational materials. Nevertheless, the textbooks that did exist were collected and destroyed.[76] In their place, the president wanted to see classroom materials that promoted the importance of family, religion, morality, antiviolence, civic education, and stability.[77]

More generally, providing new textbooks and educational materials and hiring better trained teachers were actions that would be favorably received by many parents and communities. Moreover, these were actions that could be put in place in a relatively short period of time and that could be pointed to as proof of the government's commitment to improve conditions in the country. The Sandinista legacy created a further benefit for the Chamorro government—the U.S. government was willing to provide extensive resources to undo that legacy. Very early in the Chamorro administration, USAID made over $12 million available for new textbooks.[78] Within less than a year, new texts for all subjects and grades were distributed. Education specialists questioned the distribution of textbooks without a corresponding curriculum reform and raised concerns about their quality, but the goal of the government at this point was more ideological than pedagogical.

In other respects, however, the context was not so favorable for change. The teachers' union created by the FSLN could not be expected to support the anti-Sandinista tone of reform. During the last years of the Somoza era, between 1975 and 1979, unions were prorogued, thus giving the incoming FSLN government ample opportunity to organize the teachers. In accord with its revolutionary goals, the Sandinista government supported the creation of a single teachers' union. Formed in February of 1979, the Asociación Nacional de Educadores Nicaragüenses (ANDEN) required all teachers to become members. Its organization paralleled the vertical and centralized structure of the education system. Teachers were widely regarded as soldiers of the revolution, engaged in the important effort to reshape society along more socialist lines.

Under the FSLN, there was no clear line between the ministry and the union. ANDEN influenced the hiring and firing of teachers, as well as the content of the curriculum and the performance of teachers and students.[79] After the Chamorro government was elected, the union, an association of all secondary school students, and the Sandinista party could be expected to oppose changes in the structure and content of the education system and to be particularly vociferous about any changes in personnel that weakened their influence in the ministry and local schools. Indeed, these were tumultuous times in the country. In 1990, general strikes and protests were frequent and often brought paralysis of the government and economy with them.

In this context, Humberto Belli, a deeply religious sociologist who had been a Sandinista prior to 1979 but anti-Sandinista after the FSLN came to power, was appointed vice-minister of education. One of his first responsibilities was to take charge of selecting new textbooks and destroying what remained of Sandinista-inspired educational content. In the fall of 1990, his minister was asked to take on the role of overseeing technical education in a separate ministry and in November, Belli became minister of education. His job was not to be an easy one. The ministry was strapped for funds and he lacked well-qualified staff to work with him. Under his command, an initial set of activities focused on scaling down the national ministry and reducing the number of teachers in the schools. A USAID-supported program in 1991 provided incentives of up to $2,000 for teachers to resign.[80] While the proponents of these measures emphasized the evils of an overstaffed government and ill-prepared "empirical" teachers, they were met with charges of ideological cleansing. Indeed, many of those whose resignations were accepted were Sandinista supporters.

Textbooks continued to arouse controversy. While reform proponents referred to the ideological indoctrination characterizing educational materials during the Sandinista period and Minister Belli spoke of the importance of "deideologizing" education, ANDEN members and others criticized the religious and conservative content of the Chamorro textbooks. According to a union leader, there was little change in the way school curricula were being used. "In the 1980s, we had education that was ideologically partisan. In the 1990s, we had an education that was ideologically religious. . . . Confessional education became the norm."[81] Indeed, religion had a prominent place in the new textbooks, and history texts described the Sandinista era in unflattering ways.[82] Belli argued: "We are not neutral. We do have a strong ideology, influenced by strong Christian values," and he stated that new curriculum would be concerned with human rights, monogamy, and "a pro-life message."[83] Sandinistas retorted that the new textbooks were "laced with U.S. propaganda."[84]

But Belli was interested in broader reforms than those signaled by the textbooks. Autonomous schools were largely his invention, and the idea grew out of his belief that the centralization of the system was the primary impediment to improved education. Initially, he made an effort to decentralize school finances and administrative management to the municipal level, but soon became disillusioned with what he found to be "the low level of education of the mayors . . . and the fact that clientelism and *amiguismo* are so embedded in government. . . . [The mayors] are also *caciques* and want to be little chiefs of everything. . . . So real decentralization happens when you can bypass this level of government"[85] The municipalization initiative was quietly abandoned in favor of a more direct link between the central ministry and the schools.

In 1991 and 1992, the idea for the autonomous schools began to take shape. According to Belli, in late 1991, as he was preparing to participate in a meeting in Chile, he chanced to read an article about reforms in that country under the military government. He was particularly intrigued by the voucher system that paid private and public schools on a per pupil basis. "I began to wonder if this same model could be applied to public schools. You must remember that at the time, school management was a disaster in Nicaragua. The school directors were appointed by the minister and had no control over the budget . . . everything was taken care of at the central level. . . . I remember visiting a school and seeing a tap that was dripping. I asked the director how much this dripping added to the cost of water for the school. He had no idea; this was an issue only at the central level."[86] Returning from Chile, Belli decided that a grant-per-student system would solve a lot of problems by making the directors more concerned about efficiency. He invited a group of Chilean consultants to contribute to the evolving plan. At the same time, he began to build a team within the ministry that could support him as he moved forward with reform.

The minister drew on Spanish experience for the idea of the school councils that were central to the functioning of the autonomous schools. "I read about their experience with such local councils and how important the balance between parents and teachers is if you want to get parental participation. . . . So we changed the distribution of positions on the councils, giving more weight to the parents. The head of the councils was originally to be the school director. We changed that to be a parent."[87]

Under the management of Minister Belli, reform proceeded apace, despite the protests of ANDEN. In the textbook initiative, which was contested on a very public stage, he had the clear support of President Chamorro. For other initiatives, he attempted to avoid publicity and debates that would encourage confrontations with ANDEN. Thus, for example, the downsizing of the ministry and the ranks of teachers and school directors—which some claimed was a purge of ANDEN and Sandinista representatives—was carried out with monetary incentives, reducing protest to some extent. At the same time, a new union was created under the auspices of a new vice-minister, Hortensia Rivas. The Confederación Nacional de Maestros de Nicaragua (CNMN) was intended to offset the power of ANDEN and provide support for Belli's reformist agenda. Soon, however, it divided, and divided again, until there were twelve unions representing the teachers. While ANDEN remained the strongest of these, its influence was significantly reduced by the voluntary departure program, the emergence of competing unions, and the nonconsultative style of Minister Belli.

By early 1993, the autonomous school program was ready to be launched. Although it was a national program that significantly altered the highly centralized system in place at the time, its introduction was managed through administrative resolutions rather than formal legislation.[88] This was a strategic choice. Soon after taking office, the broad coalition of fourteen parties that brought Chamorro to power began to unravel, and presidential initiatives were far from guaranteed success in the congress.[89] Where it could be pursued, administrative actions rather than legislation were a short-term way to avoid political stalemate. Given the volatility of the content of the autonomous schools program—election of teachers and directors, fees, and local council oversight of performance—political stalemate was also likely to be accompanied by a high level of political protest.

In addition, Belli decided to implement the reform gradually to lessen the extent of protest against it. At the outset, a set of twenty urban secondary schools was handpicked to participate in the program. This choice was also strategic. First, inscription of these schools was quasi-voluntary, thus ensuring that those participating would be among those schools most open to change and experimentation. Second, urban secondary schools were likely to be best positioned to perform well under the new system. They served a better-off constituency of parents who would be less likely to balk at the mandatory fees. In addition, the teachers and directors were likely to be more educated and able to adopt new curricula than schools in poorer areas. Clearly, Belli had orchestrated the adoption of the program to produce "winners." The program was then opened up to other secondary schools and then to primary schools on a voluntary basis. In addition, Belli worked hard to ensure that municipal-level representatives of the ministry were selected in terms of their commitment to the autonomous schools program.

Promoting the reform was also a task taken on by the minister. He visited local schools around the country, giving speeches and answering questions. Often accompanying him were directors of already autonomous schools who could describe the way the new system worked and their experiences with it. "I had to convince the teachers and directors that I was not trying to trick them. It is difficult to start something new in a country where there is a lot of distrust of government."[90] Belli seemed well aware of the kinds of obstacles the autonomous school program would set in motion. As a committed promoter of change, he evinced little sympathy for those opposed to his plans. "The reform was *designed* to take power away from the ministry and its representatives. I knew I couldn't count on the [municipal-level representatives of the ministry appointed prior to the reform] to support it. You know, throughout Latin America, the bureaucrats are the world's best experts in sabotaging programs. And our unions of teachers are the most reactionary of all in resisting change."[91] A bulldog, perhaps, but one who thought carefully about strategy.

The Challenge of Sisyphus: Ecuador

In 1998, Jamil Mahuad campaigned for the presidency of Ecuador on a platform of strong commitment to quality education for all children in the country.[92] He linked poor education to rural poverty and growing inequality in the country, and argued that educational improvement was key to the ability of the country to benefit from rapid globalization. In his campaign speeches, he proposed that education administration be decentralized, that the quality of education be improved, and that parents be more engaged in local school decision-making. He also declared that economic reform would enable more money to be spent on education.

When the new president entered office in August 1998, he followed up his campaign commitments by first appointing a widely respected politician to the post of minister of education; when this person was needed elsewhere in the administration, Mahuad asked Rosángela Adoum, newly elected as a representative in congress, to take over the education portfolio. According to President Mahuad, she "had a real commitment to education and an ability to negotiate and move in all the intellectual circles of the country. . . . We worked together for six years [in Quito City Hall] and shared a similar vision."[93]

Adoum was a committed advocate of improving the quality and reach of education in the country, and she could count on presidential backing to promote her ideas. When she entered the ministry, she brought in a group of policy experts who would work closely with her in planning education reform. This reform team faced major challenges in responding to the weaknesses of the country's education system. Many of them were similar to the problems faced by reformers in the other case study countries. What is distinctive about the Ecuador case, however, is that reform did not happen. Ultimately, efforts to promote change in Ecuador's education system in the 1990s were swamped by bureaucratic conflict, economic crisis, and political disarray.

During most of the 1990s, education in Ecuador limped along, declining in quality and resources, despite several efforts to improve it. In 1992, the First National Consultation on Education in the Twenty-first Century brought together representatives of major groups in the country and ministry officials to discuss the education sector. At the end of this initiative, participants signed a series of agreements acknowledging the importance of education to national development and indicating a broad consensus on the need to improve its quality. A Second National Consultation followed in 1996, reaffirming the earlier agreements and emphasizing the need to decentralize the sector. Then, in December 1997, representatives of the church, economic groups, the military, indigenous leaders, nongovernmental organizations, and the teachers' union met in Washington, D.C., with the Inter-American Development Bank (IDB) to further advance consensus on the need for reform. In addition, in a new constitution written in 1998, the state was committed to decentralize the education system, involve parent participation in schools, and evaluate teachers on a regular basis.[94] However, none of these agreements was followed by concrete changes. There were "lots of plans but little action," as one UNESCO official put it.[95] A union leader reflected: "Since 1963, Ecuador has had 20 education reform projects. When you ask the most experienced teachers which of these they remember, they barely remember even two or three of them."[96]

Lack of action did not mean that change was unnecessary. In the 1990s, Ecuadoreans received an average of 7.1 years of schooling, but only 67 percent of children entering primary school managed to complete it and only 20 percent of them did so without having to repeat any grades.[97] On average, children took 8.5 years to complete the six years of primary education mandated by law. As with other Latin American countries, rural education, which accounted for 43 percent of primary enrollment and 13 percent of secondary enrollment, performed more poorly than urban education. In the late 1990s, the repetition rate for rural primary school children was 15.2 percent; in urban areas, it was 9.7 percent. The rural desertion rate was double the urban rate of 17 percent. As a consequence, only 36 percent of rural children entering primary school completed it.[98] Scores for rural children in the second and sixth grade were 15 percentage points lower in national language tests than their urban public school counterparts; they scored eleven points lower in mathematics.

Most of Ecuador's teachers were poorly trained, underutilized, and badly paid. The vast majority of primary teachers attended normal schools rather than universities, and some 30 percent had no postsecondary training at all.[99] Most worked one shift only, less than four hours daily, and absences were frequent. Efforts in in-service training generally took the form of capacity building of large numbers for short periods of time, often a waste of resources because the knowledge gained was only superficial. When teachers were posted to schools, the post became their property, to be carried with them when they were reassigned. As teacher assignments tended to proceed from rural to urban schools, and teachers were eager to gain urban assignments, this eventually resulted in an overabundance of urban teachers and a paucity of rural ones.

The Unión Nacional de Educadores (UNE) represented 140,000 of the country's 156,000 teachers. The principal public demands of UNE were for increased salaries and job security—the president of the organization characterized the income of teachers as a "salary of misery."[100] Closely allied with the Movimiento Popular Democrático (MPD) Party, the union was well-known for its revolutionary ideology. Although many teachers did not hold the same views, they generally accepted UNE's leadership as their only hope for improving their salaries. Over the years, when the poverty-stricken ministry had been unable to respond to salary demands, the union had been compensated with control over key personnel decisions. As a consequence, when UNE declared strikes, the ministry was unable to function.

A former minister of education cautioned against blaming the problems of education solely on the teachers' union, however. "The drama of education in Ecuador cannot be traced to a single factor. It is a combination of factors that results in very little progress. It is the union, but it is also the weak ministry, the low priority that education has, the poverty of the teachers."[101] The condition of the ministry was mute testimony to this perspective. Decision making about education policies and programs involved the central administration—responsible for planning and policy development and implementation—and the provincial-level offices of the ministry—responsible for regional administration, including hiring and assignment of teachers. But the central ministry did not have the information or the resources to carry out its policy-making and oversight activities. Most of its officials were former teachers who had been appointed through the patronage of UNE and the MPD; their jobs were secure and there were no incentives or resources to reward them for a job well done. In contrast, a typical minister of education could expect to be in office for eight months.

Moreover, the ministry lost resources over the course of the 1990s. From a high of about 19.5 percent of central government expenditures in 1992, it had declined to about 13 percent in 1999. In the mid-1990s, 92 percent of the budget was directed toward teacher and administrator salaries, while 3 percent was spent on materials and supplies for the schools. There was little the ministry of education could do on its own to improve financing. Its budgets were determined by the ministry of finance with little input from the education sector, and control over disbursements by the same ministry usually meant that education did not receive even the amount budgeted.[102] Not surprisingly, relations between the ministry of education and the ministry of finance were strained.

Because it was a weak and inefficient ministry in the best of times, capacity to carry out innovations in education depended on access to funds from international financial agencies, especially the IDB and the World Bank.[103] Within the ministry, internationally financed programs were the responsibility of special units composed of people hired by the program and using equipment and resources that were exclusive to it.

From the donors' perspective, these special implementation units often made sense. Frustrated by the poor incentive structure, low capacity, and poor motivation of regular ministry employees, the special unit offered the possibility of bringing bright and energetic people into the public sector, providing them with attractive salaries and appropriate equipment—computers, vehicles, and communication technology—and supplying them with the resources to make an impact on a focused problem. While they acknowledged some of the problems inherent in the special implementation unit approach, this method of operation also gave the agencies some assurance that resources would be spent as planned, expenditures monitored, and reports forthcoming to meet their auditing and contracting standards.

Looked at from the perspective of the ministry, however, the internationally funded programs were a source of considerable tension. In effect, they created two ministries, operating side by side. The "real" ministry was virtually penniless and subject to the power of the union, which over the years had assumed much of the decision-making for education, and the ministry of finance, which controlled its budget. In this ministry, the telephones often didn't work, there were few computers and those that existed were outdated or broken, desks were old and rickety, and field-workers had no vehicles to visit schools. In 1999, the minister earned about $400 a month, and other employees earned much less, making it almost impossible to attract well-qualified technical and managerial personnel.

In the "funded program" ministry, in contrast, bright people, good equipment, interesting new ideas, and much better salaries, as well as high morale, prestige, and opportunities to travel and be part of international networks, were a constant reminder to those in the rest of the ministry of what they were missing. A program director earned four times what the minister did in 1999. Chronic lack of coordination and communication between the implementation units and the rest of the ministry added to internal tensions and administrative problems. As one education adviser summed up the problem, "The ministry had all the responsibility but the unit had all the resources."[104]

Clearly, Ecuador's education system was in serious trouble by the late 1990s, and the combined interests of ministry officials and union leaders created an impressive barrier to reform. Other political and economic conditions increased the difficulty of change. President Mahuad did not have a majority in congress and, in the institutional environment of Ecuador, creating a governing coalition was much more difficult than in Bolivia; moreover, presidents were usually unable to sustain the coalitions that they managed to patch together. In addition, the condition of the economy created an uncertain environment for carrying out education ministry activities. At the outset of the Mahuad administration, in August 1998, the fiscal deficit had escalated to 7 percent of GDP.[105] Export earnings had decreased by about 15 percent as a result of the destruction caused by El Niño, and oil prices had dropped to about half of what they had been the previous year. During 1997–1998, drought and flooding caused 317,000 deaths and $2.2 billion in damage to the economy. Russia's economic collapse, itself a casualty of the Asian financial crisis, caused a sharp drop in Ecuador's growth; at the end of 1998, economic crisis in Brazil contributed to a further drop.

In September 1998, the government announced a devaluation of the currency along with a pledge for fiscal austerity; a second devaluation followed in February 1999. Shortly after these announcements, subsidies totaling $564 million were cut and replaced with more targeted programs. Prices for gasoline, cooking gas, electricity, and public transport were raised. Protest demonstrations and a general strike were the immediate response to these measures. The Confederación de Nacionalidades Indígenas de Ecuador (CONIAE) blocked main highways and proclaimed an uprising of indigenous peoples. As the currency continued to lose value and interest rates were adjusted sharply upwards, protesters continued to attack the government; Mahuad's popularity declined rapidly.

This was the situation that confronted Rosángela Adoum when she took office in February 1999—spiraling inflation, a rapidly depreciating currency, falling prices for petroleum, an escalating foreign debt, and, above all, protests, strikes, demonstrations, and violence in the streets. More-

over, early in February, about ten days before Adoum took office, the public school teachers went on strike under the banner of the UNE. Their
principal demand was that the government make good on legislation
passed by the previous administration to almost triple teachers' salaries in
three steps between 1998 and 1999. The government had had no money
with which to pay up on these promises, and the Mahuad administration
considered that the previous administration had been ill-advised and irre-
sponsible in passing the legislation. Moreover, because the new constitution declared it unconstitutional to paralyze public services, the government sent the leaders of the strike to jail. These were hardly responses
likely to satisfy the teachers, who redoubled their protest activities.

This tumultuous situation was bad enough, but worse was to come. In
early March, the sucre depreciated a further 26 percent.[106] Panic ensued
as people rushed to the banks to withdraw their money. International reserves fell precipitously to 60 percent of what they had been in January.
The government responded by closing the banks until emergency economic measures could be devised. Taxi drivers paralyzed Quito; CONIAE
roadblocks raised the price of foodstuffs in the cities. Mahuad's public
opinion ratings plummeted further. In March, only 13 percent of respon-
dents in a public opinion poll gave positive responses about the president's
performance, down from 24 percent in February; 82 percent gave him
negative ratings.[107] Moreover, with only 27 percent of the seats in congress, and with an electoral mandate of less than three percentage points
over his rival, the president faced stiff political resistance to his economic
measures. To try to keep the financial sector from being completely destroyed, the government froze bank deposits; to try to salvage the political
situation, it reduced price increases for fuel and other goods. One by one,
banks began to fail and historical divisions between the coast (Guayaquil)
and the highlands (Quito) were exacerbated as coastal entrepreneurs attacked the government for trying to destroy them.

In this context of a massive economic crisis and political upheaval, Minister Adoum was convinced that public opinion would be inclined to see
merit in the position of the striking teachers who, like many people in the
population, had seen their incomes fall dramatically during the past year.
Between February and April, UNE and the ministry carried on negotiations that eventually resulted in a compromise—the teachers would get
their money, but on a schedule that gave the government additional time
to produce the resources. Then, Adoum moved on to the design of an
innovative social protection plan that would ensure better access to education by the country's poor. She had a team to work with her to produce
such a program. Simultaneously, plans were being developed for a school
autonomy plan for rural areas, based on the idea of clusters of schools that
would share a director, education resources, and technical assistance for

TABLE 3.1
Seizing the Initiative: Leadership Strategies

| | | | | | Weaken or | | |
Case	Year	Principal Protagonist	Manage Timing	Appoint Supporters	Marginalize Opponents	Set Terms of Debate	Campaign on Issue
Minas Gerais	1991	Minister	✔	✔	✔	✔	✔
Mexico	1992	President	✔	✔	✔	✔	
Nicaragua	1993	Minister	✔	✔	✔	✔	
Bolivia	1994	President	✔	✔	✔	✔	✔
Ecuador	1999	Minister	✔	✔		✔	✔

teachers. By December 1999, the social protection plan was ready, the president was committed to it, and the IDB and the World Bank had agreed, in principle, to fund it. Then, on January 21, 2000, the democratically elected but beleaguered Mahuad administration was toppled from power by a military coup.

LOOKING ACROSS CASES: LEADERSHIP AND REFORM INITIATIVES

Each of the cases in this chapter tells a distinct story of how education reform was taken up by a political leader. Each of these reformers faced a distinct political environment, even while the opposition of the ministry of education and the teachers' union was a common theme in all of the stories. Reform leaders clearly adapted their strategies to accord with the particular context they faced. At a more general level, however, there were striking similarities among the strategies chosen (see table 3.1). Most of the strategic choices made indicated a clear effort to use the authority and resources of leadership to seize the initiative and place the opposition in a difficult situation. Because of their positions of executive authority, the reformers were able to determine, at least initially, what was to be reformed, how the reform was to be undertaken, and when it was to occur. This was a decided advantage in launching their new initiatives.

First, the ability to affect the timing of new initiatives gave reform leaders an upper hand in seizing the initiative. This was clearest in the case of Mexico's President Salinas, whose overall strategy was to introduce his reform under conditions that were most propitious for its success. In this case, he took three years to build up the reserves of his presidential power and to shape the extent to which the union and the ministry would accept change. This involved not only altering the situation of the union and the ministry, but also waiting for a midterm election to give him the constitutional majority he needed to legislate important changes. In Bolivia, President Sánchez de Lozada committed his administration to education reform during his campaign. Once elected, he quickly adopted a team that had been developing the idea of reform for several years. Then, early in his mandate, he introduced the comprehensive reform when he had a firm governing coalition in congress and could count on passing new legislation with little demur, even when there was widespread resistance to the education reform in the streets.

In the other cases, it was ministers of education who took the major responsibility for timing the reform initiative. In Minas Gerais, the governor made education reform a priority during his electoral campaign, and Walfrido Mares Guia Neto pushed hard to have a reform ready at the outset of the administration. The minister's persistence in promoting the reform through the legislature was central in its approval. In Nicaragua, the immediate post-Sandinista period opened up considerable space for new initiatives in education and insured that U.S. interest in efforts to change the ideological tone of education would be high. In introducing the autonomous schools policy, the discrete and gradualist approach of Minister Belli was a clear response to the charged political environment in which school autonomy was being tried, as was his use of administrative resolutions rather than legislation to pursue it. Ecuador's Minister Adoum believed that getting the teachers back into the classroom was a step that must precede reform. In this case, however, the timing of education reform was interrupted by a deep economic and political crisis.

Second, reformers in each case made use of their powers of appointment to promote their initiatives. When they assumed their positions, the appointment of ministers, vice-ministers, technical teams, and key implementers of the proposed plans were central to their capacity to move forward with those plans. In Mexico, Salinas first appointed a tough politician to take back control of the ministry from the teachers' union; later, he appointed a close ally to the ministerial position to negotiate an agreement with the same union. In Bolivia, the president involved the vice president in the reform initiative, an action with symbolic value because the vice president was both a supporter of reform and represented the country's large indigenous population. In addition, the president made a critical decision in terms of the content of the reform by bringing an experienced design team into the education ministry, one that already had a well-developed idea of what the reform would look like. A team was central to the fortunes of reform in Minas Gerais, where a governor chose a minister who then chose trusted allies to head up the initiative in the ministry. Similarly, Nicaragua's Minister Belli appointed a team of sup-

porters to help him within the ministry and named municipal-level officials of the ministry who were committed to the reformist idea. In Ecuador also, the president selected a minister he thought would promote
change in the education sector; she in turn used her capacity as minister
to bring in a team of policy designers who would be loyal to her.

Third, the reformers took actions to weaken or marginalize the teachers'
union in the reform process. Of course, in Mexico, a confrontation with
the dissident CNTE forced the president's hand because of demands that
he unseat the powerful union boss, Jonguitud Barrios. Nevertheless, he
used this situation to assert his own power and to promote his own agenda
by replacing the union leader with someone who would be beholden to
him and thus likely to be ready to negotiate a deal in the future. His
education minister at the time was instructed to ensure that the ministry
was controlled by the government rather than by the union. He also low-
ered the resistance of SNTE by adjusting salaries upwards in response to
strong demands to improve the economic condition of the teachers. In
Minas Gerais, where UTE was in favor of some parts of the reform, the
school directors were a more direct threat. In this case, the minister mobilized supporters of the reform to testify in the public debate about the
benefits of reform, and the governor provided key public support to offset
the resistance of the directors' association. Moreover, by identifying distinct interests of those who were hostile to all or part of the reform, the
minister was able to play one off against the other in the debate.

In Nicaragua, Belli created a new union that could be used in the interests of the ministry and that he hoped would become a countervailing
force to ANDEN, the Sandinista union. A buyout program to reduce the
number of teachers limited the number of pro-Sandinista teachers. Further, Belli skirted the union in introducing the reform school by school
and by taking to the hustings to appeal directly to teachers and school
directors. In Bolivia, the president confronted the union with a fait accompli through congressional approval to go forward with the reform, marginalizing the unions from the approval process. Only in Ecuador was the use
of negotiations with the union unaccompanied by efforts to weaken it; in
that case, the issue was defined as simply getting the teachers off the streets
and back into the classroom.

Fourth, it is notable that in all of the cases, executive leaders sought to
set the terms of debate about reform. In Mexico and Bolivia, presidents
linked the reforms to the importance of modernizing their countries, im-
plicitly suggesting that those opposed to reform were opposed to modernization. They were also clear that education was central to the alleviation
of poverty and to the growth of the economy. In similar terms, the president of Ecuador proposed reform during his campaign as a way to alleviate

poverty and make the country more competitive internationally. In Minas Gerais, the new minister of education focused great attention on the defects of education in the state and its inefficiencies and injustices. He referred to the reform in terms of a commitment to the student, the family, the teacher, the school, and those who served the school.[108] Moreover, he was careful to introduce local election of school directors, the most controversial part of the reform, as a process in which well-qualified and locally responsive school heads would be "selected."

In Nicaragua, where an ideological battle over the content of education was implicit in all discussions of reform, positive values of family, peace, religion, and stability were invoked in promoting change. As in Minas Gerais, the autonomous schools policy was justified in terms of the bureaucratization, inefficiency, and centralization of the existing system. In addition, the minister of education sought to portray the reform as one in which teachers, school directors, and parents would all be winners. In all five cases, reform proponents, by seizing the initiative, were able to claim the high ground early in the discussion of change, at the same time implying that those opposed to change were opposed to such positive goals as modernization, poverty alleviation, choice, and responsiveness and supportive of negative conditions like centralization, poverty, and bureaucracy.

In addition, in Bolivia and Ecuador, education reform was promoted through party platforms as contenders campaigned for the presidency. In Minas Gerais, education reform was stressed throughout the 1989 campaign for governor. This was clearly the major way that education reform got on the public agendas in those countries. Once again, this allowed new administrations to seize the initiative in proposing reform and set the terms for debate over the issue. At the same time, reform proponents tended to keep their well-advertised commitment to change vague on specifics, providing greater room for executive prerogative after the elections. Further, it is interesting that while reformers sought to raise public awareness and interest in education and the need for change, in none of the cases did leaders actively encourage the creation of organizations in civil society to demand change and support new initiatives. Nicaragua's Belli came close to such action in the creation of a new union, but this had more to do with marginalizing the existing union than mobilizing more broad-based support for change.

Thus, as indicated in table 3.1, these cases suggest that the principal role of reform leaders is to raise the profile of new ideas, select the moments most propitious for introducing a new plan, promote the fortunes of those who support change initiatives, and weaken opposition to them. Their positions of executive power provided important resources for taking on these activities, capitalizing on their institutional resources to offset many other institutional factors that favored the status quo. In taking the initiative, they were attempting to improve the odds in favor of reform. In addition, among the most important things leaders in the five cases did was to empower design teams to generate the ideas they championed. The next chapter takes a closer look at design teams and assesses their role in the promotion of educational change.

Chapter Four

DESIGNING REFORMS: PROBLEMS,
SOLUTIONS, AND POLITICS

FOR MUCH OF THE 1990s, Amalia Anaya was recognized as the *apasio-nada* behind Bolivia's education reform. During this time, she studied, advocated, planned, argued, and promoted her vision of better public education in the country. She repeatedly faced mobilized protests and personal attacks, and periodically lost and regained high-level political support. Indeed, the story of how Anaya and her team crafted a reform proposal demonstrates the dogged determination that reformers need if they are to introduce new policies. More significantly, however, her story is about the process of policy design and the strategies reformers use to keep their proposals alive. In the Bolivian case, the strategic use of political resources enabled a small team of reform designers to promote policy change across three different political administrations. At the same time, however, strategic choices about the process of designing a new policy—and the characteristics of the opposition and the institutional context—contributed to the team's inability to reach accommodation with the teachers' unions or to bring all of the teachers along with their initiative. These problems, perhaps inevitable, slowed the implementation of the plan.

Design teams such as that headed up by Bolivia's Amalia Anaya played significant roles in other cases as well. In Minas Gerais, the education design team faced fewer obstacles because it had strong political backing from the beginning, but it was no less important in shaping the contents of the reform and foreshadowing the conflicts that were to meet its introduction. In these two cases, design teams worked well together and agreed on the shape and scope of what they believed needed to be done to enhance the quality of education in their countries. Indeed, design teams need to function well together or reform can be sacrificed. In Ecuador, high-level political support could not compensate for constraints on new initiatives when reformers did not agree on a common approach to a problem and when two design teams became more embroiled in conflict than in promoting a solution to education deficits. Moreover, design teams do not always make good choices about managing the politics of change. In Mexico, a small team of reformers in the ministry of education badly misread public tolerance for changing the contents of nationally provided textbooks. As a consequence, the reformers were forced into retreat.

The actions of design teams in these four countries help explain what solutions were chosen and what political interactions were set in motion by efforts to design new policies. Of course, design teams are not always important players in the politics of reform. Appointed by executives, they are subsequently dependent on political leadership in determining how central they will be to the process of reform. In Nicaragua, a ministerial team was cast in a secondary role to the minister and was more an implementer of his reform idea than a creator of it. Thus, the experience of the design team in Nicaragua is not explored in this chapter; it focuses instead on Bolivia, Minas Gerais, and Ecuador, and then provides a brief account of what occurred in Mexico.

At the outset of reform processes in Bolivia, Minas Gerais, Ecuador, and Mexico, executive leaders appointed design teams to study the issues, define the problems, and then focus on finding solutions to them. Who was appointed to design teams, what tasks they were asked to take on, and how they carried out these activities were important determinants of the contents of reform initiatives. In this work, the teams were neither politically neutral nor insulated from political pressures. Not only policy definition but also political support building and conflict management were central to their work. Although each of the four cases tells a distinct story, the most effective design teams concurred on the importance and goals of reform, had the support of political leadership at critical moments, determined who would be consulted during the design process, made use of intra-governmental networks to promote their proposals, and sought allies among international agencies.

From another perspective, the four cases suggest that education reforms of the 1990s were often elite projects, generated by small, executive-based teams. Their mandates derived from political leaders, but the teams had considerable freedom in developing solutions to problems, as they understood them. Thus, these cases reiterate what has been discovered in case studies in different countries and in different policy areas—that small groups located in the executive are central actors in defining reform initiatives.[1] Moreover, how these teams decided to organize their activities—how open or closed their deliberations, with whom they consulted, what issues they were willing to negotiate, how they announced their recommendations, how they sought the commitment of political leaders—were important in generating political support or opposition to their plans. The cases of Bolivia, Minas Gerais, Ecuador, and Mexico suggest that, above all, the work of design teams is an important part of the political economy of reform.

DESIGN AND SURVIVAL: BOLIVIA

Education reform in Bolivia was notable for the persistence of a committed design team across three political administrations.[2] As we saw in the previous chapter, at the outset of the decade, education in the country resembled that of many other Latin American countries—poorly trained teachers, high repetition and dropout rates, inequity in providing services to rural populations, discrimination against cultural minorities, hard-to-reach populations, low esteem for the teaching profession, dominance of abstract curricula and learning by rote. Although a 1955 education reform law had succeeded in providing widespread access to education, the challenge more than thirty years later was to improve its quality and equity. Amalia Anaya was at the center of a design team that took on this challenge.

Anaya began her political career as a university leader, and in 1980, during the short-lived dictatorship of General Luis García Meza, she became an activist in the Movimiento de Izquierda Revolucionaria (MIR). With the return of democracy in 1982, she continued as a party activist, becoming a member of the party's national board in 1985. In 1987, she was put in charge of formulating the party's social policy platform for the elections of 1989. When the MIR's Jaime Paz Zamora became president in 1989, Anaya became undersecretary of social policy in the ministry of planning. In that capacity, she traveled to Quito, Ecuador, in November 1989 to attend preparatory meetings for the World Conference on Education for All and then later attended that meeting at Jomtien, Thailand, in March 1990. During these activities, which were critical in turning her attention from social policy in general to education in particular, she began to forge relationships with development advisers in international agencies—UNICEF, the World Bank, and the Inter-American Development Bank.

As a consequence of her discussions with social sector specialists in international organizations, Anaya established contact with Jorge Quiroga— later to become minister of finance, then vice president, and then president of the country—who at the time was undersecretary for public investment and development cooperation in the ministry of planning. This relationship was important because it brought education reform onto the agenda of discussions between the government and international organizations. Thus, when World Bank officials came to Bolivia in May 1990 to assess the country's social adjustment program, the issue of funding for education reform was discussed with the minister of education. In separate discussions with Anaya, bank officials indicated that funds might be made available for the preparation of a project proposal. Anaya indicated interest in developing a technical design unit to spearhead the reform. In a follow-up trip to Washington to meet with World Bank and Inter-American Development Bank officials, she continued these discussions; gradually, World Bank interest increased for funding what was to become the Technical Support Team for Education Reform, ETARE.

Anaya had little faith in the capacity of the ministry of education to promote reform.[3] In her assessment, "The ministry was a huge bureaucracy. It employed 600 people, most of whom were teachers and most of whom were appointed by the unions. Its leadership didn't want to work and was strongly motivated to keep things as they were and to avoid conflict, particularly with the unions."[4] She believed that nowhere in the ministry were there people with training or motivation to undertake a technical analysis of education and use it as the basis for designing a reform policy. Instead, the team found a home in the ministry of planning. This ministry offered the advantage of a sympathetic minister and a direct relationship with international funders through Jorge Quiroga. By early 1990, and with $250,000 from the World Bank, the design of an education reform for Bolivia could now begin in earnest—or so it appeared. Despite the promising beginning, the minister of education and allies in the MIR succeeded in discrediting Anaya and she was forced out of the government in January 1991.[5] Disillusioned, she resigned from the MIR.

Because World Bank funding existed, the government established ETARE in May 1991 and named its first director but was not supportive of its mandate. Moreover, the director was skeptical that real reform could be carried out in the country, and the small unit did little more than hire consultants to undertake studies and needs assessments. Indeed, some Bolivians were convinced that education reform at this time was solely a World Bank initiative, a charge that gained some credibility in November 1991 at the Consultative Group meetings of the international financial institutions, where the government presented a general proposal for education reform. The plan focused on inefficiencies in the education system and recommended a reduction in the budget, an administrative reorganization, and improvements in teacher certification and evaluation.[6] Not surprisingly, as soon as the proposal became public, it was roundly criticized by those who perceived it as simply another instance in which World Bank technocrats, focused solely on structural adjustment, imposed belt-tightening measures on the public budget, regardless of their social consequences. The proposal was quietly shelved.

The cause of education reform was given a boost, however, when a newly appointed minister of planning, an economist deeply aware of the role of education in creating human capital and alleviating poverty, brought Anaya back into government to take charge of ETARE in April 1992. In short order, twenty-two professionals with a variety of technical specializations were identified and hired to staff the unit. Anaya also brought in politically prominent individuals who could establish a bridge to political parties in the country. Among those persuaded to join the team were Enrique Ipiña, former minister of education and member of the MNR, and Victor Hugo Cárdenas, an educator, Aymara Indian, and leader of a small indigenist political party, the Revolutionary Tupac Katari Liberation Movement (MRTKL). He was later to become vice president of the country. She also brought in Juan Carlos Pimentel, a union and party leader who represented the Free Bolivia Movement (MBL) party, as a consultant to the team. Such additions helped promote the bilingual education agenda of indigenous groups, NGOs, and others. Yet, hiring across party lines earned Anaya animosity from MIR party activists, who wanted these posts for party loyalists.

Among the first large projects undertaken by the ETARE team was an education census of schools, teachers, and students. Although the teachers' unions objected to this effort, a communications effort by the team persuaded most of the teachers to register.[7] Using this information, a Basic Education Map was developed that allowed the planners to base their planning on more accurate data than had been available before. Gradually, the ETARE team began to develop a vision of reform, and by October 1992, it had a plan to present to a mission composed of the World Bank, the IDB, and several bilateral donors interested in reform.[8] The plan included the curricular and pedagogic features that were missing in the 1991 proposal and touched on virtually all aspects of education in the country, including the introduction of bilingual education, one aspect of the reform that enjoyed some grassroots support.

Overall, however, political support for this proposal was minimal. The design team could continue to rely on the staunch support of the minister of planning as well as that of the minister of finance, Jorge Quiroga. But these two important ministers faced the strong opposition of the minister of education as well as other ministers who were concerned about the political costs of the reform. Not surprisingly, the ministry of education continued to be hostile to a reform plan that originated outside its walls and that affected so many of its interests. The teachers' unions voiced their strong opposition to reforms that would diminish their power and impinge on the status and activities of teachers. When invited to meetings to discuss the reform, they chose not to attend.

The ministry and the unions sought allies in opposing the new plan. A National Congress of Education, sponsored by the ministry of education at the end of October 1992, brought together 625 delegates to criticize what was characterized as a closed-door process pursued by the planners.[9] The ETARE team was not invited, and at the meeting, participants attacked what they called the neoliberal contents of the education plan.

They saw in the design to decentralize education a more sinister plan to privatize public education in the country and a response to the pressures being exerted by the International Monetary Fund.[10] At the end of the meeting, the congress recommended the establishment of a National Education Council (CONED) to continue to bring together interests opposed to the ETARE group. This organization was duly created by the ministry of education in May 1993 and was composed of representatives from the ministry, the unions, and the Church.[11] Together, they formed a powerful opposition to the reform program being developed in the ministry of planning.

In the period leading up to the 1993 elections, the council developed its own reform plan, containing a large number of proposals, among which were the obligatory teaching of Catholic religion and the inclusion of references to "national liberation," "revolutionary education," and "esteem for manual labor" in the reform text.[12] At the urging of the cabinet, these revisions were incorporated into the legislative proposal that Anaya and her team were developing. No political progress could be made in the planning ministry proposal, however, because President Paz refused to support it publicly.

As we saw in chapter 3, Gonzalo Sánchez de Lozada, who became president in August 1993, adopted the ETARE proposal as his education initiative. He asked the vice president—and former ETARE member—Victor Hugo Cárdenas, to promote the reform, and the super-minister of human resources decided that ETARE should become the Education Reform Support and Follow-up Unit (UNAS) and should be part of the education ministry, now headed by Enrique Ipiña, also formerly of ETARE. In February 1994, UNAS was initiated under the direction of Amalia Anaya.

Meanwhile, CONED presented its alternative proposal for reform to the president, who then met with Minister Ipiña, Anaya, and a member of her team to consider what should be done about the counterproposal. The reformers saw the CONED plan as little more than platitudes and a wish list of unrelated ideas—a compendium of "something for everyone" participating in the council. According to Anaya, "We told [the president that the CONED] proposal would not result in a reform. The choice was clear: either you do a reform or you don't. Don't pretend you're doing something when you're not. So he told us to get working on our own legislative proposal."[13] This the team did, meeting often with the president, who became deeply familiar with the plan and a committed proponent of it. Although the unions were invited to meetings to discuss the proposal, they refused to attend. In July, the education law was approved by congress and, with $150 million of funds from multilateral and bilateral agencies, it was initiated.

CONED was not pleased with this outcome. According to an education activist, "Our initiative represented a broad consensus among all important groups in society. Sánchez de Lozada took it and said he would get back to us . . . the next thing we heard, a law for education reform was being debated in congress and it was passed without our participation."[14] "They threw everything we did in the wastebasket," complained a member of the executive secretariat of one of the teachers' unions, CTEUB.[15] His view was echoed by the president of the Episcopal Commission for Education, the Church organization that participated in CONED. "Instead of talking to us, Sánchez de Lozada sent his own law to Congress."[16]

Indeed, controversy swirled around the reform initiative during the remainder of the Sánchez de Lozada administration. Its opponents charged that it had been designed by technocrats in central offices, under the tutelage of the World Bank, with little or no attempt to develop a consensus with the unions, the Church, the universities, and other powerful institutions.[17] Many, including high-level leaders of the governing MNR party, rejected bilingual education as the teaching of "dead languages."[18] The unit's weakness was clear when Vice President Cárdenas failed to defend the reform and its important initiative in bilingual education. The ministry of education began to search for accommodations with the unions and the Church, and made agreements with them that parceled out authority over appointments and the use of funds. Plans to publicize the reform and increase public support for its objectives were scuttled when they were taken over by the ministry of social communication and when UNAS's Director Anaya was told to lower her profile in the national news media.

In February 1995, Anaya, the center of dissent about the new law, was asked to resign by the new super-minister of human resources, erstwhile reformer Ipiña. Despite his close association with the design team, Ipiña was also close to the Catholic Church, which was upset at a provision in the law that the government would appoint all administrative personnel in publicly funded schools, which included some Church-run but state-financed schools. Moreover, the parties in the government's coalition questioned why a former MIRista held such an important post. After Anaya left, Ipiña initiated negotiations with the unions, agreeing to changes that significantly undermined the intent of the new law. Neither political nor technical leadership was available to promote the reform between 1995 and mid-1997, even though another former ETARE consultant, Juan Carlos Pimentel, became minister of education in 1996.

But presidential elections again altered the fate of the reform. Jorge Quiroga, undersecretary and then minister of finance in the Jaime Paz administration, became a vice presidential candidate; he asked Anaya to prepare a plan for education reform as part of the campaign platform. As might be expected, the party proposal closely resembled the 1994 law for education reform. When Hugo Banzer and Quiroga won the election, the new vice president took a special interest in the law that had been passed in the previous administration. "In 1997," he recalled, "my role shifted from being the technical supporter of reform that I had been in the Jaime Paz Zamora administration and I became the political supporter of reform."[19]

The new minister of education and culture, Tito Hoz de Vila, was also expected to add impetus to the reform process. A politician with a national reputation, strong links to the media, and extensive legislative experience and political weight, his appointment marked a difference with prior practice because he was "someone not at the end of his political career but someone who still has his career to make."[20] At the urging of Quiroga, who wished to ensure that there was a strong reform presence in the ministry, the president encouraged Hoz de Vila to appoint Amalia Anaya to the vice-ministry of preprimary, primary, and secondary education.

Back in the government, she worked to resuscitate the reform by strengthening internal management and communication in the vice-ministry and expanding coverage of the schools that were using the new, learning-oriented curriculum and pedagogy. She postponed for the present the changes that caused the most opposition by the teachers' unions—those that affected the teaching career and the power of the unions. She promoted bilingual education, in alliance with indigenous groups, and encouraged programs to promote girls' education. According to one of her top-level aides and a member of the design team since its inception, Anaya's return allowed the team to "find our way again. We rediscovered the objective of the reform."[21] The reform had, remarkably, survived across three political administrations and, although Amalia Anaya was out of government from time to time, many of her technical team remained in office. In August 2001, Hugo Banzer resigned because of ill health and Jorge Quiroga became president of Bolivia. Among his first actions was to appoint Anaya minister of education.

CO-OPTING THE MINISTRY OF EDUCATION: MINAS GERAIS

In contrast to the tense relationship between the ministry of education and the planning team in Bolivia, many of the designers of school autonomy in Minas Gerais came from the state-level ministry of education and sought to use their ties within the ministry to strengthen their proposal. They were aided by a ministry that had traditionally been staffed by many professionals with technical expertise. In this case, the placement of the design team in high-level positions in the ministry, as well as the characteristics of its members, gave them considerable advantage. Indeed, the composition of the team ensured that it could soon agree on central elements of what was needed to change education in the state. Early in the process, it made a strategic decision to focus on a few key ideas related to the management and performance of elementary schools.

As indicated in chapter 3, the reform of the state's education system emerged as a priority issue during the gubernatorial campaign of Helio Garcia in 1990.[22] During the campaign, Walfrido Mares Guia Neto paid particular attention to education. He was joined by economist and academic Paulo Paiva, who coordinated an education sector analysis for the campaign and who later became minister of planning, a key post in supporting the implementation of the reform. Together, they organized a coordinating group on education under the leadership of Ana Luiza Pinheiro, a civil servant who had worked in high-level positions for many years in the state-level ministry of education. She was asked to do a diagnostic study of the problems in the education sector and to make recommendations about how the system should be changed.

Using her contacts in the ministry, Pinheiro recruited a team of competent officials and also brought in researchers from a prestigious state-supported research institute, the Fundação João Pinheiro, and some well-regarded school superintendents who were knowledgeable about policy implementation and evaluation. The team worked quickly. It was in considerable agreement about what the problems were and what needed to be done about them—as Pinheiro recalled: "We all agreed which way was north."[23] By June 1990, the team had developed a set of basic guidelines for education reform and these ideas, stressing the need to decentralize education and to improve its quality, were incorporated into the PRS party campaign document, "Minas Gerais in the Twenty-First Century."

Like Mares Guia Neto, Pinheiro was a firm supporter of decentralization, but only when it was based on the idea of school autonomy and only when it would have an impact in the classroom. Simple deconcentration of the administrative system, bringing it closer to consumers of education, would not work, she believed, as this only created more bureaucracy and impeded real change from happening. "If we want to change education," she wrote, "we have to change the school."[24] She believed that local schools should determine their own schedules, generate local content for the curriculum, and work with students and teachers to develop a teaching program. They should become responsible for their performance.[25] Moreover, once they were no longer attending to the day-to-day management of schools, national or state-level administrators should focus their efforts on establishing norms for education, providing financing, developing teaching as a profession, managing information, and evaluating performance. These ideas were evident in the plan that emerged.

In late 1990, governor-elect Garcia established a series of commissions to work on the legislative program for his new administration. Mares Guia Neto hired Pinheiro, now the head of an education consulting firm, to develop a working plan for the new government. She brought with her several former ministry officials who had been part of the earlier campaign group and who had then joined her in the consulting firm. Initial activities involved developing basic data about the teachers in the system, the number of schools, and information about student performance.[26] Their ties to the ministry helped in gaining access to whatever information it had, and they incorporated this with new data they were generating about the education system. In addition to the team that Pinheiro put together, Mares Guia Neto asked assistance from João Batista Araujo e Oliveira, a nationally known education expert who was soon to became vice-minister of education for Brazil; a number of university and foundation researchers; and Claudio de Moura Castro, an education expert from the Inter-American Development Bank.

The evolution of the reform design was influenced by the professional backgrounds of those who worked with Pinheiro.[27] They drew on their knowledge of the problems of education reforms undertaken during the 1980s and of the deeper problems in the sector, such as the politicized system for selecting school directors and high turnover rates in these positions. Initially, the team was uncertain about how directors ought to be selected, but they agreed that current practice was fraught with problems that diminished the quality and reach of education in Minas Gerais. Eventually, they agreed that school directors should be accountable to the local community, but should also be well-trained professionals. The idea of setting qualifications for candidates through a test and then providing school assemblies with the ability to vote among several candidates, emerged as the team discussed their ideas more fully.

Team members were also concerned about the lack of coherence in the overall system, given different standards and operations among state and municipal schools, and the failure to provide schooling for more children. They knew enough of the financing of school expansion to understand the need to remove infrastructure planning from political influence. Henceforth, they believed, supply needed to respond to demand, not to the importunities of politicians. They were also united in wanting the school system to produce more and better information about performance and were particularly interested in an evaluation system. They hoped that the World Bank could be engaged in providing more resources for education. Among other benefits, they believed that an internationally funded project to support the quality-enhancing reform plan in Minas Gerais would help commit future governments to improved education.[28] Indeed, the World Bank became the principal funder of teacher and school director training programs, although financing for the reform remained primarily Brazilian.

In March, when Helio Garcia assumed the governorship, Mares Guia Neto became minister of education. He appointed Pinheiro to be his vice-minister and Zila de Almeida, who had previously worked in the ministry and who was part of the transition team, to work directly under her as head of administrative affairs, where she would be in contact with the day-to-day operations of the ministry and the schools, their teachers, and their directors. Iris Goulart, who also had a long history in the ministry, was asked to take on responsibility for educational affairs, where she would be responsible for curriculum, testing, and teacher training. In these appointments, the minister was creating a system that would free him to devote more of his time to managing the politics of the reform and that would give Pinheiro space for more technical matters. Newly appointed officials in turn appointed other experienced civil servants to assist them, putting considerable emphasis on their technical rather than their political credentials, and again drawing on those who had been part of campaign and transition planning. They were from different political parties, but Pinheiro insisted that they all belonged to the Education Party.[29]

Indeed, under Mares Guia Neto, for the first time, the ministry was led by those appointed primarily for their technical rather than political qualifications. The minister and vice-minister sought out those experienced in the ministry because both were convinced that reforms in prior administrations had suffered through lack of attention to implementation and lack of knowledge about how the bureaucratic system worked.[30] Mares Guia Neto gave orders that requests from politicians for schools and positions had to meet technical criteria before they could be complied with.[31] Such policies brought opposition from the politicians, but the minister, Pinheiro, Almeida, and Goulart could count on strong gubernatorial support when complaints were made against them. Moreover, the minister became actively engaged in discussing the reform with political leaders, the unions, school directors, and the governor.

Given prior study by Pinheiro and her team and a clear interest of the minister in a reform that would depoliticize the management of schools and the school system as well as provide more autonomy to the schools and their stakeholders, the education reform proposal was not long in the production phase. The World Bank provided funds to hire consultants to consider particular aspects of the reform. Pinheiro's team met weekly with the minister to consider progress on the plan and to discuss issues they confronted. They also used the meetings to agree upon a common "message" about the reform that was to be shared with other ministry officials, the press, teachers, school directors, and politicians.[32]

Mares Guia Neto and Pinheiro agreed that the plan should be relatively simple—not so many changes that they would overwhelm the system but enough to make a significant difference in the education system of the state. In short order, the central elements of the reform—professionally qualified school directors who would be locally elected, training, evaluation of student progress through testing, and the integration of state and municipal schools—were agreed upon. These parts of the reform were seen as mutually reinforcing; they therefore needed to be implemented as a package, rather than introduced one by one.[33] Mares Guia Neto, in discussing his ideas with the governor, announced that he would resign if he were not given a free hand to introduce the full reform, particularly the plan to introduce professional qualifications and election for school directors; for him as well as for Pinheiro, this was the linchpin of the overall reform. He was given full assurance of the governor's support. With this backing in hand, the reformers went public with their proposal.

They organized a day of public debate on the legislative package in April 1991, during which Mares Guia Neto presented a strong defense of the new plan. Unions and associations of educators were divided in the extent to which they supported or opposed the reform, and there was considerable lobbying of the legislature by politicians who benefited from the patronage afforded by the old system and by the school directors, who were strongly opposed to the new selection procedures.

In a meeting of legislators and other political leaders at the end of May, the governor announced that education reform was a critically important priority of his administration, thus giving greater political support to the legislation that was before congress.[34] Because Brazil's state governors were extremely powerful and controlled considerable resources and patronage, Helio Garcia was thus quite persuasive. Reportedly, he told party leaders, "If [the law] doesn't pass, be sure that I will reintroduce it next year. And you will have got yourselves into a *serious* fight with me."[35] The clear support of the governor significantly shifted the balance of the legislature in favor of the reform, and, despite a lively debate, it was approved on June 29, fifty-three votes to three.[36] According to the minister, "However qualified my team, however strong my leadership, nothing would have happened without the governor."[37]

CONFLICTING VISIONS OF PROBLEMS AND SOLUTIONS: ECUADOR

Ecuador's ministry of education was less amenable to change than Minas' ministry. As related in the last chapter, when the new minister of education, Rosángela Adoum, took office in February 1999, she was met with a teachers' strike and a deep economic crisis. Moreover, her task of leadership was complicated by disarray within the ministry. In particular, there was significant division between the "real" ministry and the "funded project" ministry, as each had its own reformists and each held a distinct vision of what needed to be done to improve education in the country. The competition between these two units helped undermine reform in the country.

Before Adoum took over leadership of the ministry, two quality-enhancing programs for reforming education in the country were the World Bank–funded EB/PRODEC and the IDB-funded PROMECEB.[38] Both used the concept of clusters of schools organized into a network. EB/PRODEC focused on networks of urban schools in marginal areas and PROMECEB on networks of rural schools; both sought to promote decentralization of education and enhance school autonomy. Under PROMECEB, the network program grouped rural schools into units that shared socioeconomic and cultural similarities, with an average of twenty schools in each network. The network was assigned funds to finance teacher training, deliver didactic material and technical assistance to teachers, and upgrade the physical infrastructure of local schools. In accordance with traditional practice, parents and local communities assumed responsibilities for maintaining and improving school infrastructure.

These programs did not have a fair chance to prove their potential, however. Frequent changes in the leadership of the ministry and political instability more generally made it difficult to implement them as designed. An evaluation of PROMECEB indicated that education centers were rarely staffed with qualified people, and decision making about the content of the program and its implementation continued to be centrally controlled.[39] Project resources added to top-heavy administration rather than to local-level problem solving. During the initial period of the program, the implementation unit employed some 250 people; its administrative costs were high and its productivity low. Moreover, the PROMECEB networks did not provide increased autonomy of decision making at the school or network level and did not include local control over financial or human resources. As with other internationally funded programs, it tended to operate as a "micro system" at the margin of the larger system, which continued along virtually unchanged.[40]

Despite these drawbacks, some networks performed well when they had parents and communities actively involved in monitoring teacher performance and providing feedback to parents on academic issues related to their children.[41] Reform advocates in Ecuador and in the funding agencies continued to believe these programs were based on a good idea—the school network as the central unit of a system for decentralized management and increased local autonomy. Indeed, the head of the special implementation unit for PROMECEB in the education ministry, Samia Peñaherrera, was convinced of the importance of giving local communities real decision-making power and control over resources and increasing the participation of parents in school affairs. These were fundamental, she and her team believed, to improving the quality of education in the country. "In our education system, the school has no decision making power. It has reached the point that at the school level people won't even change a light bulb without first asking higher authorities about it. There is no responsibility of the parents, and there is no integration of school and home life. They are completely separate realms."[42]

Moreover, the PROMECEB team believed that local autonomy and participation were the only ways to ensure the sustainability of quality-enhancing reforms. "To the extent that there has been decentralization of investment in the schools, sustainability is a real problem. Everything is done through a project and the projects aren't sustainable unless the parents are involved. We need to go beyond projects and beyond the ministry to involve communities, universities, the Church, civil society."[43] Thus, the program implementation unit believed it could overcome its poor relationship with the rest of the ministry, and even the crippling power of the unions, by spearheading a society-wide reform initiative. At the same time, by targeting the unions, the teachers, and the rest of the ministry as enemies of the reform, the unit's leadership quickly earned the animosity of these groups. The distance between the unit and the ministry grew even more when its director made public remarks about the low quality of education officials and disparaged the unions and the teachers.

As they began to envision a more radical successor to PROMECEB, the design team became intrigued by the 1993 school autonomy initiative put in place by Nicaragua's education minister, Humberto Belli. He was invited to Quito, and the design of what was to become the "Network of Friends" schools owed much to his influence.[44] In addition, the team brought in consultants from El Salvador, Minas Gerais, and Chile—all places where significant school autonomy reforms had been put in place—and Mexico. With additional technical assistance from the IDB, the team developed a plan to deepen the PROMECEB approach. The new program would continue to use the idea of a network of about twenty schools. Now, each network would be responsible for hiring, firing, and evaluating teachers, directors, and administrators, making decisions about curriculum, and resolving problems that emerged at the level of the school and the network. In addition, echoing the Nicaragua reform, each network would have a council representing parents, teachers, and community members; parents and community representatives would have majority representation.[45] Along with personnel decisions, the council would develop a strategic plan for improving the quality of education within the network. In these ways, the new program gave real power to the networks and went far beyond PROMECEB in promoting local autonomy.

The Network of Friends plan was finished in the final months of the Fabian Alarcón presidency (1997–1998). Although the president was ready to commit to the program, the PROMECEB team believed it would be better to wait for a new administration to sign an agreement with the IDB, thus providing the program with relatively assured political support for a longer period and allowing the reformers to benefit from a "honey-moon" period that the new administration could expect. Thus, on September 22, 1998, just a month after Jamil Mahuad became president, Minister of Education and Culture Vladimir Alvarez signed the agreement with the Inter-American Development Bank, and a newer and bolder use of the school networks could be put into operation.[46]

As attractive as many believed the Network of Friends program to be, it was not without its critics. Among the most outspoken opponents was the teachers' union, UNE, which lambasted the decentralization scheme as an effort to privatize education. The union claimed that the government, in pursuing a neoliberal approach to social sector expenditures, would gradually shift the burden of financing education to parents and local communities. Its leaders pointed to the Nicaraguan example, in which parental fees were an explicit part of the reform. Moreover, the new program, UNE's leaders claimed, sought to destroy the union by robbing it of its role in representing teachers. Nor did the union trust the reform leadership. Peñaherrera was a lead architect of a comprehensive education reform law that had been strongly criticized by the union and that had been rejected by congress. Moreover, when UNE called the strike in February 1999, she was the strongest advocate in the ministry for taking aggressive action to break the power of the union.

Less public but no less important criticisms of the new networks program charged that it had been developed within the ministry by a technocratic elite with little effort to generate allies or put together a reform coalition among those who supported educational change. In this regard, the project was called to account for "treating teachers, school directors, local officials as enemies of change rather than change agents."[47] The new plan was also attacked for ignoring local governments as participants in reform and creating a new kind of clientelism between the central ministry and the networks for distributing money, textbooks, training, computers, and other inputs. On a more substantive basis, the reform was questioned because it focused more on organizational changes than it did on pedagogy or curriculum.

Minister Adoum joined in the skepticism of the program, for many of the same reasons. "I was very critical of the networks program. . . . We had an international advisory group in to assess how this program was working and I remember one academic telling me that the Networks of Friends were a very good way to get popular participation in the schools, but not a good way at all to improve quality or to use resources more wisely. Communities were simply not prepared to use the resources well or to make good decisions. The plan worked directly from the national level to the level of the networks, with no intermediary. I believed there should be an intermediary and that we should be decentralizing adminis- tration to the municipal level."[48] On a more personal level, she was aware that the unit's director had publicly criticized her management of the min- istry and her approach to the conflict with the unions. Within the minis- try, the networks team had visibility, resources, and power—it raised the disturbing question of who, in fact, was the leader of the organization.

After negotiating the teachers back to the classrooms, and as the eco- nomic crisis of March continued into April and May 1999, Adoum and her team of advisers began to wonder if the ministry should be thinking in terms of social protection rather than education reform at this particular moment. Among the factors that encouraged their interest in such an ap- proach were statistics on the impact of increased poverty on education. According to government figures, those living in poverty—defined as liv- ing on less than two dollars a day—increased from 31.8 percent of the population in 1995 to 37.9 percent in 1998. In rural areas they increased from 52.5 percent of the population to 57.3 percent.[49] A quality of life survey carried out in 1998 indicated that 340,000 children between the ages of six and fifteen were not in school (13 percent of all children in this cohort). Some 71 percent of these children lived in rural areas. In the coastal region, 150,000 children were not registered in schools in 1999– 2000. At the same time, the number of working children increased from 8.3 percent to 9.7 percent of those under fifteen years of age. In the poor- est quintile of the population, 24 percent of children deserted school to work. Studies suggested that even with economic improvement, school deserters tended to continue in the workforce rather than return to school.

Adoum believed that parents were probably making rational choices to send their children to work rather than to school. "In the midst of a crisis," she argued, "you have to keep the children in school *first* and then you can get on with improving the quality of education. A person dying of hunger can't be expected to be concerned about quality."[50] If increases in poverty caused by the economic crisis were encouraging parents to send their chil- dren into the labor force rather than to school, the team members believed that they had to look for ways to compensate for the income foregone and spent when children were sent to school. They calculated that a child in the labor force could earn, on average, three dollars a month to contribute to family income. They further calculated that the costs of attending school were about two dollars a month, when transportation, school uniforms, shoes, notebooks, pencils, and food were included. Thus, they believed, a scholarship of five dollars a month for each child (up to three children per family) would compensate the family for the opportunity cost of sending a child to school as well as pay for the costs of schooling.

In July, meetings with staff from the IDB were useful in bringing shape to the idea of a scholarship program to encourage parents to keep their children in school during a period of economic crisis. Adoum's team became familiar with the experience of an education protection program in Brasilia. The Bolsa-Escola program provided a stipend to encourage poor families to keep their children in school. Its purpose was to reduce the incidence of child labor in the district and to reduce the number of wayward children roaming the streets. Although it was implemented only in some neighborhoods, the Bolsa-Escola demonstrated positive results in school enrollments and income transfers.[51] The Adoum team was also impressed by what they heard about its impact on parental involvement in the schools. According to one member of this group: "In the Brazilian case, women began to become more insistent about the education of their children; their situation was improved and they began to speak out and to pressure the schools and to get control of the teachers."[52]

Adoum became convinced that school retention should be the highest priority of the ministry. "I believed that it was critically important to attend to the urgent issues in education and not the structural ones. We were seeing how the crisis showed up first in education—the mothers took their children out of school and the teachers took on other jobs to make ends meet."[53] Her team designed a program of scholarships for the poorest 20 percent of families to protect the development of human capital in the country and to counteract the tendency for increased inequality in the life chances of the better- and worse-off populations during a time of sustained economic crisis.[54] By December 1999, a plan was ready, the president was committed to it, and the IDB and the World Bank had agreed, in principle, to fund it.[55]

Despite the enthusiasm of the minister and her design team, some thought that the scholarship program was an inappropriate adaptation of the Brasilia experiment. One management expert argued: "The Brazilian program was a small plan in just one municipality and it was directly managed by the local government. There was also a lot of community participation in it. Those who wanted the program here never thought about the fact that this is a very large country and that it would be a massive program administered by the central government."[56] Others were concerned that this two-year emergency scholarship program could eventually be seen as an entitlement by recipients and encourage demands for unsustainable subsidies in the future. More insistent criticism came from the Network of Friends team. For them, it demonstrated that the minister was not serious about real education reform, only with showcasing a short-term program that would be popular with poor people. "We had a good proposal for reform and the scholarship program was not relevant to it. It was not relevant to improving the quality of education. How could we be trying to stimulate participation on the one hand and then turn around and *pay* parents to send their kids to school? It is contradictory."[57]

In response, Minister Adoum defended the program vigorously. "[The scholarship program] had nothing to do with improving the quality of education in the country. Of course it didn't! But we were in the middle of a crisis and people were dying of hunger. And, at times like this it is important to remember that 'the worst school is better than no school at all.' "[58] But here also, the networks team had a response—high dropout rates were a result of the washed-out roads and schools destroyed and closed by El Niño, not the consequence of the economic crisis. Peñaherrera also thought the "crisis" of working children was overstated. "There is an issue about children who work," she argued, "but there are really only about 300,000 of them. This is a lot, but it is only 10 percent of the total number of children. The response to this should be to think of some targeted program for reaching them but spending most of the effort on improving the overall quality of education. . . . It doesn't make sense to stop everything and focus on the temporary crisis."[59]

Thus, throughout much of the summer and fall of 1999, Ecuador's ministry of education was caught in a serious conflict. Plans for two programs existed; one was already in operation and the other was almost certain to be funded. The debate raged on, drawing in education specialists from the international agencies, partisans of each team, the president, and other high-level officials. The conflict was often personal. The Network of Friends reformers blamed Adoum. "The minister was completely blind to the idea of education reform. She only wanted to survive in office and get on well with the MPD. . . . She was the main obstacle to the reform program proceeding ahead."[60] Adoum's team was just as harsh about the network group. "The resistance to the plan came from the education reformers. . . . It was like they had blinders on in terms of understanding our point of view. It was all motivated by a fear of losing their preeminent position within the ministry, a personal thing about being known as reformers."[61] According to the super-minister for social development, there was little intellectual reason for the conflict. "I never saw any reason for there to be any conflict about it—one was a short term response to an emergency and the other was a long term plan for the sector."[62] Many believed the conflict was first and foremost about power and "turf" in the ministry.

Finally, the level of internal conflict became so great that, in mid-December 1999, President Mahuad asked the head of the networks program to resign, along with members of her team. Before any action could be taken on the education scholarship program, however, the president was toppled from power by a military coup. The vice president, Gustavo Noboa, was selected by congress to take over the presidency. With a new leader in power, most ministries changed hands. Rosángela Adoum was replaced, and after several weeks devoted to filling positions with new appointees, the ministry of education began to assess the options for moving forward with its programs. By March 2000, it had decided to continue with the Network of Friends program and was still reviewing the education scholarship program with the IDB and the World Bank. The teachers' union continued to resist the networks program, focusing its message on the specter of the privatization of public education.

STRATEGIC ERRORS: MEXICO

Most of the attention of reformers in Mexico was focused on negotiating an agreement with SNTE and the governors to allow decentralization to go forward. While there were other aspects of the reform—the teaching career and the design of new curricula and teaching materials, in particular—they were clearly secondary to the concern with restructuring the administration of education. But these other changes did receive attention from teams within the ministry of education. The teaching career issue was dealt with as part of the larger negotiation with SNTE, and curriculum reform became the responsibility of a small team in the ministry of education. Its task was to develop new textbooks and materials that would modernize learning in classrooms throughout the country.

At the time of the reform, Mexico could look back on a long history of providing all schoolchildren in the country with free textbooks. Introduced in 1959, this policy had roots in presidential concerns about expanding educational opportunities, particularly to the poor, and ensuring that all children were receiving similar content in the education they were receiving. From a political perspective, the free textbooks had been extremely popular and were looked on by many as an important way in which the PRI regime affected local communities and individual voters. Indeed, while the demand for textbooks was often not fully satisfied, the government had demonstrated considerable capacity to reach even remote rural areas with at least a portion of the materials needed.[63]

The problem for reformers in 1992, however, was that the textbooks had last been fully revised in 1972. Seven years later, they were partially altered. In history and social studies textbooks, in particular, those revisions echoed themes important to the politics of the period—the cold war, national sovereignty vis-à-vis the United States, hostility to international business, a statist approach to economic development—that were anathema to the goals of the Salinas economic modernization project. According to one proponent of change: "The textbooks refer to the world hunger caused by the multinational companies, the evil of foreign investment, the great revolutionary traditions of China, Cuba, and Chile, and the exploitation caused by capitalists and the capitalist systems of the world. You can imagine the problems this creates as we are now trying to encourage foreign investment and move toward a market economy. How confused the students must be! And it is clear that they are not being effectively prepared to play a role in the new economic system that is emerging."[64]

When Ernesto Zedillo became minister of education in January 1992, he brought a number of young technocrats with him from his previous position as minister of programming and budgeting. These officials shared characteristics with many others who were extensively recruited into policy design units during the Salinas years. Although well-trained, they were often more skilled in technical analysis than in understanding the complex political dynamics of the PRI regime. Most were imbued with a sense of mission to promote the modernizing vision of the president and the minister, and they believed they could take risks because of the support they enjoyed from these two impressive sources of power. When Zedillo asked them to put together plans for various aspects of the overall education reform, they responded with alacrity.[65] "So we moved ahead with an integrated reform in . . . three areas—decentralization, going back to basic and simple education that is relevant, and making it possible for someone to have a professional career in teaching."[66]

One group was asked to consider how the free textbooks could be rewritten to give children an education more relevant to the late twentieth century. It was to generate teaching materials that encouraged students to reason rather than to rely on rote learning and that were more practical and less abstract than what was currently being used. They knew that time was of the essence in early 1992, when the National Agreement on the Modernization of Education was being negotiated with SNTE. The government was eager to resolve as much conflict as possible during this period and to move on to implement the reform as soon as the negotiations were over. Moreover, it was important to get new materials into the classrooms by the beginning of the 1992–1993 school year.[67] Particularly with regard to history texts, the design team anticipated that there might be some conflict, as the aspects they wanted to change were related to deeply held beliefs by significant numbers of people in the population and by important actors, including the still powerful old guard of the PRI. Moreover, any retelling of history could easily challenge the beliefs of all those who had been educated with the older textbooks. Despite the possibility of a reaction, within a month and a half, the team had a diagnosis of the problem in hand and was ready to move on to the selection of new texts.

Although the 1992 agreement specified that new history texts would be written by a distinguished team of historians, teachers, and designers, in fact the team followed a different process. Rather than seeking to rewrite existing texts, which would require a significant commitment of time and resources, it decided to put out a bid for new books. Pressured by time, the team did not allow for much consultation about the content of new materials and made the critical choices about which texts—and which interpretations of history—would be adopted. In the event, the introduction of the new books was met with a strong negative reaction that played out in daily newspapers, protests, and meetings.

The new history texts were decried for paying too little attention to the great sacrifice of the Niños Heroes of Chapultepec, the young military academy cadets who died in battle rather than surrender to invading U.S. forces in 1847 and whose actions represented one of the finest hours of nationalist defense against the "Colossus of the North." The new texts also officially recognized, for the first time, the student movement of 1968 although not the government's use of force to quell a demonstration in Tlatelolco, a district of Mexico City. The military was not pleased with the discussion, and former presidents went directly to the president with complaints about the way their administrations were portrayed.[68] The dictatorship of Porfirio Díaz, long presented as a corrupt and greedy dictator, was remembered in the new texts for the sustained period of peace and economic growth he brought to the country in the late nineteenth and early twentieth century. Critics saw an implicit reference to the Salinas administration, which was frequently accused of promoting economic growth at the expense of democracy. In addition, in making reference to the 1988 elections, which were widely suspected of being fraudulent, the texts simply described the results as having been very close.[69]

The public furor caused by the new texts left Minister Zedillo exposed to considerable public criticism and his resignation was called for. In the event, Salinas stood behind the minister while at the same time ensuring that the offenses against martyrs, the military, and former presidents were corrected. The government abandoned the distribution of the offending textbooks. The following year, the ministry called for a public competition to select the texts and a panel of judges was asked to make the selection. Those that were selected, and whose authors received substantial prize money, were more in accord with the government's newfound desire to avoid controversy. Ho Chi Minh, Fidel Castro, and Mao Tse-tung were pictured as leaders of national self-determination and decolonization. A fifth grade text ended the discussion of the country's history in 1964, avoiding the discussion of the student protests and the election.[70] The ministry argued that the country had not yet had time to come to terms with its more recent history.[71] Nevertheless, criticism of the new books was as strong as those in the previous year, in part because they sidestepped so many issues. In August 1993, echoing the previous year, the ministry of education announced that there would be no new history texts for the fourth, fifth, and sixth grades. The announcement was made just before the beginning of a new school year and left teachers uncertain about what to do.[72]

The design team that dealt with the issue of the textbooks was responsible for a political brouhaha that might have been avoided through a more consultative process of selection or at least closer attention to the political importance of the way historical events were treated in the texts. Certainly they caused the government to look uncertain and ineffective, and they also dimmed, at least for a while, the presidential ambitions of the minister. The case of Mexico signals the extent to which issues of reform design are intensely political.

CONCLUSION: THE POLITICS OF POLICY DESIGN

In the political economy literature on policy reform, solutions are often portrayed as being technically necessary or obviously appropriate responses to particular problems. Describing the problem—an overvalued exchange rate, high inflation, the fiscal burden of state-owned enterprises, low achievement in schools, overcentralization of decision making, and so forth—often substitutes for an analysis of the origin of particular proposals. While the work of design teams is sometimes mentioned, their role is generally viewed as the application of technical expertise to particular problems of public policy, removed and insulated from politics.[73]

But the cases of design teams in Bolivia, Minas Gerais, Ecuador, and Mexico indicate that the contents of policy reforms cannot be taken as given. In these cases, design teams concerned themselves centrally in defining a problem, devising a solution, and engaging in political conflicts. They had choices and options as they set about defining the broad nature of the reforms as well as the detailed mechanisms for how the changes would work in practice. The choices they made were influenced by the preferences and composition of the design group, suggesting that similar problems might generate distinct solutions depending on who is sitting at the table when reform options are considered. The cases also indicate how the choices made by design teams prefigured the political conflicts that surrounded reform initiatives when they became public. That there are winners and losers in reform initiatives is clear, but exactly who wins and who loses and how much they win or lose can be determined by the decisions of design teams.

TABLE 4.1
Design Team Characteristics and Strategies

| | | Reform Team Characteristics | | | | Strategies | |
Case	Year	Single, Like-Minded Team	Placement/ Composition Important	Create Networks within Government	Create Networks with International Funders	Limit Entry to Discussions	Rely on Executive for Political Managements
Minas Gerais	1991	✔	✔	✔	✔	✔	✔
Mexico	1992	✔	✔			✔	✔
Nicaragua*	1993	✔			✔	✔	✔
Bolivia	1994	✔	✔	✔	✔	✔	✔
Ecuador	1989		✔	✔	✔	✔	✔

* For evidence relevant to Nicaragua, see the discussion of executive leadership in chapter 3.

The cases also cast doubt on the view that reforms occur only when they are pressed upon decision makers by politically mobilized interests. In the education reform cases explored here, specific proposals for reform were hatched in the executive, often in the absence of mobilized pressure for them. In general, interest groups were reactive rather than proactive in the process of defining changes. Similarly, only in limited ways could reform contents be understood as the consequence of conflicts among group interests. Important group interests were active in supporting and opposing the reforms, but not until after the design teams had defined the issues around which conflict would revolve. Interest group politics were not the primary dynamic responsible for the content of these reform initiatives. Indeed, a frequent criticism of the reforms was that they were designed by small groups of technocrats who carried out their activities with little consultation of broader interests. To the interest groups concerned about education, these reforms seemed much more like elite projects than broadly negotiated policies.[74]

At a more specific level, the process of policy design in Bolivia, Minas Gerais, Ecuador, and Mexico revealed a series of commonalities (see table 4.1). First, each of the teams developed a common understanding of the problem of education in the country and how to go about resolving it. Reformers, whether political leaders or heads of design units, no doubt selected people for these teams who held similar perspectives to begin with. But each of the teams also went through a process of problem diagnosis that helped engineer a common vision of what needed to be done. Indeed, the considerable stability of the composition of ETARE/UNAS in Bolivia helped the reform initiative survive and protected the coherence of its contents. The professional backgrounds of those who designed the Minas Gerais reform helped them come to rapid agreement on how to understand the problem of education in their state as well as how to resolve it. The background of those in the Mexican ministry responsible for new textbooks no doubt also helped in reaching agreement, but kept them from anticipating the public outcry against the texts that were selected. It was also important that these design teams had no competition. Just how important this factor was is clear in the case of Ecuador, where rivalry between two design teams—each one of which had a clear and coherent idea of how to proceed with reform—undermined efforts to promote any kind of change in education.

Second, in Bolivia, Minas Gerais, and Ecuador, it made a difference where the design teams were located in the government bureaucracy. The case of Bolivia is clear: early on, reformers decided they had no chance of stimulating educational change from within the ministry of education, so they became part of the ministry of planning. From this position, they enjoyed ministerial support, but reaped additional problems in the jealousy of the education sector and the charge that they were, like others in the planning ministry, aloof technocrats. Only when they were placed within the ministry of education were they in a stronger position to promote their reform. In Minas Gerais, on the other hand, the path from analysis to plan to approval was much shorter because the design team was located in the ministry and enjoyed the unwavering support of the minister. In Ecuador, of course, the ongoing conflict between the regular ministry and the well-endowed project implementation unit signaled placement problems within a ministry. As indicated earlier, the composition of the teams was important not only for their work, but also for the political advantages and liabilities they created.

There was considerable commonality among the cases in limiting access to discussions of reform until the design team had worked out a detailed plan of what was to be undertaken.[75] This was certainly a strategic choice, as the design teams also made decisions about which interests would be consulted and under what conditions. Of course, relatively closed design processes had mixed results in terms of promoting education reform. For example, the Bolivian team carried out much of its planning in camera, and this gave their initiative significant coherence as a proposal. At the same time, it also resulted in a high level of party and union animosity toward the team and its later exclusion from CONED. Public discussion of the Minas Gerais reform was not encouraged until after the reform design was prepared, and a similar closed process characterized the development of two plans in Ecuador. Certainly the decision to limit entry to the discussion of textbook reform helped the Mexican team misjudge the extent to which change would generate criticism and tension in the political system. In these cases, the decision to work behind closed doors also meant that when specific interests were consulted, it was at the behest of the design team.

The cases indicate the extent to which the power of the design teams was circumscribed by the readiness with which political leaders became advocates of change and were willing to manage the public politics of reform. Thus, the cases demonstrate the ways in which design teams are dependent on the willingness of political leaders to take up their recommendations and commit themselves to gaining legitimacy for them.[76] In Bolivia, it was very clear that the reform design so carefully put together by Amalia Anaya and her team was fully dependent on the support of the president of the day. The lack of interest by Paz Zamora kept it on the shelf during his administration; it was adopted by Sánchez de Lozada but then abandoned as other priorities pushed it to the sidelines of national politics; and it regained life under the presidencies of Banzer and Quiroga. In Minas Gerais, the strong support of the governor and the minister was critical to the design team headed by Ana Luiza Pinheiro. In Ecuador, neither of the reform proposals could move ahead without presidential support, and both teams eagerly sought that support. And in Mexico, the support that Zedillo and his team had from Salinas no doubt saved their jobs, although they were forced to backtrack on the issue of the textbooks. At the same time, however, by the time their recommendations were appropriated by political leaders, design teams had already determined the allocation of winners and losers and had foretold the form that political reaction to change was to take.

The creation of reformist networks was an important way in which the design teams promoted their ideas.[77] This was clear in Bolivia where Anaya and her team consciously created networks across government agencies and political parties and where individuals who were part of the networks emerged at various points in important positions to promote the fortunes of the team and its initiative. In Minas Gerais, a series of networks drew the reformers together with important political and academic figures. Moreover, design teams in Bolivia, Minas Gerais, and Ecuador established and maintained close connections to international agencies that were interested in funding their innovations. Technical assistance from the international agencies promoted ideas about reforms that were being introduced in other contexts and also provided the funding for the work of the design teams.[78] Indeed, the international agencies had considerable influence at this phase of the policy process, where they were able to work closely with design teams. In contrast, during the agenda-setting process, they were more distant from decision-making arenas.

Ultimately, these reformist initiatives were fragile and so, too, was the capacity of design teams to be a fulcrum of change. Bolivia provides the clearest example of this vulnerability. At no point in the long process of promoting educational change was that country's reform ensured. Even when it was passed into law, political opposition to it meant that little headway could be made in putting it into practice. Throughout the process, convinced that its approach was the only one that was both specific and comprehensive, the team was unwilling to make significant alterations in its plan to appease the opposition. And, within government, the leadership of the design team was critically important but also extremely vulnerable. Amalia Anaya was removed from office repeatedly, and her absence threatened the survival of the initiative. The case of design teams in Ecuador is also testimony to the fragility of reform proposals and their proponents. Specific choices made by the design teams no doubt added to the difficulty of the reform, but it is quite possible that even with more astute decision making, reform would have fallen victim to the larger context of economic and political turmoil. In the next two chapters, the fragility of the reforms is emphasized in the analysis of those in the forefront of opposition to change, the teachers' unions.

CONTESTING EDUCATION: TEACHERS' UNIONS
AND THE STATE   collier ; collier '91

QUALITY-ENHANCING EDUCATION reforms such as those introduced in Latin America during the 1990s required that teachers develop new skills, use new curricula, demonstrate professional competence, and respond to community and parental interest in their performance. Indeed, none of the reforms could be successful without the active commitment of the teachers in the classroom.[1] Yet, the organizations that represented teachers were generally not at the table when education reforms were designed.

Thus, when new plans were announced, rather than rallying to support them, teachers' unions objected to what they viewed as the work of technocratic elites, unwanted interference by international development agencies, invidious efforts to privatize public education in accordance with neoliberal ideology, hostility to the rightful claims of public sector workers for decent wages, and hidden agendas favoring cost saving and union breaking. Unions underscored their opposition to reform plans with strikes, marches, demonstrations, media campaigns, votes, and other forms of political pressure.[2]

In most of Latin America, the gulf between reformers and unions was wide and deep. Reformers pointed to a legacy of union power that produced patronage, malfeasance, and unresponsiveness to national or local interest in improving education. Unions were derided for corruption and abuses of power that helped place education systems in crisis. Union leaders consistently replied that teachers were miserably paid, received few benefits for the difficult work they did, were systematically excluded from discussions about change, and were publicly disparaged by the reformist elites who sought to impose unwanted burdens on them. Indeed, in many countries, against a backdrop of a decade or more of economic reform policies that produced unemployment and recession, that imposed austerity, and that were planned and executed by remote and faceless technocrats in executive bureaucracies, public sector workers had little reason to trust that the reformist measures being proposed would be beneficial to them. All too frequently, then, reform proposals generated "us versus them" conflicts that plagued the process of reform approval and implementation.

As this chapter demonstrates, virtue and fault can be found on both sides of the conflict. The reformers did systematically ignore the claims of

the unions; the unions responded with obstructionist activities. Reformers tried a variety of ways to weaken the hold of the unions on education
policy; unions used their political alliances to maintain influence in ministries of education. Reformers sought to reach teachers directly rather than
through their unions; the unions drew on teacher loyalties by demanding—and at times delivering—higher salaries, better conditions, and
more respect.

Such conflicts were critically important to the fate of education reform
in Latin America. This chapter places Latin America's teachers' unions in
the institutional structure of national politics by describing their history
and the dynamics of their relationships to government, ministries of education, and political parties (see table 5.1). These relationships, formed
over decades, created legacies that shaped how the unions reacted to education reform initiatives. The chapter also considers the grievances that
the unions regularly articulated in their conflicts with the state. It suggests
that the unions rejected reform not only because their basic demands were
not being met, but also because they objected to the ends, means, and
values of the reformers' proposals. At times, of course, union leaders selected courses of action that were not supported by all teachers. Nevertheless, the grievances of the organizations were critical ingredients in the
unsettled relationship between the teachers and the state. The subsequent
chapter returns to Bolivia, Ecuador, Mexico, Minas Gerais, and Nicaragua
to explore how education was contested in those countries.

TEACHERS' UNIONS: THEIR POWER AND STRUCTURE

Teachers' unions in much of Latin America emerged and grew in strength
as part of initiatives to expand the influence of the national state over
economic and social affairs. In this regard, teachers' unions tended to reiterate a more general history of labor mobilization in the region.[3] At the
same time, the emergence of the teachers' unions was marked by a special
relationship to national projects for the centralization and expansion of
education. In most countries, the unions promoted the development of a
welfarist state as its bases were established in the 1930s, 1940s, and 1950s.
In this process, they forged ties to political parties, ministries of education,
and national states.

In Mexico, for example, the centralization and secularization of education in the 1920s was a cause taken on by schoolteachers and their incipient organizations. This early history created an enduring legacy of close
association among the unions, the national ministry of education, and
what was later to become the PRI.[4] In Venezuela, teachers' unions
emerged in the late 1930s and 1940s. They fought against authoritarian

Table 5.1

Teachers' Unions in Latin America in the 1990s

	Ar	Bo	Br	Cb	Co	CR	Ec	Me	Ni	Pe	Ve
Number of important organizations in sector*	3	2		1	1	3	1	1	4	1	7
Number/% of workers represented in sector	200,000/ 73%	92,000/ 100%		101,000/ 75%	300,000/ 65%	40,000/ 100%	170,000/ 90%	1,103,000/ 100%	30,000/ 70%	200,000/ 100%	200,000/ 65%
Decade of initial unionization in sector	1900s, 1940s	1930s, 1940s	1930s	1920s	1950s	1940s	1930s	1910s, 1940s	1980s		1930s
Structure: H/M/L** centralization	M/L	H	L	M	M	H	H	H	L	H	M
Ministry relationship: H/M/L confrontation	M	M	M	L	L	L	M	L	L	H	M
Party relationship: H/M/L identity	H	H	L	L	M	M	H	M	M	H	M
1990s trajectory of power: ↑/↓***	→	→	→	←	←	←	→	→	→	→	→

Sources: Arnaut (1998a); Arnove (1995); Bellei (1999); Broda (1999a, 1999b, 1999c, 1999d, 1999e, 1999f); Casanova (1998); Draibe (2002); Iquiñiz Echeverria (2000); Loyo, Ibarrola, and Blanco (1999); Murillo (1999a, 1999b); Ornelas (1988); Ortiz de Zevallos (n.d.); Street (1998); Taliercio (1996); Tiramonti (2000); Trejos (1999): author's survey.

* Unions, federations, or confederations.

** H/M/L = high/medium/low.

*** ↑/↓ = increasing/decreasing.

governments and supported parties that were committed to a national
and centralized education system. Later, they were incorporated into na-
tionalizing and centralizing political parties as federations and became
subordinate to those parties.[5] In El Salvador, the dynamic was somewhat
different, as parties mobilized unions of teachers and incorporated
them into their organizational structures.[6] In Bolivia, teachers were part
of a mosaic of nationalist and revolutionary groups that organized against
an authoritarian and elitist state in the 1930s and 1940s. At the time of
the Revolution of 1952, rural and urban teachers, in alliance with radical
left parties, sought to incorporate peasants and workers into national
school systems and to inculcate a revolutionary ideology among the
young.[7] Similar concerns encouraged these parties to gain control over
teacher training schools.

Throughout the region, Latin America's teachers were no strangers to
national politics. In Argentina, teachers' organizations with anarchist and
socialist orientations emerged early in the twentieth century; they were
part of national struggles against the oligarchic state and the exclusion
of workers from politics. In the 1940s, disparate unions and professional
associations were incorporated into the Peronist state as a national guild.[8]
In later years, political parties competed for the allegiance of the teachers,
a dynamic that weakened the capacity of the unions to represent their
constituents in negotiations with the state. In Nicaragua, after a period
during which unions were banned, the creation of a national teachers'
association as part of the Sandinista revolution set the bases for later conflict with non-Sandinista governments. In Chile, the state largely pre-
empted a close identification of teachers with particular political parties
through top-down efforts to organize them. This weakened their capacity
to oppose government policies. In Brazil, while influential unions emerged
in some of the states, at the national level, they were fragmented, their
presence weak, and their influence modest.[9]

The Union/Ministry Nexus

The 1950s and 1960s, when many countries expanded their educational
systems in response to demographic pressures and reform initiatives, were
important decades for the unions.[10] During this period, the goals of the
unions—to represent teachers in negotiations over salaries and conditions
of work—coincided with government interests in labor peace and expansion of the teaching corps. Not surprisingly, corporatist relationships with
ministries of education developed as the unions were invited to help devise
norms, regulations, and statutes that were an important aspect of more
inclusive national systems.[11] Indeed, ministries were often willing to ac-
cede to union demands and to union participation in policy decision mak-

ing and implementation as budgets grew and there was need for interlocutors to ensure labor peace and coordination in the sector. When they were unable to meet union demands for salary increments, they traded union quiescence for control over education policy and positions. Union colonization of ministries of education and control over teacher education, assignments, and promotions were common results of this relationship.[12]

In Mexico, Ecuador, and elsewhere, unions developed informal but well-recognized rights to name high-level officials within the ministry and at times had a say in the selection of ministers. In Chile, Argentina, and Colombia, teachers' unions became part of corporatist structures that were regularly consulted on issues related to education and teachers. In Costa Rica, the union representing primary school teachers prepared lists of candidates deemed qualified for teaching positions and sat on the teachers' national pension board.[13] In Venezuela, an office of union affairs in the ministry was a central part of an exchange of patronage and benefits.

In Chile, the posting of teachers in the ministry of education meant that "in some sense, the teachers became the ministry and the ministry became the teachers."[14] In the 1990s, a legacy of disenfranchisement under the Pinochet government and the return of rights to unionize under the newly installed democracy in 1990 encouraged a cordial relationship between the Colegio de Profesores and the government. Confrontation with government was relatively low, and most issues were negotiated according to regular schedules and discussions.[15] Unions in Costa Rica, after a bitter and conflict-ridden strike in 1995, reverted to their more normal and cordial relationship with the ministry in subsequent years.[16] Even where governments and unions were often at loggerheads, close relationships usually continued between the unions and ministries of education. In Ecuador, for example, despite an extremely hostile relationship with government, the teachers' union continued to dominate the ministry. Under such conditions, unions were able to extend job security for their members, ensure that union members would hold supervisory roles in the school system, lighten teaching burdens, minimize monitoring of teacher performance, and create jobs in the government for union members and leaders.[17]

The Union/Party Nexus

The relationship of the unions to political parties shaped their activities vis-à-vis government, even while their relationships to education ministries tended toward mutually beneficial exchanges of influence for labor stability. In some cases, parties, unions, and the state were closely aligned. The SNTE in Mexico is an extreme example of the connections among them. By the 1990s, this union had been part of the corporatist structure of the PRI for decades.[18] Its officials ran for public office under the PRI banner, and its leaders were important in the internal power structure of the party. Through a corporatist pact, the union maintained limits on internal dissidence and labor demands. It mobilized teachers to campaign and vote for PRI candidates.[19] SNTE officials ran for public office, held positions in the ministry of education, and gained power within the PRI.[20] The union occasionally called strikes, but at least until the late 1980s, these generally ended with the close working relationship to government intact.

In some cases, however, union-party affiliations created a more hostile environment for governments. In Bolivia, Ecuador, Guatemala, and Peru, for example, teachers' unions were closely associated with small leftist parties always identified with the opposition.[21] In other cases, parties and unions changed dance partners from time to time. In Argentina, the Unión de Docentes Argentinos (UDA) was closely allied with the Peronist Party and integrated into the Peronist peak labor confederation, the CGT (Confederación General del Trabajo). CTERA, a federation of provincial unions created in 1973, brought together teachers with a range of political affiliations. In the 1980s, Peronists gained control of CTERA, but in the early 1990s, union leaders aligned with the reformist FREPASO party and joined in an effort to create an alternative labor confederation.[22] Brazil's often ephemeral and personalist political parties encouraged frequent changes of union-party alliances. In the state of Minas Gerais, however, the teachers' union, UTE, was mobilized by the Partido dos Trabalhadores (PT) in the 1980s, and its ideology was forged in the struggle for the return of democracy after two decades of military rule. It remained closely allied to the PT and its political objectives. And in Mexico, with the traditional power of the PRI in decline in the early 1990s, SNTE sought to increase its political leverage by ending its formal relationship with the party.[23]

Structures of Dissent

It was this legacy of relationship among unions, states, ministries, and parties that set the stage for labor conflicts in the reforms of the 1990s. By that time, teachers' unions tended to be highly aggregated; in many countries one national organization represented the teachers. At times, these were single unions representing all education workers, as was the case in Mexico, Peru, Chile, and the Dominican Republic. In other cases, such as in Argentina, Colombia, and Bolivia, regional and local unions were brought together to form a small number of federations or confederations. As indicated in table 5.1, Venezuela was unusual in the fragmentation of its union sector with seven different federations representing teachers.[24]

TABLE 5.2
Teachers as a Proportion of the Formal Labor Force

Country	%
Bolivia	9
Brazil	7
Chile	4
Colombia	6
Costa Rica	3
Ecuador (urban)	9
El Salvador	5
Honduras	8
Panama	6
Paraguay	5
Uruguay (urban)	2
Venezuela	3

Source: Liang (1999:3), based on national household surveys in ten countries and urban surveys in Ecuador and Uruguay, 1995 and 1996.

Note: Those categorized as teachers varies by country.

In most cases, these unions, federations, or confederations brought together teachers from all levels of schooling, as well as educational administrators.[25] In Mexico, clerical and service workers in education ministries also belonged to the teachers' union. The organizations were large, representing over 1.1 million members in Mexico, and 200,000 to 300,000 members in Argentina, Colombia, Peru, and Venezuela. Similarly, the national organizations represented a very large proportion of workers in the education sector, from virtually all of them in Bolivia and Mexico to over 70 percent of them in Argentina and Chile. Teachers were also a sizable part of the labor force in most Latin American countries. In Bolivia, Brazil, Colombia, El Salvador, Honduras, Panama, and Paraguay, for example, they represented between 5 and 9 percent of the formal labor force (see table 5.2).[26]

The size of the teachers' organizations often meant that they controlled significant financial resources. In most countries, union members paid 1 percent of their salaries as union dues; generally this amount was deducted automatically from paychecks.[27] Some wealthy unions owned businesses that catered to their membership, such as hotels, hospitals, pension funds, and mortuaries. In addition, the number of paid positions within some unions was impressive. In Mexico, for example, there were two thousand

% % gov't employment

union positions; teachers appointed or elected to these posts were freed from all other responsibilities so they could commit themselves full-time to organizational activities.[28] In Venezuela, the fragmentation of union federations created between two thousand and three thousand jobs.[29]

Although most of the national teachers' organizations were federations or confederations in the 1990s, national leadership cadres had considerable power to make binding decisions, control funds, and influence the choice of leadership at other levels of these organizations. This degree of centralization was not surprising, mirroring as it did the centralization of national education systems. The decisions most important to the unions, relating to pay and conditions of work, were generally made at national levels.

Centralization also made it possible to create and maintain close ties to national political parties and facilitated patronage and other exchanges between unions and political leaders. Moreover, centralization helped the teachers' organizations become significant actors in national labor confederations. In Mexico, for example, the SNTE held great power within the National Confederation of Popular Organizations (CNOP), and in Bolivia, rural and urban teachers' unions were a fundamental pillar of the COB (Central Obrera Boliviana). Where teachers' unions were fragmented, as in the case of Venezuela in the 1980s and Argentina in the 1990s, their power was consequently circumscribed.[30]

nvt wrt teachers unions

Despite a high degree of centralization, Latin America's teachers' unions were from time to time shaken by internal dissent.[31] In Colombia and Mexico, for example, there were conflicts in the 1980s about the extent to which union leaders could be held democratically accountable by their members.[32] In other cases, conflict over strategies to counter reform initiatives created internal tensions. In Nicaragua, leaders struggled and disagreed over whether to decentralize activities to the school and community level, where many decisions about personnel and pay were being made in the wake of reform, or to maintain a centralized decision-making system as a way of maximizing influence in national politics.[33] In Argentina, internal dissent weakened the capacity of the teachers to contest a decentralization initiative.[34] In Peru, the national teachers' union, SUTEP (Sindicato Unico de Trabajadores de la Educación Peruana), also suffered from internal divisions, although it was able to mobilize successful resistance to education reform in 1992.[35]

Overall, teachers' unions were powerful political actors when quality-enhancing reforms were introduced. However, they were often less powerful than they had been. Reflecting in part the impact of austerity, adjustment policies, and internal dissent, teachers' unions began to experience a decline in their traditional power in the 1980s, a trend that continued into the 1990s.[36] This meant decreased capacity to win concessions from government and to influence state policy. Decentralization and school autonomy reforms increased this tendency, and at the end of the decade, the unions had more distant and more contentious relationships with government than had generally been the case in the past.

UNION GRIEVANCES: PAY, INTERESTS, PROCESS, AND VALUES

In many stories of education reform, unions are presented as organizations with extensive vested interests in the status quo and considerable power to make reform initiatives short-lived.[37] Rarely are their grievances taken seriously in such accounts. Teachers' unions have also been the subject of studies of social movements seeking to increase the democratic accountability of leaders and to limit authoritarian control over these organizations.[38] Surprisingly, however, while such studies take teachers' grievances seriously, they rarely consider the implications of these complaints for public policy about education. Equally important, the negative portrayal of the unions by reformers and their allies, as well as their absence from most reform design initiatives, discouraged systematic analysis of their grievances. Indeed, a large number of studies making the case for the importance of education reform make no mention of the unions.[39] Union grievances, however, were central to the conflicts over reform in the 1990s.

The Problem of Pay

The 1990s education initiatives threatened the power of the teachers' unions. In fact, much of the interaction between governments and unions during this decade had to do with power—the power to appoint union members to positions in government, to place people in teaching positions, to determine the content of education policies, to halt reform initiatives considered inimical to teachers' interests. Over and above these issues, however, concerns about salaries and employment conditions—contractual conditions, benefits, promotion systems, evaluation procedures—loomed extremely large in the relationship between government and unions.[40]

By and large, the reforms of the 1990s ignored issues of teacher remuneration except to promote the association of pay with performance. In addition, they sought to alter employment conditions so that school supervisors, parent councils, or local governments would become agents for hiring, promoting, and firing educators. These latter issues threatened strong union commitment to collective bargaining at national levels and union control over the teaching profession. When reformers ignored the salary issue and sought significant changes in employment conditions, they inevitably encouraged union opposition.

From the perspective of the unions, the issue of teacher salaries was simple—teachers were underpaid. Some studies suggest that union positions on this issue were correct. A comparative study of sixteen developing and transitional countries at the end of the 1990s found that, on average, beginning teachers earned about 1.2 times GDP per capita. In the Latin American countries in the sample, however, teachers earned 0.8 times GDP per capita in Argentina, 0.7 times in Brazil, 1.1 times in Chile, and 0.9 times GDP per capita in Peru.[41] But other researchers have looked more closely at the issue of teacher remuneration, taking up the charge of underpayment and asking questions such as: underpaid for what? underpaid by what criteria? underpaid relative to whom? As they have asked these questions, they have come up with contradictory answers. Some report that teacher pay was comparable to that of others with similar characteristics in the labor force.[42] Others report that teachers were overpaid in some countries and underpaid in others.[43] The answers often depended on how salaries were measured.

A 1999 study of teacher salaries in twelve Latin American countries, for example, determined that, based on annual incomes of teachers compared with a non-teaching comparison group, teachers earned less than others (see table 5.3).[44] In Bolivia, Brazil, and urban Ecuador, in fact, teachers earned 35 to 38 percent less than those with comparable levels of education, and in Chile and El Salvador, they earned about 20 percent less. However, table 5.3 shows that, on average, teachers worked significantly fewer hours than the comparison group. In Brazil, Colombia, El Salvador, Honduras, Paraguay, and Uruguay, for example, teachers worked an average of twelve to fourteen hours less per week than the comparison group. In Bolivia, teachers worked an average of twenty-eight hours a week while non-teachers worked fifty hours a week. Using the same data, but controlling for the average number of hours worked weekly, the table indicates that teachers in seven countries earned more than the non-teacher comparison group. Yet again, if teachers' salaries are calculated on the basis of hourly wages adjusted for vacation time, they were paid considerably more than the comparison group. Table 5.3 indicates that in Bolivia, Colombia, Costa Rica, El Salvador, Honduras, Panama, and Venezuela, for example, they earned 33 to 44 percent more than those in other jobs when this measure is used.

The same study also found that teacher salaries varied less than those of other groups, reflecting the greater stability of employment they generally enjoyed. Women were shown to earn less than men in six of the twelve countries, largely reflecting the lower average number of hours worked by women compared to men. In Chile, they were paid 8 percent less, in El Salvador 20 percent less, and in Paraguay, 25 percent less.[45] Finally, differ-

TABLE 5.3
Teacher and Non-Teacher* Salaries in Twelve Countries

	Teacher Annual Income as a % of Non-Teacher Income	Average Hours Worked by Teachers as a % of Non-Teacher Hours	Hourly Wage Premium of Teachers without Adjusting for Vacation**	Hourly Wage of Premium of Teachers Adjusting for Vacation***
	%	%	%	%
Bolivia	62	56	NS	37
Brazil	35	70	-7	11
Chile	81	81	NS	18
Colombia	95	73	20	35
Costa Rica	NS	79	15	38
Ecuador	63	81	-27	NS
El Salvador	78	72	9	37
Honduras	NS	73	29	44
Panama	95	80	12	33
Paraguay	NS	75	NS	29
Uruguay	86	69	10	29
Venezuela	91	85	8	37

Source: Liang 1999:4, 6, 7.
* Controlled for education, experience, and other labor market characteristics.
** Assumes teachers and non-teachers work same number of days.
*** Assumes teachers work 25% fewer days than non-teachers.
NS—Not significant.

entials in pay among teachers, controlling for gender, were largely determined by years of experience.[46]

A study of Bolivian teacher salaries reached similar conclusions about their pay. If total earnings were considered, then teachers in that country were not well paid; if, however, hourly pay was calculated, teachers fared much better.[47] In a second study of Bolivian teachers, researchers also concluded that the fairness of their wages depended on how the comparison was made.[48] This study found that gender and ethnic inequalities among teachers were much less than among non-teachers and that teacher pay did not increase as much with experience as did that of other occupations. The researchers concluded, "The earnings profile for teachers starts out higher [than that of non-teachers], but has a flatter shape."[49] All three studies found that far more teachers held second jobs than was true of comparison groups.[50]

TABLE 5.4
Changes in Public Sector Teacher Real Salaries, 1980s and 1990s
(index 1980 or 1985 = 100)

Country	Level	1980	1982	1985	1988	1990
Argentina	Primary	100	69	95	59	45 (1992)
Bolivia	Primary/secondary	100	34	23	73 (1987)	
Chile	Primary	100	133	105	70 (1990)	120 (1993)
Colombia	Primary	100	103	102	102 (1987)	
Costa Rica	Primary	100	74	72	75	96 (1990)
El Salvador	Primary	100	78	62	43	32 (1992)
Guatemala	Primary	100	90	70	54 (1987)	
Mexico	Primary	100 (1981)	82	58	22	40 (1993)
Panama	Primary/secondary			100		98 (1993)
Uruguay	Primary/secondary			100		184 (1983)
Venezuela	Primary	100			70	

Source: ILO (1996:46).

Such studies are valuable in bringing research to bear on the frequent claims by unions that teachers are underpaid. There is certainly empirical evidence to suggest that this is not always the case. But at another level, this research misses much of the point of the teachers' grievances. For them, levels of pay are associated with increases and decreases over time in their salaries and standards of living. In the volatile conditions of the 1980s, teachers in many countries suffered significant declines in their salaries and purchasing power. Indeed, ILO calculations indicate much decreased salaries in Argentina, Bolivia, Chile, Costa Rica, El Salvador, Guatemala, Mexico, Panama, and Venezuela (see table 5.4). A separate study of teacher salaries in Chile showed them to have declined by 32 percent between 1981 and 1990.[51] To the extent that teachers are comparing their earnings not with any particular reference group but with their own salaries and standards of living in the past, the issue of pay takes on very different meaning.

Unions were quick to respond to these salary losses. In 1989, for example, Mexico's SNTE demanded that teacher salaries be raised by 100 percent, a level at which (they argued) teachers would have recouped the losses they experienced during the 1980s. In Chile, teachers claimed that they were owed increases in salaries because of the "historical debt" owed to them for the losses they incurred in the 1980s.[52] Between 1981 and 1990, public school teacher salaries declined by an average of 7 percent a year, a trajectory encouraged by the banning of unions under the Pinochet dictatorship.[53] In Peru, economic crisis also had severe implications for the salaries of teachers.[54] In some countries, fiscal crises meant that teachers could not count on receiving their pay on a timely basis. In Ecuador, for example, teachers at times did not receive their salaries for as much as three months in a row. Overall, teachers in many countries had reason to feel aggrieved in terms of the trajectory and reliability of their salaries.

These perceptions were important in understanding the relationship of the teachers to the unions that represented them. It is certainly true that teachers' unions were often led by corrupt officials, just as the reformers charged. It was also frequently the case that these leaders were more interested in their own power than in the welfare of their memberships. It is true that some unions were allied with political parties whose ideologies and positions were not shared by the bulk of teachers. At the same time, however, most unions consistently proclaimed the importance of raising teachers' salaries and protecting their security of employment. In the context of governments that sought to reduce these benefits in the 1980s, and reformers who ignored such claims in the 1990s, it is not surprising that teachers continued to believe that their unions were fighting for their interests and protecting them from the negative impact of a range of new policies. They gave allegiance to their unions because the unions had been able to deliver in the past and because no one else was advocating for their interests. As indicated by one education activist in Bolivia, "the unions are the only protection the teachers have."[55]

Contesting the Ends of Reform

Unions wanted better pay for teachers. They also demanded security of employment. In most countries, teacher appointments had generally meant lifetime employment, with salary increases consistent with experience. Union officials in Ecuador, for example, argued that national policy should result in "better working conditions, a just salary policy . . . and substantive legal changes."[56] They believed that improved salaries had to be the basis on which all discussion of quality enhancement would take place. They argued that governments were giving priority to paying the external debt and helping out bankrupt bankers.[57]

Even in the exceptional cases in which unions supported reform, pay and work conditions were still central to their actions. Colombian teachers who were part of the Movimiento Pedagógico in the 1980s, for example, supported merit and hardship pay and merit hiring of teachers along with a limited form of decentralization. Nevertheless, as union members, they were frequently hostile to government and believed that salary increases would only be forthcoming in the wake of strikes.[58] In Brazil's state of Minas Gerais, the teachers' union continued to advance the cause of improved salaries for its members, even while supporting some aspects of the government's school autonomy reform.

Reformers, on the other hand, were much more concerned about standards for teaching and the performance of teachers in the classroom. For them, automatic and across-the-board increases in teacher salaries and the persistence of personnel policies that rewarded seniority and stability promoted the poor performance, shirking, and lack of professionalism that they were battling against. They believed strongly that teachers should be held to certain standards and that increments in pay should be tied to improvements in performance and training. Given that low performance was the norm, they did not believe that general increases in salaries would have any impact on the quality of the education delivered.[59] Many believed that without reform, teachers were receiving the pay they deserved—low quality rewarded by low pay.

In addition to salaries and conditions of employment, unions and reformers differed about the legitimate power of the unions. Union leaders were clearly concerned that the national unions remain strong and influential and that they continue to be the interlocutors for teachers with the government. They were particularly hostile to government initiatives to decentralize education, and particularly to those mechanisms that would give governors, mayors, local school officials, school councils, or others the capacity to set salaries and conditions of employment.[60] They had reason to be concerned. In Argentina, for example, decentralization successfully placed decision making about teaching conditions at the provincial level, and union organizations found themselves dealing with numerous provincial governments rather than with one central government.

In contrast, resisting decentralization helped unions remain influential. In Chile and Mexico, unions were able to maintain national-level collective bargaining agreements for salaries and teaching conditions despite significant decentralization initiatives. Similarly, in Colombia, the Federación Colombiana de Educadores (FECODE) supported administrative decentralization to the state level, along with centralization of collective bargaining, in opposition to a government initiative to d municipal level and encourage school autonomy.[61]

Decentralization initiatives, and particularly those pro tonomy, along with pay linked to performance and the councils, were interpreted by unions as clear evidence efforts to weaken the unions or destroy them. Indeed, tion and school autonomy initiatives were undertaken with this intent. The reformers argued that with centralized and powerful unions, it was impossible to introduce effective incentives to encourage teachers to perform better in the classroom or to see students and their parents as the most important clients of their activities. The resistance of the unions to such measures confirmed the reformer's view that the unions were seeking to advance their own power at the cost of improved schooling in the country.

The conflict between the reformers and the unions was also embedded in distinct views about expertise and control in the classroom. The unions, as representatives of the teachers and beneficiaries of centralized governments that structured curricula, selected learning material, and decided on teaching methodologies, were committed to the idea that teachers, supervisors, and ministries had command of the classroom. They believed that teachers had developed professional expertise through their training and that nonexperts should not be in a position to judge their performance. Reformers, on the other hand, frequently believed that parents and local communities, as consumers of education, had the capacity to assess the effectiveness of teachers and school directors and should have opportunities to do so.

Contesting the Means of Reform

The ends of reform were hotly debated between unions and reformers in the 1990s, but so too were the means through which the reforms were generated. Unions complained about their exclusion from efforts to design reforms and from discussions about their merits and realism. In most cases, they believed that the reforms had been devised behind closed doors by technocratic elites who did not appreciate the views of the unions or the perspectives of the teachers. Union leaders in Ecuador, for example, reflecting on the large number of reform proposals that had come out of government, lamented that "the voice of the teacher corps was scorned and ignored."[62] International agencies contributed to this situation. These organizations, whose financial support was critically important to the reformers and whose ideas helped frame the contents of the policy changes, "cast public sector unions and professional associations as the villains in stories of attempted reform . . . to be avoided, circumvented, and undermined."[63]

Indeed, some unions sought to demonstrate the failings of the closed-door proceedings by contrasting them with broadly consultative processes to generate alternative reform proposals. In Peru, in addition to strikes, marches, and work stoppages, the union organized seminars throughout the country to discuss the implications of new education laws with teachers and parents.[64] In Bolivia, as we have seen, a national congress and then a national education council brought together a broad range of important interests to devise an alternative reform proposal. In Nicaragua in the late 1990s, the unions supported a national consensus document about education.[65] In Ecuador, UNE presented a widely consulted reform bill to the legislature in September 1999.[66] That these proposals often amounted to little more than general statements about the importance of education in national development was much less important than demonstrating that a consultative process was a much more appropriate way to go about education reform.[67]

In attacking the process of reform development, unions were protesting against a radical change in their relationship to government. Unions had long been partners with ministries and staunch advocates for education, closely associated with projects for expanding access to schooling, and they had become accustomed to controlling some parts of education policy. In the past, the unions knew about proposals for change because they were early participants in discussions of them. In the 1990s, they often learned of plans to reform education when they were officially announced.

Contesting the Values of Reform

The reactions of the unions to change proposals went deeper still, challenging fundamental values. As unions, they were committed to principles of solidarity, representation, and collective bargaining. From their perspective, teachers had political presence through the union. Thus, any changes in the condition of teachers or of education should involve consultation and negotiation with the union. Often, however, reformers sought to attract teachers to their proposals as individuals, directly providing them with teaching materials, opportunities for training, salary increments, and other benefits if they adopted the reforms in the classroom and in interactions with parents and local officials.[68]

Similarly, teachers' unions in almost all countries were deeply committed to public education and to the privileged position of the state in providing education. For them, many reforms challenged such commitments. Efforts to encourage private sector and NGO involvement in education were a central characteristic of the Chilean model of reform, for example. By 1990, the voucher system had created a system in which almost 40 percent of primary school students were enrolled in private schools (see table 2.8). Because this initiative preceded others by a decade or more, unions in the later reforming countries used it as a rallying cry about what could happen to public education systems.

Union leaders in Nicaragua used the Chilean example to revile the autonomous schools and the formalization of school fees as the first step toward the privatization of education, in which parents would eventually be responsible for paying the salaries of teachers in the local schools and providing textbooks and infrastructure.[69] In Ecuador, the president of the national teachers' union was adamant about the intent of the government. "What self-management [school autonomy] really means is privatization. The government is going to make the parents pay for schooling, for taking exams, for the teachers. They will make them pay for all of it. . . . The government is getting out of education and leaving it to the NGOs, the parents, the private sector. They are asking these sectors to adopt education."[70] In Argentina, 1999 was proclaimed the "Year of Defense of Public Education" by CTERA, and its leader complained that "never did we think that public education would be at risk" and went on to attack education reform for creating this condition.[71]

Indeed, the rhetoric of privatization was a powerful means for mobilizing resistance to change. In Peru in 1992, faced with the surprise announcement of a Chilean-style education reform emphasizing vouchers, community education councils, and decentralization, SUTEP immediately responded with a protest campaign. Its cry that the government was intent upon privatizing education won enough public support that President Fujimori backed away from supporting the proposal.[72]

For the unions, many reforms were an attack on "the public character of education and the role of the teacher as a bearer of a universal rationality superior to particular interests that could only be carried out by public servants."[73] They therefore attacked what they saw as the primary commitments of the reformers to efficiency and market-oriented solutions to national problems. For union activists in Ecuador, education was an "inalienable human right . . . [that was] an undeniable obligation of the state."[74] For the leader of CTERA in Argentina, "knowledge and the public school were going to be subjected to buying and selling in the national market," if reform succeeded.[75] Unions similarly decried the influence of international agencies such as the World Bank, which represented the intrusion of global forces and ideas into an arena of strong nationalist concern. State versus market, neoliberalism versus nationalism, state responsibility versus privatization were potent lines along which education reforms were debated throughout the region.

Two Different Worlds?

Conflicts between the unions and the reformers were about real issues with very concrete consequences for the lives of teachers and the power of the unions that represented them. But they also represented fundamental disagreements over the role of education in public life, the role of teachers in the classroom, the role of the state in education, and the role of unions in representing the teachers. At times, the discourse between the unions and the reformers suggested that they were living in two distinct worlds.

The case of Bolivia, where unions and reformers collided for more than a decade over interests, process, and values, vividly demonstrates how far apart they could be. The country's teachers' unions were opposed to education reform from the time that it began to be discussed publicly. The reformers early on identified the unions as the enemy of any reform initiative. Their positions on key issues, summarized in table 5.5, never varied.

Many parts of the reform initiative impinged directly on the interests of the unions. As discussed in chapter 3, the 1994 reform would end the monopoly on teacher training enjoyed by the country's normal schools; it would introduce merit-based systems for evaluating and promoting teachers; and it would make union membership voluntary and end the automatic salary deductions for union dues. The reform had no provision for raising teacher salaries. To union leaders, too much of the reform looked like a deliberate effort to weaken and destroy the teachers' unions and to undermine the power of the teachers in their claims against government.[76] A member of the executive committee of CTEUB, for example, complained, "How does the government fail to understand the reason we fight so much—we want to participate. But the reform has been done behind a closed door and by rejecting us. Their purpose is to weaken us. The government doesn't want to build consensus or dialogue."[77] The unions argued that teachers could not support their families and that many teachers worked additional jobs to make ends meet.

Beyond differences of interests between the unions and the reformers in Bolivia, there was also a clash of cultures. For the most radical union leaders, tied to Trotskyite and orthodox Marxist parties, the issue of education reform was secondary to promotion of the revolution that would destroy not only "bourgeois education" but also the state itself. A proper education, they claimed, must be "antiimperialist, antioligarchic, and antineoliberal."[78] They believed that the goals of the reformers were "principally to save the government money, follow the lead of the international organizations, and privatize education."[79]

According to a leader of the urban education workers, "This is all part of the flexibilization of labor in an international economy in which the

TABLE 5.5
Main Areas of Conflict between the Teachers' Unions and Reformers in Bolivia

	Reformers	Teachers' Unions
Reform and education objectives	−Increase enrollment −Improve quality −Equity: reduce education differences −Efficiency in resource use and allocation −Improve productivity for the country's development and modernization	−"Strengthen class consciousness for the defense of the nation's sovereignty, self determination of the Bolivian people and the interests of the exploited classes" (CTEUB 1991)
Organization of the education sector	−Unify the education sector −Decentralize education	−Continue the urban and rural division −Maintain centralized education system
Teaching career	−Open access, that is, all who qualify can be teachers −Certification tests for access and promotion −Salaries tied to results and provision of incentives −Voluntary union membership, without the government automatically deducting the union fees from payrolls	−Access to teaching career only to graduates of the normal schools −Maintain guaranteed employment for teachers −Improve salaries, without links to productivity and without differentiation −Mandatory unionization with automatic payroll deductions
Parents' participation	−Active, through the "Juntas Escolares" and "Proyectos de Núcleo" −In the school management as actors of the education process	−Limited and determined by teachers' needs −Continuation of the monopoly of the ministry and the teachers' unions
Pedagogical proposal	−Constructivist −Centered on learning and the student −Changes in the classroom	−General philosophical principles about the "new Bolivian man" −Diffused and not structured
Formulation process and immediate objectives of the reform	−Gradual and as a process initiated by the ministry of planning in 1990 −Restructure the education sector and make it efficient and appropriate for the model of development	−From the top to the bottom, without consultation* −Imposed by the World Bank and the IMF* −It pursues "the destruction of a free public education, its delivery to imperialism and to the private sector, as an instrument of greater alienation" (CTEUB 1991)*

Source: Contreras (1999c).
*Reaction of the teachers' association to government actions or proposals.

great international corporations can go on gaining profits by taking money from the backs of workers."[80] Another union leader described the neoliberal ideology that "reproduced the ideology of the dominant class that gives priority to individualism and egoism."[81] For these leaders, the reforms were "intended to destroy Bolivian education . . . [they are] the first step toward the eventual privatization of public education in Bolivia."[82] Parent councils were described as having been set up to police the teachers, and the government of Hugo Banzer was accused of being "fascist, intent on destroying the unions." But, "all the government's actions are creating greater discontent among the people that will result in a social convulsion."[83] While many rank and file union members no doubt took exception to such rhetoric, there was little question that these organizations and their leaders had little trust in government.

The reformers, on the other hand, viewed the unions as anachronistic. According to one: "Once, we went over to discuss the reform with the unions. But when we came out of the building sometime later, I looked at my colleague and said, 'Jeez, these guys are paleolithic.'"[84] Amalia Anaya remembered the recommendations of the National Education Congress in 1992 as "fantastic—many had to do with international relations and things that had nothing to do with education."[85] According to another reformer: "The tragedy of the unions is their ideology. It is what is destroying them."[86] Regularly, the unions were described by these reformers as irrational in their positions. The fact that over 40 percent of teachers were from indigenous groups, while most of the reformers came from more elite backgrounds, no doubt added to the distance between them.[87]

The unions, following established Bolivian custom, consistently favored direct action, protest, and public mobilization rather than negotiation. This was anathema to the reformers:

> When I was first appointed vice-minister [of education, the unions] took over the building and held some staff people hostage and destroyed furniture and equipment and files. They even threw dynamite into the building. . . . I called the police and threw the protesters out by force. I told them they were not going to treat me or the ministry this way. . . . I closed the security blinds and put two guards at the door checking the credentials of everyone who came in. The unions told me I couldn't close a public building like this; I replied that I had an obligation to guard the security of the public's business. They threatened me with an uprising, but I told them I wasn't going to tolerate this kind of threat. (Interview, February 16, 2000, La Paz, Bolivia)

Oddly, despite the confrontational rhetoric and action on both sides, some believed that the ministry and the government might reach an accommodation. While Bolivian unions declined in power during the 1990s, the teachers' unions could "still mobilize a lot of people for a strike or a demonstration and they [controlled] critically important votes, particularly in La Paz."[88] Thus, in any confrontation, the unions anticipated that the government would capitulate, particularly on non-salary issues, because it always had in the past. According to a minister of planning who supported the reform, "The idea was that if the ministry gave them things, the unions would stay off the streets."[89] When strikes and protests oc-

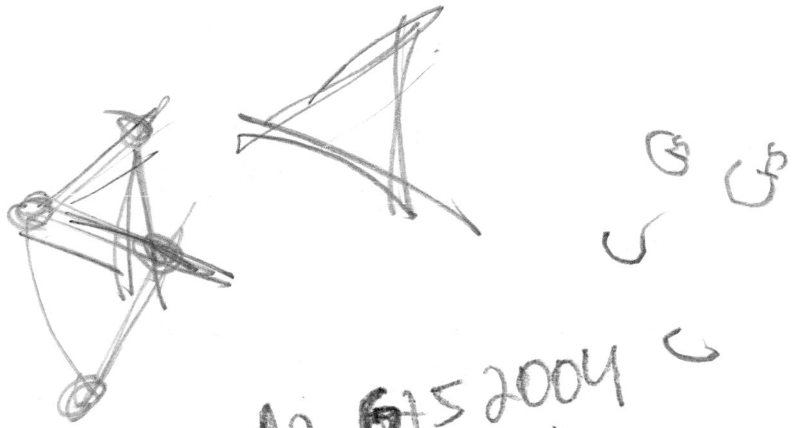

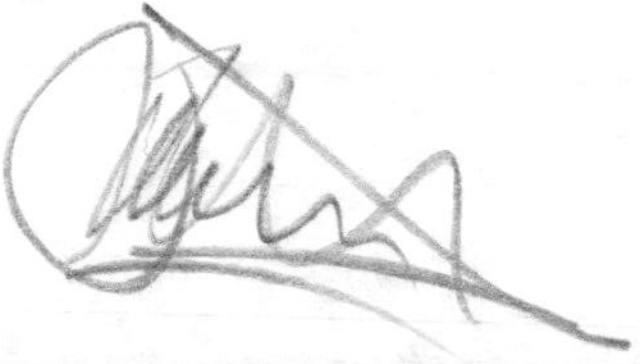

ry for the confusion...

ave always been lucky and had someone to give
cording the scenario & choice and re-bundling the
the discussion a bit (but probably not much). It

curred, salaries were still paid and those detained by police were let out of jail. In the past, "there were no costs to the unions for striking. They always got concessions from the government as part of the settlement."[90] These expectations for the 1994 reform were not realized, however, as the next chapter indicates.

CONCLUSION: THE CORE OF RESISTANCE

With very few exceptions, teachers' unions formed the core of resistance to the education reforms of the 1990s. They were powerful political opponents, even if they had seen their influence diminish over the course of the 1980s and 1990s. Institutionally, they continued to be well positioned to confront government policies, making their demands known through strikes and protest actions and using their links to ministries of education and political parties to challenge the power of the reformers. They had the capacity to bring national ministries and school systems to a halt. They marshaled significant numbers of votes. Their close connections to political parties meant that their leaders were frequently important figures in party decision making and the distribution of government largesse when those parties were in power.

As previous chapters indicated, reformers were able to rely on institutional sources of policy initiative to set national agendas, to initiate new quality-enhancing education ideas, and to take the lead in designing them. Once their plans were made public, however, the interests of the unions became much more central to debates about reform and their command of political resources easily matched that of the reformers. The unions also could communicate important messages to public opinion and potential allies. In addition to claiming that the reforms ignored many bread-and-butter grievances, they could also criticize policy changes on the grounds of process and values—that they were technocratic, neoliberal, impractical, and antinational, and that they sought to impoverish teachers and communities alike. As indicated in the next chapter, while the conflicts had their sources in interests and institutional sources of power, the resolution of those conflicts had much to do with the actions and choices available to union leaders and reformers.

Chapter Six

CONTESTING EDUCATION: TEACHERS'

UNIONS VERSUS REFORMERS

MATERIAL INTERESTS, exclusion from the discussion of reform, and fundamental differences in outlook almost certainly ensured that most teachers' unions would oppose education policy initiatives in the 1990s. But opposition to reform did not always play out in similar ways. In a few countries, education reformers and unions negotiated their differences and new policies were implemented within a context of relative labor peace. In other cases, new policies were put in place in the context of strident union opposition. And in some cases, union opposition helped scuttle reform.

In previous chapters, I argued that reformers had considerable capacity to shape when and how reform proposals were given priority on national political agendas and also had considerable control over their contents. Thus, reformers largely determined the timing of agenda setting, framed the discussion of change, and managed the policy design process. In the case of the debates and conflicts that swirled around these proposals once they had been announced, however, reformers were more constrained. Certainly it was true that opponents of change had been placed on the defensive by earlier actions. In addition, as this chapter indicates, reformers made critical decisions about whether to negotiate with the teachers' unions or to confront them. But, in these decisions, proponents of change were clearly making calculations about the relationship of the unions to broader structures of power. In particular, they were sensitive to the relationship of the unions to political parties and the dependence of the governments in power on those parties. In some cases, this calculation gave reformers some freedom to determine how to handle opposition; in other cases, they were convinced they had little room to maneuver.

In Mexico, where the SNTE was large, well organized, and closely integrated into the PRI, the president believed that it was important to sit down with the union and negotiate about the contents of the reform. This was a strategic choice; previous presidents had chosen to confront the union, and their reforms had languished as a consequence. In Minas Gerais, where the teachers' union was relatively weak and tied to a minority party that was not important to the government, reformers had more capacity to hold firm on their proposals, even though they negotiated with UTE on other issues. At the same time, the association of UTE with the Partido dos Trabalhadores encouraged some meeting of minds over aspects of the reform. In Bolivia, where unions were tied to small parties that were adamantly opposed to the governments in power, reformers reached the conclusion that it was impossible to negotiate with the opposition; instead, they opted to try to break the power of the unions. In Nicaragua, reformers came to a similar conclusion about the Sandinista union and followed strategies to confront, weaken, and maneuver around this organization. And in Ecuador, given the volatile economic situation, there was probably little that the reformers could do to offset the opposition of UNE and its party ally, the MPD, because teachers formed part of the growing opposition to the government's economic policies. Indeed, neither a response to their demands nor an attempt to undermine the union's power was effective.

In all cases, unions influenced the advance of education reform. In Mexico, where an agreement was reached, the reform that went forward was less bold than the kinds of changes that were implemented in other countries. In Minas Gerais, the reform went forward rapidly in the context of concessions to union demands for improvements in salaries and working conditions. In Bolivia and Nicaragua, reformers successfully undermined union efforts to defeat their proposals and were able to push ahead with them. They did so, however, in the context of continued contention that influenced how the reforms were implemented. In Ecuador, of course, reform was undercut by an economic crisis that provided the teachers' union an opportunity to join other organizations in attacking the government and ultimately in contributing to its demise. In this chapter, therefore, case studies of the interactions between reformers and unions indicate how institutional constraints set bounds on what could be attempted and accomplished in education reform. At the same time, however, the case histories suggest that the process of reform provided opportunities for strategic decision making about how to move new policies forward.

Negotiating among Titans: Mexico

The Salinas administration opted to negotiate the education reform with the union rather than to confront it. Ruefully, a lead government negotiator explained that this path was a necessity. "If you had asked any of us where we wanted the union, we'd have said, three meters underground. But the reality was that we needed them."[1] Indeed, the decision to negotiate rather than to confront the union recognized the important political role of the SNTE. Moreover, the Salinas administration, tied as it was to the PRI, decided not to turn its back on the largest union incorporated into the party. In deciding on this approach, the reformers differed from past administrations that had pursued education reform without support from the union.

These negotiations began almost immediately after Ernesto Zedillo was appointed minister of education in January 1992. Although the resulting agreement was a tripartite consensus document—the national government, the union, and the state governors—from the beginning, the negotiations centered on the government and the SNTE. Most governors, given their preferences, would have actively resisted taking on responsibility for education for fiscal and political reasons. They feared increased political and administrative burdens with the transfer of responsibility for large numbers of new teachers, schools, and students. They also anticipated great risk in central government revenue sharing formulas that could be altered at the whim of the president or the ministry of finance. But they were in a weak position. All but one of them from the PRI, there was little they could do to stop a determined president who had already deposed several governors in bids to emphasize his power. Indeed, according to one official in the ministry: "The agreement was signed [by the governors] because Salinas said 'Sign!' Many of the governors did not want to touch it."[2] Another education official characterized the reform as "a decision made by a strong president to make the governors accept new responsibilities."[3]

At the outset of the negotiations, SNTE was already on record as being firmly against decentralization. The central issue for the union, of course, was that of annual negotiations over teacher pay and benefits. The governors' authority over such decisions would hit at the heart of the national power of the union, replacing its central role with annual negotiations focused at the state level and on the governors and state-level ministries of education. But the government's decision to refer to the "federalization" of education was something that could be discussed without loss of face and that would enable the union to agree to negotiate. Indeed, Elba Ester Gordillo, the secretary general of SNTE who owed her position to the strong support she had received from Salinas, had already begun to speak of the importance of "modernizing" the educational system, providing another platform on which both the union and the government could agree.[4] Moreover, during the course of the negotiations, the government was careful not to portray the union as an enemy of change; instead, it was referred to as an important interlocutor for the teachers.[5]

Gordillo strengthened the union's position by establishing the Fundación SNTE para la Cultura del Maestro Mexicano. This think tank was staffed with well-regarded academics, some of whom had held important positions in the ministry of education. The foundation gave greater technical credibility to the union's positions by bringing in people who were not identified with the movement in the past. It produced studies and reports that argued for the importance of modernizing education, provided alternatives to the government's proposals, and encouraged greater dialogue about the contents of the reform.[6] According to Gordillo: "The proposal of the SNTE was focused on three points: the reoganization of the system, the redesign of educational contents and improved social and political respect for teachers and the teaching role."[7] Moreover, in a "Declaration of Principles," SNTE announced it was no longer officially connected to the PRI. This move had little immediate practical impact because relations between the union and the party continued much as usual, but it served to increase the autonomy of the union to negotiate directly with the ministry.[8]

A team of ministry negotiators, headed by education vice-minister Esteban Moctezuma, along with Carlos Mancera and others, began meeting daily with groups designated by Gordillo to consider how the education initiative would go forward. For the government, the most important issue was to make decentralization happen and to end the stranglehold of the union and ministry bureaucrats on efforts to improve the system. The minister, given the expectations of the president, was focused on making sure the negotiations proceeded ahead. He was ready to step in and deal personally with SNTE's leadership when needed. Similarly, he could count on the support of the president. Indeed, according to one of the lead negotiators, "Zedillo had exceptional support and trust [confianza] from the president. This was so apparent that he had considerable autonomy to carry out the negotiations without oversight from the office of the presidency."[9] At the same time, the president was clearly and frequently on record in support of the ministry team. This was important for the negotiators. "The ministry [team] had no base of support in the PRI and really didn't have political weight. It was the president who made it happen by signaling his strong commitment very frequently."[10]

Strategically, the government negotiators sought to make clear that the discussions were about a larger package of reforms, not just about decentralization. According to the chief negotiator for the government, "It was important that they realize that if they said no to federalization, they were saying no to a whole package of things, some of which they wanted."[11] Implicit throughout the discussions, of course, was the promise of an increase in salaries if agreement could be reached. In addition, there was the proposal for a status and salary enhancing *carerra magisterial*, a career ladder that would allow for greater mobility within the teacher corps and increases in salaries with movement on the ladder.[12] In the background of the negotiations was also the protest movement of 1989, when striking teachers had caused significant alarm in governing circles.

From time to time, as issues arose, the minister and the president met personally with Gordillo to move the agreement forward. Throughout, the union leader maintained a good relationship with Minister Zedillo. More important, however, was her relationship to Salinas. "The relationship of Salinas to Elba Ester was key to the ability to put through the reform. . . . He couldn't have succeeded if someone else had been [leader of the union]. And, of course, behind Elba Ester was the role of Salinas in the conflict with Jonguitud," according to one negotiator.[13] In brief: "He helped her in the leadership struggle in '89 with Jonguitud, and she paid him back three years later by backing the agreement of '92."[14] Thus, alongside the formal negotiations, a set of informal meetings helped smooth the way toward agreement. According to Salinas:

> Secretary Zedillo had asked me to intervene directly with the leaders of the SNTE because, within the organization, there was great resistance to the agreement's proposal, in particular, to decentralization. I spoke first with the Secretary-general Gordillo. I trusted in her and in her integrity as a leader. She explained clearly to me all the areas that concerned her: The SNTE leadership believed that decentralization would tear the union apart. The decision to decentralize could mask the federal government withdrawal from its obligations to educate the youth of the country. Teaching salaries at the federal level varied greatly compared to those at the state level, and this would generate tension at the time of decentralization. Many states had no administrative or political capacity to take over the process of decentralization and paying teachers. Finally, she noted, various leaders of union locals believed it was necessary for my administration to postpone the decision to decentralize . . . for the teachers' leaders themselves to explain to me those and other issues so that we could debate these matters openly.[15]

A subsequent meeting of SNTE union locals with the president, the minister of education, and the mayor of Mexico City resulted in a presidential promise to increase spending on education in the remaining years of his term of office.[16] Eventually, four months of difficult negotiation resulted in an agreement that allowed SNTE to continue the practice of annual discussions between the ministry of education over increments for the base salaries of teachers and the package of benefits that all teachers were entitled to. State governors would have the opportunity to increase salaries and provide improvements in work conditions, and the teachers would be ensured of a national minimum set of rewards and conditions. As part of this settlement, the teachers were granted a large salary adjustment that boosted their average income to second highest for public sector employees.[17]

A sticking point in the negotiations over the *carerra magisterial* was a government-proposed proficiency examination for teachers. The union was adamantly opposed to such a test, but eventually agreed to it when a formula was worked out that assessed proficiency along with seniority.[18]

In addition, the agreement reaffirmed SNTE as the rightful representative of the teachers in labor matters, set the bases for curriculum and textbook reform, and promised improved training for teachers.[19] Although largely sidelined during the negotiations, the governors were able to insist that the government be more specific about the terms of the fiscal transfers that would come their way in the aftermath of decentralization. They were also delighted to have the central government continue to be in charge of negotiating salaries with the union.

Some aspects of the existing system did not change. Technical education, a strong fiefdom within the ministry of education, was successful in resisting the decentralization initiative. In addition, teachers of the federal district, a strong group within SNTE, refused to be part of the new plan. The national government remained in control of this large bureaucracy as well as curriculum, the national program of free textbooks, and the standards set for student performance. And of course, the agreement did not resolve all issues. As we saw in chapter 4, an initiative to introduce new content into the curriculum through newly designed textbooks created a major confrontation between the ministry and critics who decried its treatment of important historical events.

More generally, however, the negotiations and the resulting package of reforms were clearly a milestone in the relations between the government and the union. In the years following the agreement and its ratification through a constitutional reform in 1992 and the 1993 Law for the Modernization of Education, SNTE continued to focus its attention on basic salaries and work conditions for teachers. From time to time, the teachers went on strike, and annually, protests and marches interrupted traffic around the ministry of education building in central Mexico City. Indeed, these actions became normal aspects of politics in the country, annoying for ministry officials and drivers, but not threatening to the political system. Even after 2000, when control of the presidency passed from the PRI for the first time in seventy-one years, the basic relationship between SNTE and the ministry did not change much. The union continued its demands for salaries and the ministry continued to maintain a relatively close working relationship with the union. More broadly, the union continued to guarantee a large measure of labor peace for the government even while it found that some decisions now focused the attention of its locals on state-level negotiations.

NEGOTIATING AMONG INTERESTS: MINAS GERAIS

The politics of education reform in Minas Gerais were more complex than Mexico's, in large part because the structure of interest representation was more pluralistic. A large number of professional and community associations were invited to discuss school autonomy and how it should be achieved. There was little agreement across these organizations about which aspects of the reform advanced their interests and which were antithetical to them. Moreover, the teachers' union was supportive of some of the aims of the school autonomy reform promoted by Minister Mares Guia Neto and his team. This provided the education reformers with considerable room to maneuver in gaining approval of the policy they had so carefully designed. In particular, they were able to play interests off against each other.

UTE, representing teachers from the state and municipal school systems, was not in a strong bargaining position in the spring of 1991, when the proposal was announced and sent to congress.[20] While the union had been in the forefront of the democratization movement in the early 1980s and had been led by strong and capable leaders, by the 1990s, the issues that drew it together were more mundane—salaries and conditions of employment—and its leadership was less dynamic. The first generation had been committed to democratic transition and workers' rights, but by the 1990s, leaders were more likely to view their role in the union as a stepping stone to other positions.[21] Moreover, while in the earlier period, as many as fifty teachers were able to take paid leave from their jobs to work for the union, this number was reduced to three in the late 1980s. This meant that the union was forced to rely on a much smaller staff to recruit members and mobilize them around issues of importance. Just as important, while UTE was the only union to represent teachers, a competing professional association that was close to the government sought to attract the loyalty of teachers. Nevertheless, the relationship between the union and the PT remained strong. UTE's president, Rosaura Magalhães, was part of the leadership of the PT in the state, and the alliance was important to both.

Despite its weakened position, the union continued to seek increases in salaries and benefits for its members and to speak out on issues of importance to it.[22] Indeed, when the school reform was being debated publicly and in the legislature, the teachers were on strike, called out of the classroom and onto the street by UTE. Of course, that teachers were on strike was not unusual in Minas Gerais. Each year, as part of salary negotiations with government and whenever a new administration assumed office, job actions were common. In 1991, however, the scope and length of the strike was unusual. Initially, most expected that it would affect about half the public schools. In the event, 82 percent of the schools were closed for an action that lasted eighty-six days; 433 municipalities were affected—not a bad showing for a union that represented considerably less than half the teachers in the state. Virtually all schools in the large metropolitan areas were closed.[23] Union protests stopped traffic in the state capital, Belo

Horizonte. Strikers scuffled with police, set up tents in the downtown area of the capital, occupied the ministry, and sought to gain legislative support for their demands. The press covered the strike action avidly.

The teachers were adamant about their demands, but most of these were not about the reform proposal. In March, UTE sent the government a set of demands: that teachers receive increased wages; that they receive the year-end bonus that had not been paid in December 1990—the so-called thirteenth month of salary—that the government hire those who had already passed the qualifying examination to be teachers; and that the state transfer resources to community-controlled schools.

The union also wanted a career system for teachers and went so far as to design a proposal that was submitted to the ministry for approval. This issue signaled an important difference between the union in Minas Gerais and those in Mexico, Bolivia, Nicaragua, and Ecuador. In those cases, the unions were the primary beneficiaries of patronage appointments for teachers and other school personnel; in Minas Gerais, politicians had long monopolized this right and the union had little influence in hiring, promotion, and firing procedures. For the teachers, changes in political leadership, particularly at the municipal level, meant extensive turnover in teaching jobs. Thus, UTE was making a claim for greater job stability and seeking to eliminate the clientelist system that it believed victimized its members.[24]

In the context of union demands on the government, UTE and the reformers agreed on some issues. The teachers' union, tied as it was to the PT and its democratizing agenda, was in favor of greater community control over the schools and wanted to see the government push harder for the creation of general assemblies and school boards and for them to take on greater responsibilities in the management of the schools. It believed that this was the only way to end the political manipulation that went into the selection of directors and the only way to increase the capacity of the PT to have greater local influence. While the reform team supported these aspects of local control out of belief that they would lead to better management of the schools, and while UTE and the PT were more concerned about strengthening local democracy, they agreed on the mechanisms that would lead to their distinct goals.[25] Even with this commonality of interests, however, the union criticized the "nondemocratic" orientation of the reformers, even after their project was approved by the legislature.

Despite considerable meeting of minds about some elements of the Mares Guia Neto reform, one aspect of it did concern the teachers a great deal. This was the proposal that school directors first pass a qualifying test before they could be candidates for election by the general assembly of the school. For UTE, which had a history of militancy for increased democracy in Brazil, the test represented a barrier to democratic school management. This was central to the union's position and to the position of the PT. Indeed, when the union occupied the ministry in Belo Horizonte, its banners proclaimed: "If anyone can be president of the republic, why can't anyone be a school director?"[26] When appealing to legislators, UTE used the same logic to make the comparison between them and school directors. Important political calculations were also embedded in this issue. If a qualifying exam were approved, party and union leaders believed that it would be difficult for ordinary teachers and party loyalists to become school directors. Those already in the system who had experience in such positions would end up as the most likely to do well on the test. On this point, then, the union had strong support from the PT and its representatives in the legislature.

At issue for the union was also its capacity to represent the teachers of Minas Gerais. While UTE claimed to be the only teachers' union, the Associação de Professores Publicos de Minas Gerais (APPMG) claimed the loyalties of a significant portion of the teachers. APPMG, which promoted itself as a nonpolitical professional association, not a union, generally worked closely with the ministry in the pursuit of its goals. While it had similar concerns to UTE about salaries and benefits, it usually was not confrontational in its demands. Not only did APPMG support the reform, but the reformers were able to use this organization in its lobbying efforts in congress.

Indeed, the number of organizations concerned about the reform—and its relative weakness in representing the teachers—limited the capacity of UTE and other opposition groups to derail it or alter its content. The focus of greatest contention was the issue of how school directors were to be selected. While the teachers' union wanted elections but not a qualifying text, the school directors' association, ADEOMG, led the opposition to their election. This association had allies in the Associação Mineira de Inspetores Escolares (AMIE) and the Associação Mineira de Supervisores Pedagogicas (AMISP), both of which argued that school directors should be selected on the basis of merit.[27] For those opposed to this position, of course, "selection on the basis of merit" was a code word for the clientelist system of political nomination for filling these jobs. If elections were not approved, they believed, the governors, mayors, and legislators would continue to use their patronage to staff local school leadership positions.

Meanwhile, the negotiating team, headed by Minister Mares Guia Neto, was firm about directors being elected after a qualifying test. He and the reform team in the ministry believed that this was to be the linchpin of the reform; without it, they argued, local school autonomy was not likely to improve the management of the schools. In the face of adamant pressure from the ADEOMG, the minister held firm. When the school directors confronted him, Mares Guia Neto remembers taking a very hard line.

"[They said] 'We are going to knock you off your high horse,' so I said, 'Every time you knock me off, I will get back up. You are going to get tired of knocking me down and seeing me get up again!' "[28]

ADEOMG and other groups that argued against the election of school directors had an important argument on their side. According to Article 196 of the state constitution, school directors were to be selected through a competitive process on the basis of their knowledge and experience.[29] Those opposed to the idea of the election of directors therefore claimed that this meant the government's proposal was unconstitutional. This was a powerful position and one that was important to some of the parties in congress. It diverted attention from the interests of ADEOMG and the politicians and embroiled the reformers in a fight over constitutional interpretation. The reformers, of course, took issue with the constitutional claim. They believed that the idea of a qualifying test met the requirement for knowledge and experience and that the election met the requirement for a competitive process. At least part of their position found willing support from UTE and the PT, which joined Mares Guia Neto in arguing that even if direct elections were not foreseen in the constitution, the legislature could amend the constitution to make it possible.[30]

Overall, then, the organized interests that represented the education sector were in disarray. The government sought to use this situation to gain its points. The minister offered to meet with the groups, but then arranged to meet with each separately. He did the same with the party leadership that was important in the legislative arena. In these meetings, Mares Guia Neto encouraged disagreements among the unions and the parties. He used their arguments about democracy against them. "I responded to PT representatives in the legislature and to the union [by saying], 'We beat you in the election in the first round and in the second round, and now you want to govern by confrontation? We've been democratically elected [to promote this reform].'"[31]

In addition, the minister sought interlocutors for the teachers and directors who differed with the union positions; certainly APPMG was one such organization, and it stood firm with the minister in support of the reform. In similar fashion, he revived an organization of school directors formed in the 1980s but fallen in disuse, the school directors' board.[32] This board, originally created to increase communication between the ministry and the schools and to act as a counterpoint to ADEOMG, was brought into the negotiations to undermine the association's claim to represent the directors. Not surprisingly, the board supported the government's position.[33] The government team also invited the Federação dos Associaçãos de Pais e Alunos das Escolas Publicas de Minas Gerais (FAPAEPMG) to be part of the discussions. This organization, originally created by APPMG, had been set up in the late 1980s during a protracted teachers' strike to provide a communication channel between the ministry and the schools and communities and was now a handy organization to provide support to the government. In addition, the Federação dos Associaçãos de Moradores de Belo Horizonte (FAMBH) was invited to express its support of the democratic control of local schools through the election of their directors.

The disarray and differing positions among the organizations representing the teachers and directors weakened opposition to school autonomy. At the same time, reformers could agree to several strike demands in exchange for carrying the day on issues they cared greatly about. Thus, by the end of June, the minister had reached an agreement with the union on guidelines for the reform. While these guidelines were quite general, they did include an agreement on the importance of school autonomy and local democracy as an important feature of the management of education. More important to the teachers, the government agreed to an 88 percent salary increase and the payment of the thirteenth-month bonus from the previous year. It also agreed to increase transfers of funds to schools that were already managed by local communities and to encourage more local schools to set up general assemblies and school boards. The government further agreed to appoint teachers who had passed the qualifying exam and to ensure that teachers would have greater autonomy in the classroom. At the same time, Mares Guia Neto was firm that there would be no negotiating over the qualifying test and direct election for school directors. He also rejected the plan for a teaching career.

According to the president of UTE at the time, negotiations with Mares Guia Neto, particularly about the issue of the selection of school directors, were difficult. He was very clear on what he wanted and, "unlike other [people in the ministry], a decision made by Walfrido was decided."[34] She reflected on how the union had been outmaneuvered. "As a negotiator [to deal with], Walfrido was horrible. Only he spoke and he wouldn't let anyone else speak, and he didn't listen. Worse, he tried to undermine [the UTE leadership] right at the negotiating table. He tried to distract us in order not to resolve the issue. Our own teachers started fighting with us to press just for the salary increase. Negotiating with Walfrido was complicated. It was very complicated."[35]

These negotiations were important in the public airing of the issues and they led to the end of the strike. The critical issue of legislative approval for the reform, however, was not directly affected by them. It was, in fact, the strong intervention of the governor, discussed in chapter 4, that caused the vast majority of legislators to vote for the reform bill on June 29, not the pressure from ministry reformers or unions. The day after the law was approved, the strike ended. In November 1991, just eight months after the Helio Garcia administration assumed office, the first elections for school director took place. The reform battle was not yet won, however, as ADEOMG continued to resist this way of selecting school leaders, basing its opposition on their claim that it was unconstitutional. Ultimately, the school directors were successful and the direct election of school directors was declared unconstitutional.[36] Nevertheless, the practice had acquired some support in local communities by that time, and the practice continued on an informal basis in a number of schools.

In Minas Gerais, then, negotiation with the unions was a complicated affair, made so by the numerous actors brought to the fore by the government and by disarray among opponents in terms of their interests. The issues on the table involved the bread-and-butter concerns of the teachers as well as important elements of the reform, particularly those having to do with how school directors would be selected. The government was in a strong position in these negotiations, in part because of the weak position of the union, but also in part because it was able to control the discussions. In particular, by dealing separately with the various interests and exploiting differences among them, it was able to increase the collective action problems that stood in the way of presenting a united front to the government. In the end, the reformers got what they wanted, even while offering concessions to UTE on pay, benefits, and issues related to school financing and management. Given the political resources the governor was prepared to put into supporting the reform, the marginal position of the PT in the legislature, and UTE's support of several aspects of the proposal, Mares Guia Neto and his team might have been able to ignore the union; they chose instead to find accommodation on issues that did not affect the reform, hoping no doubt to create a more positive environment for implementing it.

FACING DOWN THE UNIONS: BOLIVIA

In Bolivia, there was little possibility for negotiation between the unions representing teachers, CTEUB and CONMERB, and the government.[37] From the beginning, the unions—and particularly the urban teachers' union—opposed the reformers' ideas and joined with the ministry, the Catholic Church, and others in developing an alternative plan more to their liking. They denounced the reform as elitist and identified it as one of the "three damned laws" of the Sánchez de Lozada administration. For them, it was yet another neoliberal plan to privatize education and allow the state to get out of the business of providing education. They were particularly adamant that they had been excluded from discussions about reform and that their alternative plan was simply ignored by the government, although in fact they had repeatedly been invited to important meetings and had refused to attend. When the reform was sent to congress, they protested loudly and publicly against it.

Thus, after their new education law was approved in 1994, the reformers began to implement it in the face of often violent union opposition. Over the course of the 1990s, the unions engaged in strikes, street demonstrations, work stoppages, and protests to make their points clear. Most of these activities occurred in February and March each year when the unions and the ministry tussled over whether the schools would open on time and whether teachers would attend their classes. In 1995, thirty-seven school days were lost to strikes; in 1996, twenty-four days were lost, in 1997, fifteen days, and in 1998, twenty-two days.[38] According to one count, between 1995 and 1996, the teachers engaged in three work stoppages, five strikes, twelve protest marches, four threats of violence, and seventeen encounters with the police. The unions calculated losses at 171 taken to jail, two dead, and sixty-two wounded in their confrontations with government.[39] With strong support from the peak labor organization, the COB, the unions demanded the repeal of the 1994 education reform law.

In February 1999, tensions between the unions and the reformers came to a head. Just as in other years, the beginning of classes marked opening day of the strike season that pitted the unions and the teachers against the government. But in 1999, the opposition of the unions was particularly problematic. By that time, some 28 percent of the public schools in the country had been selected by the ministry to be incorporated into the reform. For the reform to advance further, Anaya—now vice-minister for preprimary, primary, and secondary education—believed it imperative to move ahead with unimplemented aspects related to the teaching profession. In the year ahead, she wished to establish standards for teacher assignments, teaching credentials, and school, local, and regional education administrators; alter the career system for teachers; establish more school and regional parents' councils; and close some normal schools and transfer others to secondary schools or universities.

Anaya believed that a strong signal needed to come from the government about its commitment to the reform and its unwillingness to sacrifice it to the unions. As the vice-minister pointed out to President Banzer at a meeting in January, the "lack of initiative and firmness in government decisions" was one of the important obstacles to implementing the reform.[40] In fact, since mid-January, when the urban teachers' union, CTEUB, announced it would go on strike, the government had been taking a hard line. In response to the union ultimatum, education minister Tito Hoz de Vila announced that plans for the school year would go forward, despite the opposition of the unions.

In the following days, the minister announced two strike-breaking policies. First was a "no work, no pay" policy, in which teachers who were out of the classroom because of union activities would not be paid for the time away from their jobs. In the past, teachers had always been paid for the time they were on strike or engaged in protest. He further announced a "six days, you're out" policy, in which teachers who were absent from the classroom for six consecutive workdays for union activities would lose their jobs. Past practice had always been to allow teachers to return to the classroom, no matter how long their absence. In addition, Hoz de Vila stated that the ministry would hire retired teachers and others to fill the vacancies left by those on strike and permit teachers who had not joined in the action to teach double shifts. Several days after the beginning of the strike, President Banzer stated that the government would be firm with teachers who didn't attend classes, docking their pay and replacing them if necessary.

Then, in a summit meeting, Vice President Jorge Quiroga, Hoz de Vila, the minister of labor, and officials from the ministry of the presidency and the vice-ministry of education agreed that the government would maintain its commitment to the education reform and face down the strike by following up on the no work, no pay and six days, you're out policies. In addition, they agreed on three other measures. First, they backed a "no negotiation" policy for salary increases, in which the government would make an initial and firm offer of the actual salary increase it was prepared to make. In the past, the government had always begun with a low increase and then negotiated to a higher amount when the unions protested. Second, they agreed to encourage public opinion to support the reform and oppose the "obstructionist," "violent," and "selfish" actions of the teachers' unions. Third, they moved to implement a "local vigilance" policy, in which parents' councils would monitor the work of the teachers.[41] They decided that the principal focus of the government's communication strategy would be the right of all children to attend school for a full two hundred days each year.

On February 8, the ministry of education opened an office to hire new teachers and began accepting applications from those who had not been trained in the country's normal schools.[42] On February 10, the ministry began to send out letters to teachers on strike, announcing that they were to be replaced. By February 11, the unions had begun to discuss returning to classes; they proposed that they would return to work in return for the reinstatement of two hundred teachers who had been suspended for participating in the strike. The government rejected the deal. In reply, the unions announced that they would continue the strike. Then, on February 14, Minister Hoz de Vila indicated that teachers who returned to work immediately wouldn't be fired. On February 19, the unions announced that, due to pressure from parents, they would end the strike and teachers would return to schools. Thus, the strike ended without a deal with the government. In fact, many teachers had returned to work before the end of the strike; public opinion was also strongly in favor of ending the confrontation and getting children back into the schools.

But conflict continued. In April, the ministry of education announced its intention of transferring normal schools to the public universities, setting off a new wave of protest that lasted through July. An unusual degree of violence marked these protests, and the government was quick to take advantage of the image of teachers and normal school students rioting in the streets, breaking windows, attacking police, throwing rocks, and setting cars on fire. Television footage of rampaging protesters added to low public opinion about the teachers and their demands. The minister of education asked publicly: "What parent is going to trust a vandal?"[43] According to the vice president: "We showed images of this on television and then asked if these were *teachers*? Was this appropriate behavior for a *teacher*?" The purpose of this public opinion campaign was to drive a further wedge between parents and the unions.[44]

Marches, hunger strikes, road blockages, and crucifixions (a traditional Bolivian protest action, in which protesters have themselves tied to crosses located in strategic spots to attract support) continued, but the public opinion campaign of the government was largely successful. Finally, the protesters raised the white flag and an accord was signed with the government. In the aftermath of the strikes, media coverage highlighted how poorly educated many normal school graduates were, and praised programs for school breakfasts, the distribution of school materials, and the good results already achieved from the education reform.

In late 1999, the minister of education was named "Person of the Year" by one of the country's most respected newspapers, *La Razón*. In selecting him for this award, the newspaper lauded his contributions to Bolivian education, particularly in "normalizing" the school year by facing down the unions. More evidence of the success of the government's get tough policy came in early 2000, when the minister announced that schools would open on February 7 and, for the first time that most Bolivians could remember, the education year started on the appointed day without strikes, protests, or delays.

Nevertheless, while the publicity campaign was useful in breaking union opposition, its message led to the further discrediting of the teaching profession and left many teachers feeling abused. Low pay and low public esteem made it even more difficult to attract well-qualified people to the profession. And, protests by CTEUB and CONMERB continued, although less frequently than formerly.[45] Two broad-based strikes against the Banzer government in April and September 2000 effectively paralyzed the country; as part of this mobilization, teachers demanded a 50 percent salary increase.[46] The government agreed to most demands in talks mediated by the Catholic Church, and the teachers were promised bonuses. In April and May 2001, the teachers, in alliance with other unions, again struck over their call for a 50 percent wage increase in addition to the payment of the promised bonuses.[47] By June, leaders of the union, now in alliance with health workers, went on a hunger strike and forced the government to back down on decentralization legislation.[48] In Bolivia, then, the commitments of both unions and reformers to maintain hostile stances toward each other resulted in a zero-sum conflict that constrained how the new policies were implemented.

UNDERMINING DISSENT: NICARAGUA

Nicaragua's education reform in the 1990s was something of a one-person show. The minister of education, Humberto Belli, entered office in 1990 and remained there until 1998. In the first years of his administration, he was fortunate to have a series of conditions in his favor—the end of the Sandinista revolution under a cloud of public displeasure about its management of the country, the election of a popular president at the head of a broad coalition of fourteen parties, and extensive bilateral assistance from the United States. In the early 1990s, however, the teachers' union, ANDEN, was firmly in opposition to school autonomy.

Under the Sandinistas, the power of ANDEN had grown along with the increasing centralization of decision making in the national ministry of education. Its leadership was deeply committed to revolutionary principles, and many of its members were teachers who had entered the field under the Sandinista government and who were committed to pushing forward with the revolutionary cause through education. Its privileged role as the only union in the sector was one its leadership hoped to maintain. The union was also committed to the centralized structure of the education system, particularly with regard to labor relations. Moreover, ANDEN's ideological orientation encouraged a confrontational orientation toward the new government. According to its leaders, "The teachers are workers, they are part of the working classes and must show solidarity with them. Their conditions are those of workers. They have workers' rights and rights to have unions."[49] When there were protests by unions in other sectors, ANDEN joined them.

Thus, strikes, protests, and massive demonstrations characterized the relationship between ANDEN and the government in the early 1990s. Above all, the union wanted adjustments in teacher pay to compensate for the collapse of the Nicaraguan economy in the late 1980s. In May 1990, less than three weeks after the Chamorro government had taken office, ANDEN joined the rest of the public sector unions in a five-day nation-wide strike demanding salary increases of 200 percent. In July, it struck again, and again in September. ANDEN leaders protested against plans to fire Sandinista teachers.[50] In addition, there were sporadic walkouts by teachers in the spring of 1991 over demands for increases in salaries and employment. Then in April and May, a fifty-day national teachers' strike left schools vacant throughout the country. Teachers went back to work only when the ministry of education agreed to a 25 percent wage hike, proclaimed a "triumph for all teachers" by ANDEN's president.[51] ANDEN also strongly opposed Minister Belli's reform measures. Even before he became minister, they attacked the textbooks that were being prepared and introduced as evidence of U.S. propaganda. Later, the school autonomy reform was also rejected. "We saw it as a privatization of the schools and an effort to take the responsibility of the state for education and transfer it to the parents through the fees that were to be charged."[52]

In this context, Minister Belli sought to undermine the power of ANDEN. He asked his vice-minister, Hortensia Rivas, to establish a new union. Created at the behest of reformers within the government, then, the Confederación Nacional de Maestros de Nicaragua (CNMN) was ex-pected to be a principal pillar for restructuring the education system and to support Chamorro's government. It was also expected to compete with ANDEN for the loyalties of the teachers. These expectations were never fulfilled to the extent the reformers wanted, however, because the number of teachers' unions expanded rapidly. The CNMN split when the Confe-deración de Trabajadores de la Educación y la Cultura (CONFETEC) was created. It split again and again until there were twelve unions in the sector, each with links to particular parties. ANDEN remained the most powerful and continued to attract the most members, but it was also hit hard by the downsizing of the teacher corps in 1991.[53]

Indeed, the school autonomy reform went ahead during the decade with the unions on the sidelines. Belli ignored them and appealed directly to the local schools and the teachers who might want to join the program because it promised benefits of improved salaries and the potential for greater autonomy from the national ministry. The new program offered them a way to improve their salaries without working with the union. "[This] was a way of responding to the problem without empowering the unions. In fact, it helped weaken them," according to one ANDEN leader.[54] Belli continued to enjoy strong presidential support. In a speech before the legislature in early 1994, President Chamorro indicated her commitment to the school autonomy initiative and invoked the impor-tance of community participation in education written into Article 118 of the constitution.[55] At the same time, the government sought to increase the number of schools in the country, thus creating jobs for teachers and potential members for other unions.

Predictably, ANDEN grew increasingly hostile to the ministry and complained about being left out. Between 1991 and 1994, it led the other unions in numerous protest activities and two national teachers' strikes. In retrospect, a leader of ANDEN argued that the organization had not been strategic enough in its opposition to the reform. "We just said 'no autonomy' without understanding how the teachers would really react to it, particularly the secondary school teachers, and we didn't have a perspective that allowed us to oppose it by 'complementing' the reform with our own proposals. . . . We didn't do enough analysis of what the reform was about and how it affected teachers. And second, we didn't talk to the teachers and get their reactions. As a result, we miscalculated about how we should react. At the time, the leaders of the other unions were our enemies."[56]

Belli's strategies appeared to pay off. As indicated earlier, the progress of the reform presented a difficult dilemma to ANDEN and the other unions. If they continued to oppose school autonomy, they risked losing the support of teachers who allied themselves with the reform, in part as a way of improving their salaries. On the other hand, if they followed the government's lead and continued to devolve power to local organizations, they risked losing their capacity to have a significant voice at the national level.[57] Eventually, the unions had to face the shift in power that was occurring with the school autonomy initiative. By 1996, ANDEN had decided to decentralize and soon had 126 local unions and 19 departmental level federations. According to the president of this union, "This was our response to the repression and the decentralization of the ministry. In some ways, it was a response taken at our weakest moment."[58]

In 1998, Belli left the ministry and a new minister of education, Antonio Alvarado, worried about ongoing conflicts with the unions that made life difficult for the ministry. He set out to improve relations. To that end, he called for a national consultation, under the direction of the National Commission on Education, to develop a National Education Plan. The National Commission, originally established in 1996 to provide support for education reform in general, brought together ministry leaders and representatives from the presidency, the Catholic Church, the National Technical Institute, the National University Commission, the teachers' unions, the National Federation of Private Universities, the Private Sector High Commission, the Forum for Education and Human Development, the Nicaraguan Pedagogic Movement, and several NGOs active in the education sector.

For two years, the commission met, consulted, and debated education policy. In the end, it produced a document that committed the participants to a number of broad principles of education: education as a human right; the importance of a national education system; broader access and equity in the provision of education; higher quality and relevance in learning; greater respect and training for teachers; more participatory, transparent, and decentralized management.[59] The final document was signed by the twenty-six members of the technical committee of the commission and the heads of twelve education unions. The value of the agreement, according to many participants, was not what it committed the participants to, but the process through which it was developed. Bringing affected groups together to discuss common interests in the education system, many argued, was an important way to bridge the gaps that had been created by the Belli era reforms.

Despite such statements in favor of consultation and negotiation, the relationship between the unions and the reformers in the ministry of education continued to be difficult. The unions were weakened by internecine conflicts among them and by their inability to agree on a national federation to represent all teachers. This placed them in a further disadvantage vis-à-vis the government. A past leader of ANDEN argued, "The divisiveness and weakness of the teachers' unions keeps them from playing the role they traditionally have played in protecting the salaries and work stability of the teachers. With every change of minister and regional ministry representative there are changes in teachers."[60] Recognizing the weakness of the unions, the ministry continued ahead with additional changes without consultations. The response of the union was to resist. "They imposed the 200 days of classes without discussing it with us and without any raise in pay. So we say, no more work without more salary," in the words of ANDEN's president.[61]

The decade-long conflict between ANDEN and other unions with reformers in Nicaragua significantly weakened the unions. At the outset of the 1990s, the minister of education chose not to negotiate with the Sandinista union, believing it to be the embodiment of what was wrong with the national education system. Rather than directly confront the union, as reformers in Bolivia did, however, he pursued a longer-term strategy of undermining their importance in the education sector. By creating an alternative union and using material incentives to appeal directly to teachers, Belli was able to undermine union capacity for dissent. He was not able to put an end to labor conflict, but he managed to sideline it from much of the action about education during the decade. Ultimately, however, the continuation of labor tensions encouraged subsequent leaders of the ministry to try to bring the unions back into national education planning. This initiative offered ANDEN a bit of hope of regaining some of its former influence, although the ministry clearly retained the upper hand.

Zero-Sum Politics: Ecuador

The teachers' union in Ecuador was similar to those in Bolivia. It was tied to a small, far left political party committed to a revolutionary ideology and confrontation with government. As in Bolivia, this union-party alliance had managed to take over control of the ministry of education and the country's normal schools, even while regularly opposing government over issues related to pay and work conditions. Few teachers probably believed in the rhetoric of UNE, but they continued to support it as the only vehicle they had to improve their wages and benefits. The union opposed any measures that would alter the educational system. As a consequence, the 1990s were characterized by repeated public agreements about the importance of education for the future of the country, but little agreement on going ahead with the kinds of changes that would improve its quality.

As indicated in chapter 3, the minister of education, in the midst of a major strike by UNE, agreed to salary increases that would return the teachers to the classroom. She did so because she believed that public opinion would side with the teachers and their demands. She even had some sympathy with their position. Moreover, political conditions in the country were tense, and an agreement with the union would help in a larger effort to keep opposition to the government from escalating even further. In reaching an agreement with UNE that did not carry with it concessions on the teachers' side, however, the minister was probably acknowledging that there was little chance for reform in the late 1990s.

In all likelihood, a confrontational approach to the union would also have failed. A reform initiative in 1998 demonstrates how difficult reform would be in the conflicts of the time. An education law, prepared by consultants to the ministry of education in 1997 and 1998, was submitted to congress in March. The purpose of the law was to address the most egregious problems of the sector—the poor quality of the teaching profession, the power of the union, the centralized decision-making structures, and the lack of parental involvement in local schools. It had been designed without the participation of the union and without much participation from the ministry of education because the designers assumed, with probable cause, that they would be met by intransigence.

When the proposal was sent to congress, UNE regarded it as an effort to break the union, destroy the teaching career, and privatize public education. The union denounced its contents and the administration that sponsored it. Moreover, because it formed part of a package of structural adjustment measures to deal with a devastating economic crisis, the teachers were in a good position to attack it as a neoliberal plan to diminish the state's role in providing free and universal education. In this denunciation,

TABLE 6.1
Teachers' Unions Responses to Education Reform Initiatives

	Strikes	Demand Better Salaries or Benefits	Claim Attack on Union Integrity/ Solidarity	Claim Exclusion from Discussion and Design	Claim Privatization of Public Education/ Neoliberalism	Provide Counter- proposal	Denounce Government More Generally
Negotiated settlement							
Minas Gerais	✔	✔		✔	✔	✔	
Mexico	✔	✔	✔	✔	✔	✔	
Confrontation							
Nicaragua	✔	✔	✔	✔	✔	✔	✔
Bolivia	✔	✔	✔	✔	✔	✔	✔
Ecuador	✔	✔		✔	✔	✔	✔

UNE joined a broad group of unions, parties, and movements that were adamantly opposed to the adjustment measures. Protest was widespread and political leaders in the legislature responded to it. The education bill, along with the economic measures, was rejected.

Although the 1998 reform was defeated, the legislative initiative left UNE even more bitter and suspicious toward those who wanted to make changes in the education system. They attacked the government for excluding them from the design of the reform, they claimed that government was trying to privatize education, and they denounced the government for a host of other sins. The law, of course, was as much a victim of the economic crisis as it was of the intransigence of the union. Nevertheless, the difficulties and risks of pursuing significant changes in education were clear to any erstwhile reformers. In Ecuador, at least in the late 1990s, small changes could be introduced in specific programs, as indicated in chapter 4, but national policy for education was at an impasse.

CONCLUSION: UNIONS, PARTIES, AND CONFLICT

Teachers' unions in Mexico, Minas Gerais, Bolivia, Nicaragua, and Ecuador followed similar strategies in opposing education reform (see table 6.1). All used strikes to assert their power and to make demands on the government while the reforms were being publicly discussed. Usually, salary and benefit increases were central to their demands. But they addressed the reforms also, by protesting against being kept out of the discussions about reform, a claim that encouraged them to develop alternative proposals as a way of demonstrating the virtues of inclusion. In Mexico, Bolivia, and Nicaragua, the unions also charged that the governments' proposals were a direct attack on the principle of union solidarity and integrity. In particular, the efforts of the Bolivian and Nicaraguan reformers to appeal directly to teachers and to offer incentives to those willing to go along with their plans was a very sore point with union leaders. All of the unions argued that government was trying to privatize education and abandon a long national tradition of public education. By associating the reforms with neoliberalism, they sought to connect with public discontent over the range of free-market economic policy reforms that were also being introduced in the 1990s. And in situations in which the unions were aligned with parties of the left, they used the reforms as an occasion to denounce government more generally.

Negotiation or Confrontation?

Clearly, in following these strategies, the unions were using their most effective weapons against unwanted changes. The power to disrupt public life, to close down schools and ministries, to halt traffic in capital cities, to appeal to public opinion—all were familiar actions to them. The union strategies were largely defensive, even though alternative proposals were put forward. Yet, in two cases, unions engaged in negotiations with government while in three cases, they either refused to discuss reform issues or were not invited to do so.

What explains these distinct outcomes? Decisions about negotiation or confrontation do not seem to have been a result of different union capacities to spark protests and disorder in the streets or to close down national education systems. All the unions used the strike as a major weapon against the government. All the unions had the capacity to create public disruptions and to halt the actions of the ministry and to appeal to public opinion. They used these resources repeatedly. Although in a strong position in Mexico and a relatively weak one in Minas Gerais, unions were at the negotiation table in both cases. In both cases, the reformers were able to emerge from these negotiations with their most important reform plans intact. In Bolivia, Nicaragua, and Ecuador, where governments confronted or ignored the unions, the teachers' organizations also had the capacity to take over the streets and to shut down schools for extended periods of time. Thus, the power of the unions vis-à-vis the government is not enough to explain decisions to negotiate or confront.

Nor does it seem that negotiation or confrontation was a result of the structure of the unions. In Mexico, a single union negotiated with the government; in Minas Gerais, several organizations—though only one union—represented the teachers and school directors. In Bolivia and Nicaragua, where confrontation occurred, there were several unions; in Ecuador, also a site of confrontation, there was just one. The unanimity of the teachers on reform issues also varied, but did not seem to affect whether there were negotiations or not. SNTE was unified in its position, as were the unions in Bolivia and Ecuador; in Minas Gerais, and in Nicaragua after 1993, however, organizations differed in their positions on reform.

The decision to negotiate or confront the unions did respond to how reformers assessed the constraints facing them. In some cases, these assessments were affected by the relationship that had developed between the unions and particular political parties. In Mexico, the power of SNTE, perhaps the strongest labor union in all of Latin America, was underscored by its power within the PRI. In turn, the PRI was the underpinning of the power of the Mexican government. President Salinas believed that to confront the union was to destroy the chance for reform. Not surprisingly, he opted for negotiation, even though several of his presidential predecessors had taken a different approach and sought reform without union acquiescence. In Minas Gerais, reformers chose to negotiate as a way of gaining their objectives with the least residue of teacher hostility, even though they were in a strong enough position to move ahead without the union. In contrast to Mexico, UTE was not particularly strong and the PT was of little concern to the governor, and the union could be outmaneuvered relatively easily, particularly given the range of other interests that were brought into the discussions. The reformers used their strength vis-à-vis the union to push their main objectives through while generating considerable goodwill from UTE by agreeing to some of its demands.

In Bolivia and Nicaragua, union-party alliances diminished the political costs of confronting the unions. In Bolivia, the teachers' organizations were aligned with small but vociferous parties of the far left. The tradition of interaction with government was one of confrontation, even violence, at the same time that the unions penetrated and colonized the ministry of education. Legacies of past conflicts between the government and organized labor had left behind mutual suspicions and intransigence. Moreover, the government did not rely on the union-affiliated party for support nor was it a player in the coalition politics that characterized executive-congressional relations. In Nicaragua, the national teachers' union was linked to the Sandinista party, the major opposition to the coalition government in power, but one that the government was committed to marginalizing. In these cases, governments were threatened by the disruptive capacity of the unions, but not dependent on them or their party affiliations for power. In Ecuador, at least in 1998, reformers ignored the unions and the politically marginal parties that supported them, and they lost their chance for introducing change in the education system. However, given the escalating political and economic problems of the country, it is unlikely that a different approach would have resulted in any better outcome.

The Politics of Approval versus the Politics of Implementation

The politics of negotiating with, confronting, or maneuvering around the teachers' unions were rife with conflict and uncertainty. In contrast, the politics surrounding the legislative approval of the reforms in Mexico, Minas Gerais, and Bolivia were surprisingly lacking in drama. The Nicaraguan reform was not legislated, but its promotion from proposal to a policy of government was equally unexciting. Even in Ecuador, where the reform was rejected, conflict between the executive and the legislature was not about disagreements over education per se; it was instead about a range of much broader issues related to economic policy and political power.

As we saw in previous chapters, negotiating the modernization agreement with the teachers' unions was the most important part of the process from the perspective of Mexico's reformers. President Salinas, to underscore his capacity to lead the political system, waited until after midterm elections had ensured a two-thirds majority for the PRI to pursue negotiations with SNTE in 1992. The law that enshrined the agreement followed in 1993, and, given the PRI's position in the legislature, was never a topic of controversy. In Minas Gerais, the education minister hosted a set of legislative hearings to promote the reform agenda, and then the governor used his considerable control over the distribution of political resources to threaten legislators into support of it. And in Bolivia, a highly contentious reform that featured extensive confrontations in the street between the government and the teachers' unions barely raised the temperature of the congress because of a governing pact ensuring party adherence on issues of import to the president. Thus, in three cases, legislative action on education was determined on the basis of factors that had little to do with the substance of education reform.

In the case of Nicaragua, when the minister of education anticipated that party strife in the legislature would stand in the way of his reform initiative, he simply decreed the reform. The lack of legislative action did not seem to hinder the promotion of the reform, and, at the end of the decade, it had proceeded as well as reforms in other countries that had the backing of law. In Ecuador, the education reform was rejected because the majority of legislators placed themselves firmly against a broad array of economic reform measures promoted by the president and underscored this position by rejecting an education law also. In this case, conflict was an important feature of executive-legislative relations, but this conflict was not primarily about how or whether to reform education.

The primary way in which reformers were constrained by opposition, then, was in how far they could push their proposals in the face of union opposition. Some reformers were more constrained than others due to the alliances among parties, unions, and governments. Thus, the role of political parties was an important aspect of decisions about how to respond to opposition, but only so far as parties were factors in determining reformer strategies in the period leading up to decisions about whether to seek legislative action or not. In four of the five cases, legislative action did not appear to be a major strategic concern of the reformers.

Nevertheless, prelegislative conflict had a significant impact on the subsequent history of each of the reforms. Where reformers negotiated with the unions, they were forced to compromise on some issues but were able then to proceed relatively rapidly with the reforms. In two cases in which reformers sought to confront or maneuver around the opposition—Bolivia and Nicaragua—they could also move ahead with new educational policies, but they would do so in the face of ongoing and bitter opposition. In the next chapter, a discussion of the implementation of four reforms indicates how this happened.

IMPLEMENTING AND SUSTAINING CHANGE:
NEW ARENAS FOR CONFLICT

MANY OF THOSE who were active in advancing quality-enhancing education reforms in the 1990s were optimistic that, once approved, changes would be implemented effectively, they would be supported and deepened by new stakeholders, and they would be sustained across time and political administrations.[1] Certainly, earlier successes in getting education on national political agendas, formulating new policies, and gaining approval for them might have emboldened reformers to feel confident that they could also meet the challenges of implementation.

In fact, the path to implementing and sustaining reform in most countries was a rocky and uncertain one. Contention continued to characterize the relationship between supporters and opponents of change long after the new policies became official. Moreover, as efforts were made to put the reforms into practice, new arenas of conflict emerged; often these new arenas were far removed from the purview of the reformers. Indeed, by the end of the decade, the grip of new policies was nowhere fully assured.

Long after the reforms were adopted, teachers' unions continued to challenge them. As we saw in the previous chapter, some governments chose to confront the unions and push ahead with reform, despite opposition. Other governments ignored the unions while pursuing policy changes, leaving union leaders, as well as many teachers, hostile to the new initiatives. The situation was different, but no more certain, where governments chose to negotiate with the teachers' unions. Just as in countries where no negotiations took place, these organizations continued to resist their marginalization from decision-making arenas and to object to measures that impinged on the role of teachers in the classroom and the power of unions to represent them. And certainly, in all cases, the unions remained true to their members' concern by continuing to demand better pay and work conditions, at times using the reforms as hostage.

Implementing and sustaining education reforms was not only difficult because of the overhang of conflict with the teachers' union, however. When efforts were made to put the new initiatives into practice, the political arena shifted away from interaction among reformers, their supporters, and their opponents in the "high politics" of national capitals. Instead, the actors who could determine the destiny of the reforms were found deep within national ministries of education, among officials at state, local, and school levels, and among the school directors, teachers, and parents in local communities. The reforms affected bureaucratic interests; many administrators were loath to give up old responsibilities and take on new ones. Moreover, in some cases, implementing and sustaining reforms would hinge on whether state governors and mayors chose to pursue educational improvement or to build stronger political machines by capitalizing on the patronage potential of school appointments and infrastructure. Reform destinies would also be affected by efforts of mayors and local communities to gain power over teachers and directors, and the acceptance or rejection by those teachers and directors of new ways of managing education in the classroom and the school. In addition, the path of reform could be influenced by the extent of support for change from local communities and parents.

In these new arenas, action was often less public and more diffuse than the conflicts that characterized agenda setting, policy design, and approval. As a consequence, it was sometimes difficult for reformers at central levels to capture what was happening to their initiatives. Indeed, new ways of understanding reform were required, as suggested by an education administrator in Nicaragua:

> You listen to a Mass at central levels about how everything is going well, but then if you go down the ladder and visit various levels and go out to the schools as I do, you see that things are very different. The central level shows data on how many new textbooks or preschool materials have been distributed and how many new desks have been delivered. But I see schools in which preschool materials are of lower quality than those sent out by the ministry . . . and I've seen warehouses full of desks that have never been delivered.[2]

In fact, central reformers often assumed that they had more control over their initiatives than they actually had. As these reforms became dependent on the actions of middle-level bureaucrats, regional and local officials, local communities, school directors, teachers, and parents, a mosaic of successes and failures emerged. Nevertheless, while these outcomes were determined primarily in arenas removed from the direct control of the reformers, there were ways these proponents of change could try to influence what became of their reforms. With political luck, they could remain in office long enough to help institutionalize change. They could use appointments to ensure that education bureaucracies were colonized with people in strategic implementing roles who understood and supported their reform initiatives. They could get out of their offices and communicate about change at more local levels. And they could find ways to reach the frontline workers—school directors, teachers, and school

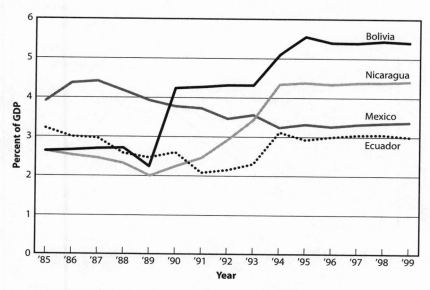

Figure 7.1. Education Expenditures as a Percentage of GDP
Source: World Bank, *World Tables*.

councils—with incentives to take on the difficult task of changing the way education was delivered.

COMPARING IMPLEMENTATION STRATEGIES

In four of the case studies—Mexico, Nicaragua, Bolivia, and Minas Gerais—reformers were able to move from adopting reforms to implementing them.[3] Nevertheless, the commitment of governments to support reform was not always as robust as the commitments of the reformers. As a proxy for overall commitment to education, expenditures on this sector as a percentage of GDP indicate that gains were substantial in Bolivia and Nicaragua, but disappointing in Mexico (see figure 7.1). It is interesting that significant upticks in funding in the first two cases corresponded to years in which reforms were introduced or the year following their introduction. When education expenditures are compared with overall government expenditures, Mexico indicates significant change (see figure 7.2).

Reformers in the four cases chose distinct strategies for implementing their plans. Much of the difference among them can be explained by government-union interactons during the approval phase of the policy pro-

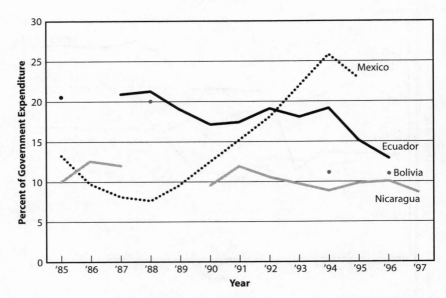

Figure 7.2. Public Education Spending as a Percentage of Government Expenditures
Source: World Bank, *World Tables*.

cess. In Mexico and Minas Gerais, where reforms had been negotiated
with the unions, they were put in place within a short time period (see
table 7.1). In Nicaragua and Bolivia, on the other hand, where the opposition of the teachers' unions was extensive, reforms were implemented in-
crementally. This suggests that the conflicts surrounding the adoption of
reform, and strategies chosen for dealing with those conflicts, had consequences for the subsequent history of change initiatives.

In addition, the cases differed in whether the objects of reform—the
states, municipalities, schools, and communities—were required to adopt
them or could choose to be part of them. In three cases, the changes were
mandatory; in Nicaragua, a voluntary process of adhesion allowed schools
to vote on whether they wanted to be part of it or not. Incentives, such as
increases in salaries of teachers who adopted the reforms or opportunities
for training, were used in Nicaragua and Bolivia, where relationships with
the unions had been particularly difficult. Countries also varied in the
extent to which they committed resources to helping state and local governments or local schools and communities develop the capacity to implement the reform. Despite these differences, the reforms shared a positive
experience—they all survived changes in political administrations—no
mean feat in Latin America's contentious political systems.

TABLE 7.1
Reform Implementation Strategies

	Timing		Degree of Choice		Use of Individual Incentives*		Capacity Development	
	All at once	Gradual	Mandatory	Voluntary	Yes	No	Minimal	Substantial
Minas Gerais	✔		✔			✔		✔
Mexico	✔		✔			✔	✔	
Nicaragua		✔		✔	✔			✔
Bolivia		✔		✔	✔			✔

*Incentives for teachers to support reform implementation as distinct from incentives used to gain approval of reform.

Implementation achievements varied among the cases. In Minas Gerais, a committed design team managed to gain approval for its school autonomy reform within a short period after a new governor was elected. In less than a year, the first elections for school directors, which reformers believed to be the central ingredient for more accountable and better performing schools, were held. A sample of 364 schools indicated that between 1992 and 1994, 85 percent of them had formed general assemblies and boards to oversee school activities.[4] During the same period, 69 percent of the state's schools had elected directors—all of whom had passed the qualifying test.[5] In addition, control over personnel and financial resources were devolved to the schools relatively rapidly and a program for testing student achievement was put in place. In 1994, the state's reform was recognized as an innovative approach to school management by UNESCO.

Implementation of the decentralization reform in Mexico was also rapid and universal. As soon as the agreement on the modernization of education was signed, states were asked to put procedures in place to receive the funds from the central government. Twenty-eight of thirty-one states did so immediately, even before the national education law confirming the agreement was passed in 1993.[6] The other three states followed suit during the next three years. In addition, by 1997, nineteen states had passed new laws setting out objectives and means for managing their education systems.[7] Table 7.2 indicates the degree to which the 1992 agreement made a difference in the structure of education in Mexico. Prior to the reform, the national government was responsible for 70 percent or more of students, teachers, and schools in the basic education system; after decentralization, it was responsible for 15 percent or less.[8] The practical implications

TABLE 7.2
Enrollment, Teachers, and Schools in Mexico by Source of Funding

	Primary		Basic Education*	
	1991–1992 Pre-reform thousands	1996–1997 Post-reform thousands	1991–1992 Pre-reform %	1996–1997 Post-reform %
Enrollment				
National	10,243	1,020	71	8
State	3,240	12,701	22	86
Private	914	927	7	7
Teachers				
National	348.1	47.3	70	10
State	102.8	441.5	22	81
Private	28.7	36.1	8	9
Schools				
National	67.3	15.9	75	15
State	13.5	74.7	19	78
Private	3.8	5.3	7	7

Source: Merino Juárez (1999:41).
*Preschool, primary, secondary schools.

of these numbers were considerable; state governments were now expected to make decisions and solve problems that used to be transferred to bureaucrats and politicians in Mexico City.[9]

In Nicaragua, reform proceeded through the voluntary inscription of individual schools, an approach that meant relatively slow implementation. Thus, by the end of 1999, of 4,554 primary educational centers, 1,797 (39.5 percent) were autonomous. This incorporated 63.5 percent of all students and 57.4 percent of all teachers at the primary level, reflecting the more urban character of reform implementation. Including secondary schools, 40.1 percent of all schools in the country, 68.5 percent of all students, and 62 percent of all teachers were part of the new autonomous school system.[10]

In Bolivia, to ease the introduction of new curricula and teaching methodologies that were central to the reform, two strategies were followed. Some schools were selected for upgrading with the introduction of new libraries, textbooks, and teacher training programs. Other schools were targeted for "transformation," the intensive introduction of new curricula and pedagogy, one grade per year, beginning with the first grade. After a number of years, transformed schools would produce a cohort of students who had been fully educated through new approaches and materials. National promoters of reform believed that incrementalism was the best way to encourage individual teachers to become part of the reform, given the opposition of their unions. They also initiated the reform in rural areas, where union opposition was less strident. Improved pay for rural and bilingual teachers also helped spur conversions to the reform goals. This cautious approach also recognized the difficulties of implementing a complex change in which each teacher and school director had to behave in new ways if the reform were to be successful. But this approach also slowed progress. In 1997, three years after the reform was passed into law, 46 percent of primary school networks (clusters of schools linked administratively) were being upgraded or transformed. Of 1.57 million students in primary school, 1.27 million (81 percent) were in schools being upgraded and 300,000 (19 percent) were in schools being transformed. Two years later, of 1.58 million students, 1.13 million (72 percent) were in schools that were being upgraded and 452,000 (28 percent) were in transformed schools.[11]

These data on expenditures and on the extent of incorporation into the reforms do not reveal much about the real fate of the reform initiatives, however, or the extent to which they were taken on by state and local officials, local schools, and communities as platforms for introducing better quality education in the classroom, or the ways they created new burdens, responsibilities, and benefits for officials, parents, teachers, school directors, and students. Recognizing that they were still in process at the end of the decade, the story of the achievements and constraints on implementing reform in the case study countries reveals the ways in which political interactions continued to affect the fate of the new policies.

UP THE DOWN STAIRCASE: MINAS GERAIS

The cause of education reform in Minas Gerais was advanced by a committed team in the ministry of education and backed by a governor who was willing to use his political muscle to ensure that the reform was adopted as planned by the reformers. Minister Mares Guia Neto argued that the implementation of the reform was strategically planned and carefully monitored. According to him: "Internally, bureaucrats were given a chance to participate, design the reform and adopt new roles—since the power to nominate principals and decide on resource allocation and daily routines of schools was gone. Extensive and permanent communications with mayors, principals, teachers and media were a key to 'sell' the reform and involve the key actors in its discussion and implementation."[12] While the evidence of previous chapters suggests that bureaucrats, except those on the reform team, were not much involved in the reform design, there was considerable effort to communicate about the reform with a variety of constituencies.

Indeed, after the law was passed at the end of June 1991, the minister toured the state with Vice-Minister Pinheiro and Edir Valadares, who had been recruited to oversee the testing and election of school directors. Their purpose was to explain the new procedures to school boards, general assemblies, teachers, and local communities and build support for putting them in place. The minister believed that the rapid and full implementation of the reform would help stymie opposition. In addition, he believed that by working quickly, new stakeholders who had an interest in better education would soon become aware that they had something to gain in sustaining the implementation of school autonomy.

At the administrative level, personnel files were relocated to the schools, and each school was assigned a fund for repairs, construction, equipment, lunches, and books. While there were complaints from time to time that these funds were mishandled by school directors, fairly strict monitoring by the ministry kept such abuses to a minimal level.[13] Many schools received new computers that helped in record keeping. Some progress was also made in ensuring that state and municipal schools met minimum requirements for per-pupil expenditures. At the level of the classroom, innovation proved more difficult. Altering pedagogy was difficult and teacher-training programs moved slowly.

The most significant change was the way school leaders were selected. In 1990, the year before the reform, 11.6 percent of school directors were elected by local school assemblies.[14] In the absence of a law legitimizing this form of selection, communities actually elected the director and then put pressure on appropriate politicians to appoint the person who had won the election. Thus, by 1991, local communities had already had some impact on altering how the patronage system worked. The old clientelist system received a body blow in 1991, however. By 1993, over two-thirds of the state's schools had elected directors. In addition, the vast majority of communities created the general assemblies and school boards mandated by the 1991 law. At this level, particularly where there was active community involvement and political support from parties of the democratic left, the implementation of the 1991 reform proceeded apace. According to Mares Guia Neto, seventeen thousand candidates competed in six thousand elections for school director in 1991, involving 3 million parents as well as teachers, students, and administrators.[15] Many believed there was no going back to the old system.[16]

Indeed, the period between 1991 and 1993 was a heyday for the Minas Gerais reform, particularly with regard to two critical aspects, the qualifying test and elections for school directors. After 1993, however, sustaining change became less certain. In 1990 and 1991, a series of supreme court decisions had determined that such elections in other states violated the federal constitution. After losing the legislative battle over this part of the reform in Minas Gerais, ADEOMG, the school directors' association, immediately challenged the constitutionality of the new law.[17] The directors won their case and, after 1993, elections proceeded without a law to back them up. As a consequence, the process would continue only when there was strong gubernatorial backing for it or when local communities insisted on it. It was therefore important to the reform that, for the next several years, leadership in the governor's office and in the ministry ensured that school autonomy received significant high-level support. Although Minister Mares Guia Neto resigned from his post in 1993 to run for vice-governor, he left Ana Luiza Pinhiero, the head of the reform's design team, in charge at the ministry. After the election in 1994, a new governor, Eduardo Azeredo, supported the continuation of the reform, no doubt influenced by his vice-governor, the erstwhile minister.

Nevertheless, even in the context of supportive governors, the link between the qualifying test for candidates for school director and subsequent elections began to unravel at the local level. As indicated in the previous chapter, the Partido dos Trabalhadores, in alliance with the teachers' union, favored elections but opposed the qualifying test. At the local level, and working through the general assemblies and school boards, the PT and UTE were at times able to promote the one and not the other. Elections as the means to select directors became hotly contested local events, and even more so when they coincided with municipal and state elections.[18] The number of school directors representing the PT increased, suggesting that the ministry's insistence on prior experience for the post was not being observed. Thus, although the union had lost in 1991, UTE was able to eat away at the full process of reform in some local communities while it was being implemented.

In 1998, Itamar Franco, a strong opponent of Helio Garcia, became governor. Soon, most of the original reform team left the ministry, convinced that the new governor would do everything he could to erase the legacy of the prior administration. In short order, under pressure from UTE, the qualifying tests for school directors were officially done away with and directors were no longer constrained to serve fixed terms in office. In addition, the degree of financial autonomy for local schools was curbed and statewide testing of students was suspended for a time, although it was later reinstated. Nevertheless, because Franco headed a center-left, pro-democratization coalition, he continued to support local elections for school director.[19] This aspect of the reform was sustained, therefore, even while other aspects of it were undermined.

At the end of the decade, school autonomy in Minas Gerais was still fragile. On the positive side, it had created new stakeholders who were important to undermining the old clientelist system and supporting more democratic local control over schools. Test scores in language, mathematics, and science demonstrated improvement in 1994 and 1996.[20] Along with this good news, repetition rates also decreased.[21] But questions remained about the sustainability of the reform. After 1998, ministry interest turned more to the issue of grade repetition, and the strong gubernatorial and ministerial support formerly seen for school autonomy clearly weakened. The extent of the reform, then, became more dependent on how local communities were responding to it. At this level, even where there was strong support for autonomy, the reformers lost the capacity to insist on the importance of demonstrated competence for school leadership positions.

DIVERGENT DESTINIES: MEXICO

Perhaps nowhere was the fate of reform more ambiguous than in Mexico. As we have seen, in the wake of the 1992 agreement between the ministry, the SNTE, and the governors, central administrators held on to considerable control over the education system through their role in finance, curriculum design, textbook design and selection, regulation of teaching credentials, base salary and benefits negotiations, testing, standards setting, and compensatory programs. Indeed, the maintenance of these activities led some to claim that Mexico maintained one of the most centralized education systems in the world.[22] Nevertheless, and despite the continued insistence on a large role for the central government, the education reform of 1992 significantly altered the preexisting system. The relationship of the states to the center, of the teachers' union to the states, and of the governors to their education systems were all altered in important ways. In some cases the structural change led to efforts to improve education; in other cases, state-level education systems continued to suffer from all the maladies that had afflicted the pre-reform national system.

With decentralization, governors became central actors in conflicts about education policies at the state level. This was an ironic outcome; the governors had been little involved in the negotiations that resulted in the agreement that bore their signatures.[23] Indeed, as we saw in the previous chapter, most state executives, given their fiscal and political preferences, would have actively resisted taking on responsibility for education. They were certainly concerned that they would be expected to bear more of the costs of education. In their one important input into the national agreement of 1992, they managed to persuade the government to define and then refine further the formula for assigning funds to the states and to introduce measures that made the transfers to the states obligatory.[24] In addition, the governors were deeply concerned about becoming targets for SNTE demands.

Whatever their concerns, decentralization happened rapidly. The reform meant that more than a half million teachers, more than 100,000 administrators, almost 14 million students, and 100,000 schools would be transferred to the states almost overnight.[25] State budgets for education automatically doubled, tripled, quadrupled, or more, reflecting equal growth in responsibilities for personnel, students, and infrastructure. In twelve states, responsibilities for education increased nine to ten times.[26] No wonder many states were ill-prepared to take on these new responsibilities and considerable chaos characterized the transfer of funds, personnel, students, and infrastructure.[27] According to one analysis: "The magnitude and rapidity of the transfers and the rapidity with which they were implemented, has caused great bottlenecks in the state administrations . . . the total of state government personnel has in many cases quadrupled, the power of the union has destabilized a number of state governments, and the lack of technical experts has often inhibited innovation at the state level."[28] A state-level education reformer characterized the situation as one of "federal disengagement proceeding faster than state engagement."[29]

The situation was complicated in other ways. Prior to decentralization, all but six states had education systems that paralleled the national system. They varied considerably in size. Thirteen states enrolled between 25 and 50 percent of all basic education students; in eight, from 10 to 25 percent of students were in the subnational system, and in seven more, from 1 to 10 percent.[30] As a consequence, after the national agreements, all but a handful of state governments would have to find ways of coordinating or combining two separate teachers' corps, two separate administrative systems, and two sets of educational infrastructure with different regulations, salary levels, and record-keeping systems. In some states, governors created new autonomous institutes to manage the transferred resources and responsibilities, in large part to provide for greater legal, administrative, labor, technical, and financial flexibility.[31] To ease the transition, a number of states opted to maintain two separate structures. By the end of the decade, however, the national ministry was putting pressure on all state-level systems to integrate more fully, especially in terms of planning, teacher training, and day-to-day administration.[32]

Given the weight of education expenditures in state budgets, newly empowered education ministers or managers of independent educational agencies became important players in state-level politics. Now responsible for the education payroll and the administration of schools, they, and the governors they served, had significant new resources. Moreover, the leaders of SNTE locals increased in importance as they focused new energies on gaining advances for teachers at the state level.[33] In some states, officials and union leaders managed to routinize a bargaining relationship; in others, they were at loggerheads; in still others, the locals of the union demanded and received positions within the new ministry leadership structures.[34] A review of several states indicates the kinds of political struggles that resulted from decentralization.

In the state of Guanajuato, a new institute for education was created for the transfer of funds, personnel, and infrastructure. At the same time, the state-level ministry of education, which had managed about 27 percent of basic education in the state, remained in control of its own resources and responsibilities. Eighteen months of intense conflict over the control of education pitted the two organizations against each other.[35] In the end, both entities were absorbed in a new organization and new leaders were brought in by the governor to manage it. Only at this point could the task of responding to education needs in the state be undertaken. In the ensuing months, and with support from the governor, a group of reformers gained power over education policy and managed to limit the power of the SNTE local. This made it possible to introduce a number of changes in the structure and functions of the education bureaucracy and introduce innovations at lower levels in the system. Despite these early successes, reformers failed to incorporate important interests in their plans and were unable to sustain the initiative in the face of rising opposition from traditional interests and passivity from schools and local communities.[36] Indeed, one study concluded that "a school reform was designed without the school," including participation of teachers, school directors, parents, or local officials.[37]

In Nuevo Leon, where the state government had been responsible for almost 41 percent of students in basic education, the intention from the beginning was to fuse the two educational systems into one. A new ministry of education was established and a new minister brought in with strong support from the governor. But within a short period of time, contention within the ministry emerged between two groups. One, known for its commitment to innovation and reform, confronted another, made up of politically oriented officials with links to the teachers' union, who sought to slow the process of change.[38] With leadership support, the reformers were able to push forward with their agenda, and "there was hardly an area of the administrative apparatus of the education sector that was not subjected—with different degrees of intensity—to important structural changes carried out with great innovativeness and in the context of real and radical restructuring of the state."[39] Nevertheless, by the end of the decade, the fusion of the two systems was still incomplete: many teachers felt orphaned by the changes; problems of implementation were interpreted as evidence of the failure of decentralization; conflicts continued to characterize the management of education; constraints on the use of funds limited the reach of state-level reform initiatives; and local participation in the reform initiative was lacking.[40]

In the state of Chihuahua, the national education agreement coincided with the election of a new governor whose party, the Partido Acción Nacional (PAN), displaced the PRI not only in the governor's office, but also in the state legislature. Almost immediately, SNTE locals—long accustomed to naming education leaders—mobilized to maintain their control over the education system. The new government announced its commitment to administrative efficiency, improved quality, social participation, and value-oriented education. Not surprisingly, between 1992 and 1995, the state was the site of serious conflicts between the PAN government and the SNTE over virtually all aspects of education. In addition, there was contention with the SNTE locals over the integration of state and federal teachers. A values-oriented addition to the mandated curriculum also engendered tension between the governor and his PAN supporters and the PRI-dominated ministry. The SNTE locals were united in their suspicion that the PAN was intent on privatizing the public education system.[41] Teachers were confused and uncertain about the scope of reform and their relationship to the ministry.[42] This difficult situation began to improve after 1995, when the PAN lost its majority in the state legislature and the PAN governor was forced to assume a more accommodating position vis-à-vis the PRI.

The state of Oaxaca was characterized by accommodation between the union and the government. Prior to 1992, Oaxaca had virtually no state education system and therefore took on new responsibilities with little organizational conflict but with a great deal of uncertainty, given its paucity of experience. At the time of the national agreement, the governor was intent on avoiding conflicts with the union.[43] During the 1980s, the union local had been active in resisting the leadership of the national ministry of education and had grown distrustful of the national system that was to be transferred to the state. At the same time, the local was a powerful organization at the state level and still important within the PRI. The governor met frequently with union leaders, provided a meeting place for retired teachers, increased retirement funds for some teachers, and promised to find land for a warehouse for teaching materials and for the normal school. In late 1992, a new PRI governor took over the leadership of the state and began building new schools and improving old ones, expanding the teacher corps, and building housing for teachers.[44] By the end of the decade, many of the changes in the state were quantitative expressions of expansion of the old system rather than qualitative changes in the kind of education children were receiving.

In contrast to many other states, Aguascalientes became well-known as a case in which new management was brought into the education system, resources were managed relatively efficiently, and innovation and creativity characterized officials in the decentralized institute in charge of education.[45] A new governor elected in 1992 was able to choose the head of this institute independently of STNE. This governor made education reform a priority for the state's development and moved ahead with a series of innovative reforms.[46] Teacher training, regional content in the curriculum, more and better classroom materials, local school councils, and further decentralization to the municipal level characterized post-decentralization activities in this small and highly urbanized state.[47] Initially, the local SNTE was sympathetic to the reforms but at the behest of the national organization, took to the streets to demand higher salaries and to protest against the lengthening of the school year, a new team-based structure of work, performance-based incentives, and openness about teacher assignments and promotions.[48] These early protests, however, gradually gave way to a more accommodating stance as union leaders were invited to join in planning the reforms.[49] Strong presidential support for the governor also helped reduce tension with the local union.

As in Minas Gerais, much of the variation among states in Mexico can be credited to the priorities of the governors, their perspectives about the importance of education, and their political party ties.[50] In distinction to the Brazilian state, however, local communities did not play much of a role in reform implementation. The Mexican initiative included social participation councils that were to be established at the school level; along with new municipal councils, these organizations were to bring together parents, local officials, teachers, administrators, and representatives of business and religious organizations. In fact, however, by the end of the decade, these councils had not resulted in effective involvement of parents and other citizens in the schools. Councils, indicated one observer, "never had a chance in the face of the union and the power of the school professionals."[51] One official argued that "traditionally, teachers have been very jealous of their rights in the classroom. . . . The constitution says the role of parents is to see that their children get to school—that's all!"[52] According to others: "The teacher decides what happens in the school" and does not invite others to share such decisions.[53] "If parents complain or put pressure on the school or the teacher, the teacher will retaliate against the child in the class. The parents know this and are very reluctant to speak out."[54]

Even beyond this hostile setting, there was really little that parents could do locally to influence school performance. Although state governments were now administering basic and normal education, and municipalities were given responsibility for the construction of schools at the end of the decade, Mexico's education system remained highly centralized.[55] Curriculum, base salaries and benefits for teachers, most of the funding, standards and criteria for educational achievement—all continued to be determined centrally. The teachers looked to national decision makers to tell them what to teach—and how to teach it—and they did not have much leeway for responding to parental demands, even if they were prepared to do so.

Local input was further limited by ambiguities in the decentralization initiative. As one observer noted: "If you go to the governor or the secretariat of education in the state and complain, they will say 'No, no, we don't have anything to do with that; you have to go to the federal government.' If you go to the federal government to complain, they will say 'No, no, that's the responsibility of the state.' "[56] Under the Fox administration (2000–2006), governors of two states, Tlaxcala and Oaxaca, declared that they were returning their education responsibilities to the central government because they did not have sufficient resources to operate the system.[57] Given the difficulty of assigning responsibilities, concerned citizens found it difficult to hold officials directly accountable for educational performance. Indeed, the legacies of a centralized system continued to haunt this initiative to improve the quality of Mexico's public schools.

SLOW BOAT TO SCHOOL AUTONOMY: NICARAGUA

School autonomy in Nicaragua was implemented through a "pick winners first" strategy. In 1993, the first twenty high schools to become autonomous were handpicked by the ministry, ensuring that the most urban, progressive, and prosperous part of the school system would be the first to experiment with autonomy. Then the program was expanded on a voluntary basis to other high schools. Primary schools became eligible for incorporation in 1995. The incremental and voluntary nature of this expansion of the reform was chosen by Minister Belli in order to stack the cards in favor of early positive results. First, by beginning with secondary schools—usually located in urban areas and attended by better-off students—the chances of demonstrating the advantages of autonomy for teachers, school directors, and parents were improved. Second, reformers recognized that resource and capacity constraints would necessarily limit what they could accomplish through retraining teachers and school directors and organizing and training school councils to take on new management and oversight responsibilities. Third, they believed that if teachers voted on whether their school should become autonomous or not, and if they had to go through some type of vetting process by the central administration, they would feel greater commitment to the success of the new policy. This was important, given that the unions and the reformers were at odds.

As the reform was implemented, incentives encouraged teachers and school directors to see the benefit of commitment to the reform, especially the potential for increased salaries, even while it would reduce their job security. International agencies ensured that there was funding for following through with promised incentives. Moreover, ministry of education representatives at the municipal level were recruited and trained by the reformers to be the local source of support and encouragement for the program.[58] In this positive and evolutionary context, it could be expected that assessments of the implementation of reform would be positive.

In fact, results after several years of implementation were mixed. Just as the state became the new focus of contestation about reform in Mexico, in Nicaragua, the local school became the site of considerable contestation about decision making, responsiveness to local communities, and accountability.[59] Contention over reform also continued at the national level, as education ministers after Belli attempted to generate more consensus and participation in national education policy. After 1998, the local representatives who had been so carefully selected and trained under Belli's administration were gradually replaced by appointees who were less committed to the reform and more interested in reestablishing some of the privileges that teachers had formerly enjoyed. School directors, school councils in which parents composed the majority, and teachers vied for influence over school-level decisions and control over the resources made available through the reform.

Implementation of the reform was also afflicted by bureaucratic and financial problems. Vague and unclear norms and regulations allowed for considerable variation in how the schools were incorporated into the reform and how decisions were reached after their incorporation. Bureaucratic procedures for inclusion in the reform program and development of the requisite institutional structures at the school level also resulted in delays and inconsistencies among schools, a characteristic that became more notable after Belli left office. Initially, in some schools, teachers in favor of reform became part of the new incentive system while teachers who did not vote for it remained in the old payroll and career systems, making it difficult to coordinate across educators within schools.[60] Given the differentials in salary, however, over time most teachers within a reform school tended to join the new system. Still, many teachers didn't understand new structures for decision making and accountability. In addition, some changes, such as the development of municipal-level education councils, were never seriously implemented and were abandoned. And, according to one reformer who spent considerable time visiting schools and explaining the reform: "There was a lot of misinformation about the [reform] at the time. The central idea [that many had] was that the government was abandoning the schools and not going to provide funding. So our principal job was to deal with the negative perceptions of the autonomous school program."[61]

Despite these problems, the reform proceeded ahead throughout the 1990s. A 1997 evaluation of the initiative, based on quantitative and qualitative research in a sample of 226 autonomous and centralized schools, affirmed that autonomous schools had the capacity to assume considerable responsibility, including decision making about salaries, incentives, hiring and firing personnel, and developing school-based goals, pedagogy, maintenance, and relationships with the community.[62] More generally, implementation of the reform was easier in larger schools and more urban centers and more difficult in smaller schools and more rural areas. Urban schools were generally characterized by better-trained teachers, more experienced directors, more engaged parents, and students with better socioeconomic conditions. In addition, the report found that the administrative aspects of the reform were more easily put in place than changes in the pedagogy used in the classroom.

Response to the reform varied at the local level. In general, school directors evaluated school autonomy more positively than did school councils or teachers.[63] As the number of types of decisions made at the school level increased, school directors believed that their degree of influence over those decisions also increased. Council members believed that their influence increased slightly, while teachers saw no difference in their influence on decisions made at the school level, regardless of how many types of decisions were being made. A separate analysis of a subsample of eighteen schools comparing autonomous with centrally managed schools concluded that autonomy had introduced more communication and interaction among teachers and school directors, better understanding of the distribution of functions and responsibilities among educators, and greater commonality of goals and missions within the school.[64] At the same time, centers differed in terms of how well teachers and directors interacted with the councils, and this in turn affected attitudes toward the value of school autonomy, an outcome that was true of the larger sample also.[65]

School directors were key actors in the initiation of the reform at the school level and in setting up the councils. In some cases, they were able to manage the selection of which teachers and parents would be on these boards and had considerable influence in determining how to spend school resources from the ministry and local fees.[66] In some cases, mayors or the municipal representative of the ministry played a role in determining the makeup of the councils.[67] Under the reform, the councils had considerable power to appoint and fire personnel and decide on what should be done with school fees. They also had input into issues related to curriculum and pedagogy. According to one study, councils at times eliminated sex education from the curriculum and favored traditional teaching techniques over those supported by reformers in the national ministry.[68] Thus, the school councils opened up democratic space for input into school-level decision making, but it was possible for representation on the councils to be less than democratic and for their pedagogical decisions to be less than progressive.

As in other countries, the issue of the engagement of the teachers in the reform continued to cause concern. An NGO leader and former leader of ANDEN summed up some of the skepticism about the reform. "We have real concerns about the teachers losing influence in schools and education, of being left out of the decisions that are made. We hear that, yes, there may be greater retention and promotion now, but we think it has to do with giving kids passing grades because teachers want to keep kids in school to get the fees."[69] Some teachers believed that the government was trying to privatize education through local autonomy.[70] Moreover, teachers frequently felt threatened by the councils because parents had the preponderance of power and they generally believed that they should be subject to their ministry supervisors, not to parents. There were some reports that teachers felt coerced into joining the autonomy initiative.[71] At the same time, they were often dismissive of efforts by parents to become more involved in the school.[72] More generally, while evaluations indicated that teacher attendance and punctuality were considerably improved because of increased parental monitoring, there were no appreciable changes in the extent to which children were learning.[73]

The payment of school fees, however voluntary, also remained a contentious issue among parents, directors, and teachers throughout the 1990s. Where parents did not contribute significant resources to the schools, the teachers often did not receive the salary increments they had been told would materialize through the autonomy program.[74] Accordingly, "Teachers in [primary] schools clearly feel that they have been deceived since they were sold the program on the expectation of higher salaries that have not materialized."[75] In interviews and focus groups carried out in the 1997 study, teachers complained that their employment security and salaries were jeopardized by the reform, even though the same study found that 69 percent of expenditures from school fees were for teacher salary increments and another 5 percent was distributed as in-kind assistance to teachers.[76] Where salaries had been increased through participation in the reform, they were likely to be more supportive.[77] Teachers often resented having to take on the administrative burden of collecting and accounting for such fees.

The fees were also a source of concern to parents. Most of them believed that autonomy was synonymous with increases in contributions to the schools and were worried that teachers would exert pressure on students to bring their "voluntary" fees to school.[78] They expected teachers to retaliate against their children if fees were not paid, and many complained that the imposition of the voluntary contributions on very poor people was unjust. Poorer communities and their teachers were well aware that schools in better-off areas were benefiting more than they were from the fee system.[79] More generally, the unions' charge that the education reform was privatizing public education often resonated with parents who resented the fees. In other ways, however, parents were more positive about autonomy. They tended to see it as a more open space for local influence over the school.[80] But when teachers were dismissive and school directors did not counteract this attitude with special attention to parents, their approval of the new system declined.

These perceptions suggest that frequently directors, school council members, and at times parents saw themselves as winners of school autonomy, while the teachers—and at times, the parents—tended to believe that they were its losers. ANDEN also considered itself a loser.[81] Teachers who voted against incorporation into the reform were often ANDEN members; adherents of this union experienced discrimination in some schools and at times were fined for not voting for autonomy. In the face of this kind of retribution, and in the context of the possibility of higher salaries, many decided to join the reform and to abandon ANDEN's position toward it.[82]

Clearly, the school autonomy initiative altered the arena in which important decisions about education were being made and introduced the possibility of considerable variability across school and community boundaries. By decentralizing power, the reformers also gave up considerable capacity to influence important local-level decisions or to control the extent of local-level conflict. With new centers of power, "local actors will interpret the rules of the game on their own and . . . principals, teachers, parents, and municipal officials and Ministry [representatives] will compete for control of the organism that is granted considerable power over school governance."[83]

STEADY, CONTENTIOUS PROGRESS: BOLIVIA

Conflict and slow but steady progress were the hallmarks of the development and introduction of Bolivia's education reform in the 1990s.[84] At the end of the decade, the reform continued to encounter and engender conflict at the same time that it continued its steady expansion in communities, schools, and classrooms. The reform was a particularly broad one, encompassing a full range of structural, administrative, pedagogic, curricular, and professional development changes. It could be expected, then, that advances and accomplishments would vary not only by the site of implementation, as we saw in the cases of Mexico and Nicaragua, but also by aspect of the reform, as we saw in Minas Gerais.

According to the ministry of education, by the end of the 1990s, the reform had achieved the introduction of a new curriculum in the first four years of primary school, the production and distribution of textbooks and other materials in four "national" languages and the creation of four education councils representing these language groups (Aymara, Quechua, Guaraní, and multiethnic Amazonia), and the training of teachers and supervisors in the design and use of the new curriculum.[85] In addition, the ministry had put in place technology for managing information, teachers, and administrators. It had successfully introduced—and maintained—a school year based on two hundred days of classes and reduced the high rate of term time turnover in teacher assignments.[86] The ministry had also managed to decrease the number of teachers without teaching credentials in urban schools.[87] It had created offices at the provincial level whose responsibilities were to promote educational management at the municipal and district level, and it had put in place a national testing program for student achievement. In 1999, the reform program invested $38.3 million in building new schools and repairing old ones.[88] And, despite extensive opposition, the ministry had managed to transfer the management of previously autonomous normal schools to the university sector.[89]

International donor agencies, which played a significant role in funding Bolivia's reform, were positive about its progress by the end of the decade. They praised the increased stability in the school year that resulted from the confrontation with the unions, the increased stability of teachers in the classroom within school terms, the ability to get new textbooks to the classrooms at the outset of the school term, the student testing program, and the transfer of the normal schools to the universities.[90] They supported the intention of the ministry to provide incentives for teaching in rural areas as a way of upgrading education quality. They anticipated improvements in the university-based normal schools and better in-service training for teachers.[91]

These were important achievements. With the exception of the curricular reforms, however, they were changes that could be instituted through central fiat rather than those requiring teachers, principals, local officials, or local communities to buy into the reforms and manage them. This second aspect of reform implementation was both more difficult and slower than reformers in the ministry had anticipated. For example, the introduction of a 1994 decentralization policy focused primarily on increasing the responsibilities of municipalities meant that local officials were to be making important decisions about investments in education; provincial (departmental) officials were to hire and fire teachers. While the education reform remained the responsibility of the central ministry, its implementation would depend significantly on the actions of regional and local officials, raising concerns about accountability and follow-through.[92]

Initial experience with implementing the reform and the new structure of responsibilities for education led to some strategic rethinking among the reformers. In 1999, their strategy changed to a focus on 85 (of 311) municipalities, carefully selected as areas where important gains could be achieved. This new strategy would initially involve $12 million, 12,500 teachers, and 15,000 parents.[93] In the following year, an additional 114 municipalities were to be incorporated into the focused implementation program, involving an additional 18,000 teachers and 20,000 parents.[94] These targeted municipalities would receive particular attention for improving the decentralization, community participation, and results-based management aspects of the reform. In addition, the curricular reform would continue to be introduced one grade at a time in transformed schools, and teacher development was to be emphasized.[95]

Reformers in Bolivia, unable to negotiate with the unions, had to find other ways to reach the teachers in the classroom. As indicated by one social scientist: "The future of the reform is going to depend on reaching teachers effectively and winning them over without working through the unions."[96] Teachers received significantly increased salaries after the reform was put in place in 1994, and their attendance as well as their term time permanence in the classroom improved at the end of the decade. Parent councils were also widely organized to keep track of classroom and school activities. These should have been important ways to attract the attention of the teachers and encourage their professional interest in the reform program. However, salary increases continued to reflect primarily credentials and time in service rather than performance, thus limiting the material incentives for adopting new behaviors in the classroom. Better salaries, if untied to performance, would have little short-term impact on the quality of education in the country, although in the longer term they might attract better qualified individuals into the teaching career.[97]

Reformers were criticized for not doing more to communicate with teachers about the content of the new measures and their role in putting them in place.[98] After completing an assessment of the reform in 1999, one researcher noted: "I am convinced, after visiting a lot of schools in a lot of different places in Bolivia that the problems are pretty much the same all over. Lack of understanding and preparation [for the reform], resistance to change in and of itself, lack of resources. The new law requires an extensive cultural change. The problems faced by the teachers are a ıway from the changes faced by people in the ministry. The teachers elt that the reform has been imposed on them."[99] She continued:

ıe materials are so different from the ways teachers are used to teaching and ᵕ ıe ways parents are used to thinking about education that it is no wonder there is resistance. The teachers receive the materials, but without any orientation in how to use them. There are all sorts of problems—the curriculum calls for teachers to put student work and other things on the walls, but many schools are double session and the students and teachers from the afternoon session abuse the stuff put up by those in the morning, and vice versa. The curriculum has all sorts of activities that require paper, string, markers, and other things, but the teachers often don't even have scissors and chalk. The parents resist paying for materials—they are used to buying a notebook and pencil for their kids at the beginning of the year, not continually being asked for money. . . . [T]he reform is a very pretty idea, but it needs to be brought down to reality.[100]

Qualitative research on new initiatives by the ministry of education, on the other hand, found that introducing merit pay, allowing teachers to teach double shifts, and providing opportunities for upward career mobility, were important for improving teacher performance and interest in further training.[101] As in the Nicaragua reform, some teachers were attracted to the reform because, through it, they received new textbooks and teaching materials, more attention from the community and ministry, and higher salaries. Some found new opportunities for promotion to positions as school directors and administrators. In Bolivia, then, the progress of the reform was affected by the legacy of conflict with the teachers' unions, yet reformers found ways to compensate teachers who committed themselves to new classroom and professional norms. Overall, by the end of the decade, the initiative made most progress in pursuing changes that did not directly involve the teachers, and it continued to promote more difficult aspects of reform municipality by municipality, school by school, and teacher by teacher.

CONCLUSION: NEW VOICES IN EDUCATION REFORM

Implementing education reform opened up new arenas of conflict long after changes had been designed and agreed to. In four of the case study countries, these arenas were likely to be at more local levels of government or within local school communities. In Mexico, Minas Gerais, and Bolivia, state and local governments became significantly involved in determining the fate of the reforms. In Minas Gerais, Nicaragua, and Bolivia, the community, the school, and the classroom became important arenas in which reforms were adopted or rejected.

The reform policies also altered the voices that were likely to be heard in debates about education. Certainly governors and to some extent mayors became more important actors in promoting or hindering reforms. In Mexico, state-level ministries increased in importance. In Minas Gerais and Nicaragua, school directors became critical in determining how well schools adapted to new curricula, pedagogy, and decision making structures. In some cases, teachers gained some capacity to be heard in discussions about school reform. And, with the exception of Mexico, parents and local communities became critically important to the outcome of reform initiatives. The emergence of these new voices was a marked change from pre-reform conditions.[102]

In promoting the new initiatives within the context of new arenas of conflict, reformers used a variety of resources to implement and sustain change. Long tenure in office, high-level support, powers of appointment, use of incentives, strategies for pacing and communicating about the reforms, and a variety of other mechanisms enabled them to make important progress. Yet it is important not to overstate the extent of change, particularly in the extent to which teachers adopted the reforms as their own and sought to put them into practice in the classroom and the extent to which parents became more effectively engaged in decision making at the school level.

Teachers often believed they had lost out in the reforms. The new policies were generally imposed on them by centralized education bureaucracies; they had little role in discussing them or designing them before they were told that they must adopt new approaches and materials.[103] When teachers did adopt the reforms, it was often because of tangible rewards such as improved salaries or materials for use in the classroom, rather than from effective training in the new methods or incentives directly related to reform objectives. In all countries, of course, there were those who were eager to adopt new methods of teaching and to use new curricula and teaching materials out of commitment to teaching and the development of the children in their classrooms. Unfortunately, the implementation of reforms at times discouraged more teachers from becoming advocates of change by ignoring their concerns, maintaining top-down communication channels, and training them superficially in new methodologies and approaches to learning and educational decision making.

Reflecting on the central place of teachers in reform initiatives, a former education official in Colombia summed up some of the ways in which reforms characteristically missed the mark. "[M]y experience in Colombia leading the Ministry of Education's Teacher and School Incentives Programs," she stated, "showed me that when educators and communities *know and understand* what the reform calls for, find an *individual and collective meaning* and *sense of mission* in its purposes, have *incentives* to engage in it, and *can do* what the reform calls for with their *personal know-how*, the dynamics and energy to get the reform going are a given."[104] The implication from the case studies was that these conditions were not generally met. Thus, a major challenge remaining for reformers in a new millennium was finding ways to improve communication and dialogue with teachers, increase their capacities to adopt the reforms in the classroom, and make them partners in the promotion of quality education in their countries.

A second challenge for the reformers was effective engagement of parents in the schooling of their children. Although parents had not been involved in discussing, designing, or approving the reforms, their role in implementing and sustaining new policies was important.[105] Certainly, a much-vaunted goal of reforms in many countries was greater participation of parents and greater community involvement in education planning, resource provision, quality enhancement, and monitoring. In Minas Gerais and Nicaragua, parental engagement was central to the new policies. But encouraging this kind of participation was not an easy task in the context of Latin America's tradition of centralized and paternalistic government. With the exception of Minas Gerais, there was little tradition of parental engagement in the schools, other than in local committees whose purpose was to encourage contributions to school maintenance and civic celebrations. Rarely were they involved in educational decision making or in monitoring teacher, director, or school performance. In addition to this legacy, parents were not immune to the perspectives promoted by the unions, that new systems were simply a prelude to privatization of education and the abandonment of public education by the state.[106] At times, they met efforts to stimulate their participation with suspicion and questions.[107]

The experience of the 1990s suggests that it is possible for new voices to emerge in the wake of education reform. These voices were likely to be those most clearly responsible for managing education programs and policies—governors, mayors, state-level ministers, and school directors, and at times teachers and school councils. Their engagement in the reforms was likely to be greater when they were expected to make important decisions that affected how resources were distributed and used, when they understood the reforms and their role in making them work, and when there were clear incentives for them to be engaged. A great challenge for further reform implementation in many countries, then, was finding better ways—and more political support—for engaging teachers, parents, and communities in efforts to improve the quality of education.

Chapter Eight

IN PROCESS: THE POLITICS OF

EDUCATION REFORM

REFORMING EDUCATION SYSTEMS is difficult and time-consuming. It involves developing new approaches to learning, putting new structures in place, and acting on the knowledge that line administrators, school directors, teachers, students, and parents must be engaged in order to produce good results. Beyond technical, administrative, and pedagogical factors, reform is difficult and long in the making because it inevitably engenders political opposition. Those who undertook to bring system-wide education changes to Latin American countries during the 1990s struggled against strongly entrenched interests; the distribution of institutional power made a difficult task even more so. In some cases, their initiatives failed.

Yet, despite the odds against them, Latin America's education reformers were neither powerless nor doomed to failure. The case studies from Brazil, Mexico, Nicaragua, Bolivia, and Ecuador indicate ways in which these actors attempted to find room for maneuver in reorganizing education decision-making structures and providing better quality services. By managing the timing of reform initiatives, using executive authority, empowering committed design teams, shaping an approval process, influencing implementation activities, and identifying new stakeholders, reformers sought to turn the tables on interests opposed to reform and to capitalize on their own institutional sources of power. Their strategies and institutional resources placed them in a relatively strong position during early phases of the reform process. In contrast, they were most vulnerable when they tried to implement and sustain new initiatives.

In this chapter, I return to the interaction of interests, institutions, and reformers in explaining policy change. Throughout this book, my interest has been in understanding outcomes that would not be anticipated because strongly mobilized interests are opposed to change and institutions are biased against it. In exploring this puzzle, I have argued that it matters how reforms are introduced, designed, approved, and implemented. Of course, reform is a slippery concept—in the case studies, those who initiated change at times whittled down their initial objectives to take account of institutional constraints and the intransigence of opponents. Even where they did not, chapter 7 indicates that what was implemented and sustained over time was often less than what reformers wanted. Moreover, not all of the cases ended in successful change. Nevertheless, many political analysts would have anticipated far less in terms of what was accomplished. Clues to the conundrum of policy change despite the odds, I believe, lie in an analysis of the political process of reform.

Before turning to the politics of the reform process, however, it is worth asking whether a reformist decade made much of a difference to education outcomes in Latin America. Given the intense activities of supporters and opponents of change, and given the emphasis on improving the quality of education, not just its reach, was education significantly different at the end of the 1990s from what it had been at the outset of that decade? Yes and no, it seems.

EDUCATION IN THE 1990s: WHAT WAS ACHIEVED?

Education became more important on national political agendas in Latin America during the 1990s as governments promised increased attention to improving its quality. Indeed, the heads of state of countries of the Americas, meeting in Miami in March 1998, proclaimed education to be a central priority of all governments in the region. Nevertheless, countries differed in their ability to deliver on such promises. Some, for example, committed more resources to the sector; others did not. Table 8.1 indicates that education spending as a percentage of GDP increased fairly consistently in Argentina, Bolivia, Brazil, Chile, El Salvador, Mexico, Paraguay, and Uruguay. In some countries, increases in spending relative to GDP correspond to the year of or the year following the introduction of reform measures. This was the case, for example, in Argentina (1991), Bolivia (1994), Costa Rica (1996), Mexico (1992) and Uruguay (1995). But the table also indicates that government expenditures relative to GDP remained generally flat in Colombia, Ecuador, Guatemala, Honduras, Panama, and Venezuela, and decreased slightly in Nicaragua.

When education spending is measured as a proportion of public expenditures, the picture changes somewhat. Table 8.2 indicates unambiguous increases in government commitment to funding education in Chile, Colombia, Guatemala, and Mexico. In Costa Rica, Nicaragua, Panama, and Uruguay, the picture was mixed and in Argentina and Ecuador, the proportion decreased. Table 8.3 provides another picture of what occurred during the decade by tracking per capita expenditures on primary education. Although incomplete, these data suggest that increases in expenditures, where they occurred, were not simply the result of demographic pressure on the school system.

TABLE 8.1
Education Spending as a Percentage of GDP

	1985	1990	1991	1992	1993	1994	1995	1996	1997	1998	1999
Argentina	1.3	1.0	1.7	1.8	1.8	1.8	1.8	3.1	3.1	3.1	3.1
Bolivia	2.6	4.2	4.2	4.3	4.3	5.1	5.6	5.4	5.4	5.4	5.4
Brazil	3.3	3.4	3.4	3.5	3.4	3.5	4.8	4.8	4.7	4.7	4.7
Chile	3.4	2.4	2.5	2.5	2.5	2.6	2.7	2.8	3.3	3.3	3.3
Colombia	2.6	2.2	2.1	3.1	2.6	2.8	2.8	3.0	3.1	3.1	3.0
Costa Rica	4.0	4.2	4.1	4.0	4.3	4.3	4.3	5.0	5.0	4.9	4.5
Ecuador	3.2	2.6	2.1	2.1	2.3	3.1	2.9	3.0	3.0	3.0	3.0
Guatemala	0.9	0.9	0.9	0.9	0.7	0.7	2.2	2.2	2.2	2.2	2.1
Honduras	1.5	1.2	1.3	1.4	1.7	1.4	1.6	1.5	1.5	1.5	1.5
Mexico	3.9	3.8	3.7	3.5	3.6	3.2	3.3	3.3	3.3	3.3	3.3
Nicaragua	2.6	2.2	2.4	2.9	3.4	4.3	4.4	4.3	4.4	4.4	4.4
Panama	4.3	4.5	4.5	4.6	4.5	4.3	4.6	4.7	4.5	4.5	4.4
Paraguay	1.2	1.1	1.8	2.3	2.7	2.8	3.0	3.5	3.5	3.5	3.5
Peru	2.6	3.4	3.3	3.4	3.4	3.5	3.0	2.5	2.5	2.5	2.5
Uruguay	2.5	2.7	2.6	2.4	2.4	2.4	2.4	3.0	3.0	3.0	3.0
Venezuela	5.0	4.7	4.8	4.7	4.7	4.9	4.9	4.9	4.9	4.9	4.9

Source: World Bank, *World Tables*.

Increases in expenditures, of course, do not necessarily reflect investments in improved education. In some cases they merely track improvement in teacher salaries after the losses of the 1980s. Indeed, in many
countries, teacher salaries did improve during the decade, although education experts continued to believe that they were too low to attract highly
qualified and motivated people to the field.[1] Increased expenditures could
also mean little more than investment in the most politically popular form
of education spending—building new schools and repairing old ones.[2]

Yet there are other indications that education was a more important
priority in the 1990s than it had been in earlier decades. Javier Corrales'
data on the tenure of ministers of education show that individuals in this
position during the 1990s could expect to remain in office longer than
their predecessors in the two preceding decades (see figure 8.1). In thirteen of eighteen countries, ministers of the most recent decade outlasted
their predecessors, and some of them by considerable amounts of time. In

TABLE 8.2
Education Expenditures as a Percentage of Government Expenditure

	1990	1991	1992	1993	1994	1995	1996	1997
Argentina			15.7	12.4	14.0	12.4		
Bolivia					11.2		11.1	
Brazil								
Chile		10.0	12.9		13.4	14.0	14.8	15.5
Colombia	16.0	15.0	16.4	17.4	16.0	18.6	19.0	
Costa Rica	20.8	21.8	21.4	20.2	19.2	19.8	22.8	
Guatemala	11.8	13.0	11.5	12.8	14.7	16.0	15.8	
Honduras					16.0	16.5		
Ecuador	17.2	17.5	19.2	18.1	19.2	15.2	13.0	
Mexico	12.8	15.3	18.1	22.3	26.0	23.0		
Nicaragua	9.7	12.1	10.6	9.8	9.0	9.9	10.2	8.8
Panama	20.9	18.9	18.9	22.9	22.2	22.1	20.9	16.3
Peru							19.2	
Uruguay	15.9	16.6	15.4		13.3		15.5	
Venezuela	12.0		23.5	22.0	22.4			

Source: World Bank, World Tables.

addition, in 11 countries, they lasted as long as, or longer, than their powerful counterparts in ministries of finance.[3]

In addition to changes in financial support for education, a number of Latin American countries made significant changes in the way decisions about education were made. In fact, structural changes, through decentralization to regional and local governments in some countries and through school autonomy initiatives in others, were perhaps the most notable accomplishment of the decade. In Mexico, the 1992 reform placed governors and state-level ministers of education at the center of education decision making after decades of systematic centralization in the national ministry. In Bolivia, local officials became more important in education decision making, and in Minas Gerais and Nicaragua—as well as in El Salvador, Chile, and Guatemala—schools took over considerable decision-making power from ministries of education.

In Minas Gerais and Nicaragua, school councils were much more engaged in such decisions than in the past. In Nicaragua, for example, school boards had "wide ranging legal authority: the power to hire and fire school staff, including the school director, to adjust teacher salaries (incentives),

TABLE 8.3

Expenditure per Primary Student as a Percentage of Per Capita GNI

	1985	1990	1991	1992	1993	1994	1995	1996
Argentina	..	..	..	..	..	..	..	8.3
Bolivia	..	..	..	..	..	..	..	..
Brazil	..	..	..	..	..	..	11.1	..
Chile	13.0	8.9	8.4	8.9	8.8	9.6	10.4	10.9
Colombia	..	..	..	..	..	..	..	..
Costa Rica	..	..	10.1	10.4	10.5	..	..	..
Ecuador	..	..	..	..	..	..	..	..
El Salvador	..	..	..	b..	..	..	7.1	..
Guatemala	..	2.8	2.7	3.0	5.8	5.0	6.1	6.2
Honduras	..	..	..	..	..	..	..	..
Mexico	3.7	..	5.0	5.1	6.6	11.0	11.9	..
Nicaragua	15.1	..	..	13.3	..	12.8	11.4	14.5
Panama	..	..	..	..	..	..	..	..
Paraguay	2.8	3.0	4.7	7.2	8.0	7.9	..	10.9
Peru	5.1	..	..	..	..	..	..	4.5
Uruguay	..	..	..	..	..	..	..	..
Venezuela, RB	4.8	..	..	2.5	2.1	6.1	2.1	..

Source: World Bank, World Tables.

set and collect student fees, to select from available textbooks, and to carry out evaluations of teachers . . . [allocating] available teaching posts and cash to any mix of school inputs, training programs, or curricular area that it sees fit."[4] Given that all such decisions were routinely taken in Managua prior to the reform, this was a significant change.

The politics of the reform process also left some important legacies. In Mexico, the powerful teachers' union was still strong at the end of the decade, but probably less so than it had been in the early 1990s. The same conclusion could be reached about less powerful unions in Bolivia, Minas Gerais, and Nicaragua, where reformers had been relatively successful in marginalizing them from decision-making arenas. At the same time, other actors—regional and local officials in some cases and the local school community in others—increased their presence in the sector. In addition, international development agencies became more deeply connected to education initiatives than they had been in the 1980s. There were political

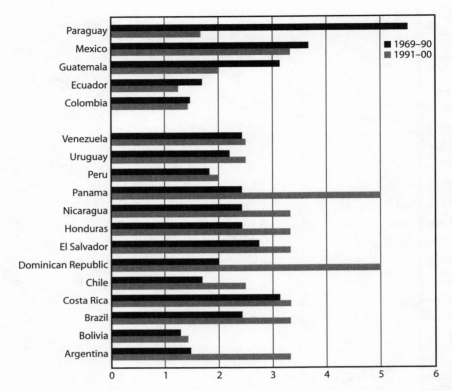

Figure 8.1. Average Years in Office of Ministers of Education, 1991–2000 versus 1969–1990 (Source: Corrales 2003:19)

legacies on other fronts also. Many teachers were better paid at the end of the decade, and a great many had received increased training through pedagogical and curriculum reforms. Nevertheless, many also felt bruised by the process of change, by the reforms that were largely imposed on them without their participation, and by new decision-making structures that made them feel threatened. Future reformers would have to deal with this legacy as they generated new initiatives for education reform.

Many of these financial, structural, and political changes were undertaken by reformers in the belief that they would pay off in better education for Latin America's children. While data on quality improvements are scarce, at the end of the reformist decade, it was not clear that reformers were correct in these assumptions. In 2001, a group of educational and civic leaders from thirteen countries in the region issued a *Report Card on Latin American Education* that found much to criticize. The report found little progress in improved test scores, reduced school dropout rates, increased equity, development of national standards, or professionalization of the teacher corps.[5] Somewhat more positively, the evaluators found that countries had expanded educational enrollments, particularly at the pre-primary and primary levels, and that they had done much to put national testing programs in place. They acknowledged that many countries had increased spending on basic education and improved school accountability. Overall, however, their report reached the dour conclusion that Latin American countries lagged behind what they could and should have achieved in improving education. From this, some might conclude that education reformers of the 1990s did much to shift the locus of decision making about education without necessarily encountering a solution to the problem of low-quality education.

Others, however, would disagree with this conclusion. Defenders of the changes introduced in the 1990s would certainly point out that improvements in education do not happen in the short term and that in some countries, reforms had been in place for a limited time. They might also point to the poor quality of data that made tracking improvements difficult.[6] Others would undoubtedly argue that the problems of education in the region were deeply embedded in more general social problems of poverty, inequity, and institutional instability that trapped children in low performance almost regardless of inputs into the education system.[7] In addition, some reforms involved administrative and structural changes that were expected to have an impact on the efficiency of school financing, decision making, and accountability, but only secondarily to affect pedagogy and learning. One study suggested that such structural changes—in particular the increased autonomy of school directors, the greater involvement of teachers, and regular evaluation of students—did have some impact on performance.[8] From these perspectives, the report card was overly pessimistic.

Nevertheless, when more and better data are available, it may be that a decade of reformism produced much less than reformers anticipated in terms of improving the quality of services delivered and the extent of learning taking place in the classroom. If this is the case, then reformers of the future may need new models of what needs to be done to improve education in Latin American countries.[9] While this book does not answer questions about what kinds of reforms lead to improved performance, it does provide insights into how education reform battles are fought out inside government, between reformers and opponents of change, and among new stakeholders in altered education structures. While the ultimate test of success must be whether education is improved, for this to occur, reforms must succeed in facing down the political challenges that confront efforts to introduce new policies. In this regard, four of the five case studies indicate relative—if far from complete—success in opening up the political process to new ways of structuring education decision making and new ways of delivering education services. In the following pages, I suggest some lessons that can be drawn from my analysis.

CONFLICT EQUATIONS: INTERESTS AND INSTITUTIONS IN REFORM INITIATIVES

Almost any proposal to alter policies will engage interests opposed to change; education is no exception to this generalization. Similarly, efforts to change policies are affected by institutional structures that distribute power within a society and within government; this is true of education policy also. In this book, I have attempted to demonstrate how reform agents maneuver among interests and within institutions to increase the potential for introducing and sustaining change. Thus, a dynamic interaction of interests, institutions, and reformers, as outlined in figure 1.1, is key to understanding reform outcomes. The case studies of education reform follow this dynamic to explore the power of interests and the impact of institutional biases.

Interests Present and Absent

The principal interests arrayed against education policy reform were the teachers' unions and the education bureaucracies. In all the case studies, the unions were particularly powerful players. Whether in Minas Gerais, Mexico, Nicaragua, Bolivia, or Ecuador, reformers approached the unions from a similar perspective—they were seen as the principal obstacles to change and as the culprits of poorly functioning education systems. The cases also indicated that the unions had good reason to oppose reform. Their power was threatened by initiatives to decentralize control over personnel policy and reward systems and their hold over ministries of education would be undermined. Even their claims to represent teachers were challenged, as reformers empowered new organizations and attacked the integrity of the old ones. In Bolivia, reformers went so far as to propose that union membership be voluntary and that unions no longer receive dues through automatic deductions from teacher salaries. More broadly, the unions were marginalized from the process of designing the reforms and often treated with scant respect in negotiations or confrontations about proposed changes.

Yet, the case studies demonstrated that the politics of union opposition to reform played out differently. As indicated in chapter 6, union structures and strength do not provide much insight into why this was so. More to the point of explaining distinct interactions, the analysis of the unions indicates that while all opposed reforms, they differed in their relationships with governments, ministries, and political parties and this affected the way reformers dealt with them. In Mexico, SNTE, the government, the ministry, and the PRI had long been joined at the hip in mutually supportive alliances, despite disagreements in the 1980s. In Nicaragua, a similar kind of relationship existed until 1990 when a new government replaced the Sandinistas; overnight, relations between ANDEN and the government became hostile, and the party link became a hindrance to its relationship with the ministry. In Bolivia and Ecuador, the relationship to government was always hostile and confrontational because of ties to left-wing fringe parties, while at the same time the unions had colonized the ministries. In Minas Gerais, the union had a less than cordial relationship with the government and the ministry, although its alliance with a party of the democratic left meant that it shared some objectives with the promoters of reform. This case also differed from others in that the beneficiaries of ministry patronage opportunities were individual politicians, not the union. *rel.s govt + land developers*

The major import of these relationships was to open up or close off options for reformers seeking to undermine the power of the unions. In Mexico, for example, the close association between the SNTE and the PRI regime meant that confronting or ignoring the union in the decentralization initiative was likely to result in the same kind of failure that previous reforms had encountered when this path was chosen. In Bolivia, Ecuador, and Nicaragua, intransigent opposition to government reduced opportunities for negotiating effectively with the unions. In Minas Gerais, the relationship with the government and the ministry and its alliance with an opposition party were not so extreme, giving reformers more options about how to deal with it. The unions, as major interests in the reform process, thus set constraints on how the reformers pursued their goals, but did not have the capacity to halt their initiatives, except in the case of Ecuador, where broader economic and political contexts conspired with union opposition to defeat change proposals.

As interests opposed to reform, ministry bureaucracies took a back seat to the unions. Nevertheless, they were important as part of the political landscape that reformers faced. In Mexico, for example, SNTE had colonized the ministry of education, and reform could only proceed when the minister had recolonized its high-level positions with supporters of change. In Bolivia, the ministry's opposition and its connections to the unions encouraged reformers to set up shop in another ministry, a factor that facilitated their early activities but that also encouraged alliances among the opposition. In Nicaragua and Ecuador, reformers initially had to proceed largely without any support or assistance in the ministry. Eventually, they controlled only enclaves within these organizations. In Minas Gerais, re-formers found like-minded people in the ministry and recruited them to be part of the reform team, even while many other bureaucrats were side-lined in the process. Overall, the obstacle of bureaucratic opposition be-came a more critical issue when reform initiatives were implemented.

With the exception of Mexico, international development agencies were also important players in the reform initiatives. In Bolivia and Ecuador, reform initiatives would not have been designed had it not been for the funding provided by these organizations. In Nicaragua, they were particu-larly important in supporting initiatives aimed as undermining Sandinista content and structures in education. In Minas Gerais, they supported spe-cific objectives of the autonomous school initiative. In all four cases, inter-national agencies influenced design teams through their ideas about what models were effective in improving education and introducing the experi-ences of other countries to these groups. In particular, the aspects of the reforms that perhaps had the most impact on decision making about edu-cation—decentralization and school autonomy—were an important part of the tool kit that international agencies brought to problems of educa-tion in the 1990s.

Yet these organizations did not dominate the process of change. They were not active in initiating reform projects, although they may have helped reformers by raising the profile of education in international dia-logues and disseminating data about the importance of education and the low performance of many Latin American countries. The case studies indicate that these institutions were most influential when they worked directly with design teams, providing funds and ideas as officials sought to hammer out the content of reform proposals. At the same time, interna-tional actors were largely absent in the approval process, except in the rhetoric of reform opponents who often demonized new initiatives as neo-liberal impositions of the World Bank and the IMF. They reemerged as important in implementing change initiatives, largely through funding specific aspects of the reforms.

At times, other interests were engaged in the reform initiatives, but they tended to be marginal to the conflicts that emerged. In Bolivia, the Catholic Church became an ally of the unions and the ministry in propos-ing an alternative to the reformist initiative. In Minas Gerais, the school director's association and other organizations joined in debates about the costs and benefits of the reform. In some cases, think tank and university-based education experts helped in the analysis and design of the projects or were appointed to high-level positions within ministries as supporters of reform leaders. With the exception of Minas Gerais, parents' organiza-tions, business groups, or pro-education civic alliances were conspicuously absent from these stories of reform.[10] While it is easy to understand why such groups might have an interest in discussions of reform, they were absent because such interests were unmobilized, or did not consider influencing national education policy as the best use of their resources, or were excluded from a relatively closed decision-making arena.

In some cases, new interests emerged as reforms were put into practice. As we have seen, decentralization to the state level in Mexico placed governors, state ministers of education, and SNTE locals in much more prominent positions. After 1992, they would be important players in determining the politics of education in the country. In Nicaragua and Minas Gerais, school directors and school boards were empowered to make decisions about education and came to play a larger role in explaining differences among schools than they had in the past. In Bolivia, because of a concomitant decentralization initiative, mayors took on new importance in education. Teachers and local school authorities also became the frontline players in how well the reforms were implemented. In most cases, the failure to engage teachers more effectively in the process of change was a shortcoming of the reform initiatives and one that held important implications for how much change actually happened in the classroom.

There were winners and losers among these interests. As predicted from the outset, the unions and central bureaucrats believed they were less well off after new policies were approved and implemented. Political parties that had long benefited from using teaching and administrative appointments to reward their clienteles also lost out where decolonization made significant inroads into ministries. More surprising, many teachers also considered themselves losers, largely because the reforms were imposed on them, their unions excoriated the changes, and they often did not understand the purpose of the new order or their place in it. Among the winners were certainly regional and local officials where decentralization gave them more influence, and school directors and boards where autonomy initiatives provided them with greater capacity to determine what was happening at the community level. In Minas Gerais, and at times in Nicaragua, parents and local communities won significant new influence vis-à-vis the local school. Elsewhere, they did not emerge as interests with the capacity to exert influence in the sector.

Institutional Sources of Power

Reform destinies were shaped not only by the interests engaged in contesting reform, but also by political institutions. To a significant degree, institutions presented reformers with formidable obstacles at the outset of the 1990s. Weak ministries of education meant that they had to begin their efforts in the absence of hierarchical authority, professional standards, information, or incentives that they could draw on. The hold of clientelism on decisions about personnel and administration was extensive in all the cases, and informal mechanisms linking ministries to political parties and unions made it difficult to know where to begin in altering current practice. Indeed, while the ministries were weak in the capacity to deliver education and respond to ministerial leadership, they were strong in the ability to resist change.

Moreover, institutions that linked the center to the periphery in the case studies helped entrench centralization, lack of accountability, and a wide variety of inefficiencies. Under pre-reform conditions, even minor issues about education had to be referred to national capitals for resolution. Parties, unions, resources, and decisions all flowed from the top down in a system of reinforcing power. The very strong presidentialist system in Mexico, for example, shaped the centralization of all other institutions in ways that benefited the ministry, the union, and the dominant political party. In Bolivia, Nicaragua, and Ecuador, centralization meant a compounding of inefficiencies in the distribution of resources and resolution of problems. Only in Minas Gerais, where states traditionally held more power and where the democratization movement of the 1980s left greater local political activism behind, was the hold of centralization in education somewhat less stifling. Even there, however, a reformist minister was as adamant as any national counterpart in arguing that centralization in a state of 30 million people was a powerful impediment to efficiency, effectiveness, and responsiveness.

Yet, the case studies indicate that reformers had some capacity to lessen institutional constraints and use some institutional resources to their advantage. They were able to spearhead reform in large part because they were part of executive institutions that allowed them to seize the initiative in setting national agendas about education and developing new policies for the sector. In particular, traditions of centralization and executive dominance in defining policy priorities and developing proposals and laws gave reformers the upper hand in deciding how to initiate and design changes and in selecting appropriate moments to take actions to promote reform. The appointment of design teams was exclusively their prerogative in all the countries except Ecuador, where internationally funded projects operated as a parallel universe within the ministry of education. In four cases, reformers significantly altered the structure of ministerial decision making through decentralization, and they continued to use powers of appointment to influence the implementation of their initiatives. Institutional constraints were important, but they were far from defining the scope of possibilities in most of the cases.

Moreover, reformers had considerable scope for locating the reform initiative within government, and where possible, benefiting from the support of others interested in change. This was clearest in the case of Bolivia, where the reform initiative survived in a hostile environment in part through its location in the powerful ministry of planning. Choices about timing were also in the hands of reform initiators. In Mexico, for example, the president and two ministers of education committed more than three years to orchestrating efforts to alter the context within which a reform would be introduced. In contrast, the minister of education in Minas Gerais moved swiftly to put a new policy in place, judging that the chances for success were best when the opposition would be caught off-guard. In Nicaragua, a reformist minister took advantage of an unsettled moment in national politics to promote his initiative as a counterpoint to what the previous government had done in the sector.

Executive prerogatives also allowed reformers to determine who would be in the room when reforms were designed and initially discussed. This was clearest in Minas Gerais, where the minister of education determined who would be invited to debate school autonomy, and in Bolivia, where the design team kept the door only partially open for such discussions. In large measure, it was such actions that placed the opposition to reform in a reactive and defensive mode when the new policies were announced. As the reforms proceeded, executives continued to have choices about who would be appointed to critical positions and they could take actions to set the terms of debate, weaken or marginalize opponents, and publicize the importance of the changes they proposed. In Mexico, it was important that the reform was about "federalization," not its twin, "decentraliza-tion"; in Mexico and Bolivia, the reforms were presented as important to larger projects of modernization; and in Nicaragua, the reform was presented as an effort to reintroduce Christian values and tradition into the classroom. Once the reforms were announced, of course, opponents of reform responded with communication initiatives of their own, charging that reformers were intent upon privatizing education and imposing neo-liberal policies on unwilling publics. Nevertheless, the capacity of the re-formers to dominate the early phases of the policy process was an indica-tion of the malleability of some institutional constraints.

Legislatures were much less important to the education reforms than the executive in all cases except Ecuador, but these institutions had some role in their destinies. Certainly, gaining legitimacy for change proposals through new laws was a valuable way in which to increase the potential to implement and sustain these initiatives. In Mexico, the decision to move ahead with negotiations with SNTE was on hold until after the midterm elections of 1991, when the PRI regained its two-thirds major-ity in the legislature. At that point, given the presidentialism of the sys-tem, there was little question that PRI representatives would rubber stamp the initiative. Thus, even through legislative action followed the reform agreement by a year, reformers sought to institutionalize it through the legislature. In Bolivia, a governing pact between the executive and legislature meant that the reform, although extremely contentious on the streets, would be little discussed in congress and then passed easily. In both cases, the outcome of this approval process had very little to do with education, and very much to do with institutional relationships that largely superceded policy.

Legislatures contributed to uncertainty about reform destinies in the other countries. In Nicaragua, the possibility that the reform would be rejected in the congress was great enough that Minister Belli chose not to risk it and instead announced and implemented the reform through administrative decree. In Ecuador, a tradition of tension and conflict characterized executive-legislative interactions and meant that reformist legislation probably had limited chances even in good times. In 1998, however, reformers chose a very bad time to send an education reform law to congress and made the additional mistake of attaching it to an omnibus economic reform package. The law was summarily rejected and reformers had to retreat to the traditional practice of introducing change through donor-funded projects. In Minas Gerais, in the context of a statewide teachers' strike, legislative approval for school autonomy was chancy until a supportive governor let representatives know that he would use his considerable power to punish them if they did not vote in favor of it. This case is also interesting because of the intervention of another institution, the supreme court, which declared the election of school directors to be unconstitutional and subsequently left the fate of this aspect of the reform in the hands of local communities.

The discussion of the role of executive and legislative institutions also indicates that party systems were intertwined with the fate of reform in each of the cases. Clearly, clientelism based in the party systems and party relationships with unions and ministries was seen by the reformers as a critical part of the problem of education in the first place. Beyond that, however, the party system influenced how reforms were managed after they were designed. Indeed, in Mexico, Bolivia, and Ecuador, the nature of the party system largely determined the outcome of efforts to legislate reform. As indicated earlier, legislative votes were an outcome of executive-legislative-party relationships, and were very little concerned with the issue of public education. The fragmented party system in Nicaragua and tensions within Violeta Chamorro's electoral coalition meant that the risks of attempting to legislate reform were considerable. Moreover, the history of party alliances had a significant impact on the fate of the design team in Bolivia, as reformers maneuvered among the parties in power to find opportunities to move ahead with their plans—and sometimes lost power when party politics worked against them.

Institutions were important in the reform stories of five cases. They helped define the problems that reformers sought to correct, and they provided both opponents and supporters of reform with resources to use in the conflicts surrounding the initiatives. They further helped define the obstacles to reform approval and implementation. Yet it is difficult to argue that institutional distributions of power determined outcomes. At the outset of the reform decade, institutional biases favored the status quo. Later, institutions provided sites and resources for conflicts over reform, but did not determine the use of those resources. Reformers had significant opportunities for restructuring institutions and altering institutional biases to be more congruent with their objectives.

REFORMERS AND STRATEGIC CHOICES

Reformers in Minas Gerais, Mexico, Nicaragua, Bolivia, and Ecuador did not represent established education interests. Their objectives were diverse, although all were committed to the idea that education was instrumental in achieving some larger goal. They took on education reform out of concern about the need to modernize their countries, increase the efficient use of public resources, improve the degree of equity in their societies, or strengthen important societal values. In this activity, they were not furthering the aims of existing ministries of education or promoting the ends of powerful actors in education. If they represented the interests of local communities, regional and local governments, or religious or economic elites, they did so in the absence of mobilized pressure or support from these entities. Throughout much of the reform process, they worked in relative isolation to promote change, and found social bases of support only after the reforms had been put in practice and were producing benefits for governors, ministers, school directors, local communities, or others.

In the case studies, interests, institutions, and reformers interacted across time. Thus, education reform was not so much about approving or rejecting policy at a specific moment as it was about a series of decisions and actions that drew reformers and antireformers serially into conflict within malleable institutional contexts. In most cases, strategic choices about how to use the resources they had determined the outcome of these conflicts. The cases also indicated that over time, the value of the resources controlled by reformers and the room they had to maneuver altered. During agenda setting and design, they were largely in the driver's seat; during adoption and implementation, their room for maneuver became considerably more constricted.

Moreover, different actors were drawn into the reform initiatives at distinct moments.[11] At the outset of the reform process, teachers' unions were present only as part of the problem that reformers sought to resolve, not as active participants in arenas where reforms were being initiated and designed. The unions became central actors in the reform approval phase, and then reemerged in the implementation arena as a further constraint on the possibilities for change. Similarly, although they were excluded from much of the process of design and approval, the ministries of education became more important to the outcome of reform when arenas of conflict shifted to implementation and sustainability.

Throughout the process, reformers had strategic choices about how to proceed. Often, they made very effective choices. They mobilized networks to develop their visions of change, they courted leadership support, they placed supporters in critical positions, they sought examples from other countries to inform and shape their own ideas, they negotiated or confronted or maneuvered around hostile unions with considerable aplomb, they sought alliances with international funders, and they created new stakeholders to enhance the sustainability of their policies. Their energy in seeking high-level political support helped some remain in office much longer than was characteristic.

They also probably made some mistakes. In Mexico, for example, had reformers paid more attention to state governors while negotiating with the union, they might have introduced more incentives for them to manage their new responsibilities in the interest of improved education. Certainly, if they had been more careful in selecting new textbooks, they might have avoided two years of furious political controversy. In Nicaragua, Bolivia, and Ecuador, if reformers had sought allies sooner in the process, they might have put themselves in a better position to face down union opposition and to ensure more effective implementation of their projects. In Ecuador, if design teams in the ministry had found a way to work together rather than to compete with each other, there was some possibility—however slim—that reform could have made more headway.

Moreover, drawing teachers more fully into the process, finding additional means to reward effective teaching, mobilizing parents around improved education for their children, using information more effectively to demonstrate the failings of the old system, promoting party identification with better education—these are all activities that might have smoothed the introduction and implementation of reform.[12] Such actions are certainly part of conventional wisdom about how to approach the politics of reform. Building consensus on what needs to be done, gaining the collaboration of social actors, developing initiatives in transparent ways, creating incentives for affected parties to tolerate or even welcome change, and investing in social marketing were frequently proposed methodologies for promoting a wide variety of changes in the 1990s.[13]

Indeed, the strategic choices made by reformers in the five case studies replicated some frequently observed pathologies of decision making and participation in Latin America. A long history of top-down decision making was reflected when teachers were largely excluded, parents were not consulted, and unions treated roughly. Moreover, they speak to a legacy of failing to take conditions faced by teachers seriously, not encouraging politicians to identify quality education as a good to be delivered to constituents, and not using information more effectively to build constituencies of support. At the end of a decade, these issues remained for a subsequent generation of reformers to resolve.

Yet there is enough serendipity in political outcomes that predicting results, whatever the process, is tricky. In four cases, change initiatives were put in place and at least partially implemented even without following most conventional wisdom about how to proceed. In Ecuador, given the larger context of crisis that surrounded different reform initiatives, it is unlikely that adopting different methods would ultimately have saved the reform initiatives. Moreover, in Bolivia and Nicaragua, efforts to create alternative proposals to those of the reformers were undertaken with widespread consultation and consensus building. Nevertheless, they generated documents that were long on eloquent commitments and very short on specific actions to improve education. It is not clear that alternative approaches to policy reform would have produced greater change. At the end of a decade of reform initiatives, best practice in politics remained subject to the vagaries of mobilized interests, institutional biases, and reformer strategies in specific countries.

Conclusion: Education Politics at the Millennium

At the turn of the millennium, an expert on education in Latin America summed up what countries in the region needed to do in order to improve the life chances of children: "Get them earlier, keep them longer, and teach them better."[14] Behind this simple formulation, of course, were very challenging tasks of transformation, a critical shortage of resources, and extensive needs for capacity building, evaluation, and monitoring throughout the education system.[15] Also behind the adage to teach longer and better was an even more arduous task—that of dealing with the deep social problems of poverty and inequality that keep so many children from performing well in school. Whatever the gains and shortcomings of reforms in education systems during the 1990s, much remained for reformers to do.

Moreover, whatever ideas, financial resources, and professional staff they would have to tackle the problems that remained, the success of reformers after the 1990s would be determined by their ability to manage political conflict over the ends, means, and process of reform. They would continue to face important obstacles to change. Teachers' unions were, on the whole, weaker at the end of the 1999s than they had been, but they still remained among the most influential worker organizations in Latin American countries. The resources needed for educational change remained limited, despite increased government awareness of its importance. Moreover, the weakest links in the capacity to reach the education system with important changes remained the teachers and the parents.

At the same time, the case studies in this book indicate that the process of introducing change in education systems was altered in a number of countries because of what occurred during the 1990s. During that period, significant structural changes brought new actors into the discussion of reform and the determination of its success. New alliances were created between the center and other levels of government and between reformers in the center and new stakeholders in local areas. A redistribution of administrative power created new contexts for decision making about personnel, planning, and the use of resources.

In other ways, as well, the politics of subsequent reform initiatives would be different. At the millennium, governments throughout Latin America were being forced to open up more to demands for democratic accountability and responsiveness. Civil society in most countries was becoming more organized and vocal and the perquisites of politicians more uncertain. Most particularly, citizen demands for better government and more effective social services had become more insistent. The politically disruptive potential of disparities in wealth and poverty, power and powerlessness, took on new meaning in the wake of unanticipated political changes in several countries. Strategies that had worked in the past might be less useful in this distinct political context. In a new era, to be successful, reformers might need to learn more about how to engage citizen interest, allow for more participation, and build support coalitions in advance of their activities. Thus, at the beginning of a new millennium, education reform remained in process.

NOTES

CHAPTER ONE

1. Argentina, Bolivia, Brazil, Chile, Colombia, Costa Rica, El Salvador, Mexico, Nicaragua, and Uruguay made substantial progress in promoting education reform by 2000; Venezuela and Guatemala were less successful reformers but did manage to make some progress in implementing significant changes. Peru, Ecuador, Honduras, and Paraguay made little progress in adopting or implementing change-oriented policies during the decade.

2. See, for examples of such arguments, Birdsall, Ross, and Sabot (1995); Grindle (2000b); Hardy (2002); Navarro, Carnoy, and de Moura Castro (2000); and Reimers (2000d).

3. IDB (1998:27). Many countries increased the years of obligatory education to conform with the recommendations of UNESCO's Education for All initiative that emerged from a global summit on education held in Jomtien, Thailand, in 1990. Even when officially sanctioned, however, many countries did not have the infrastructure of schools, teachers, or materials to put this obligation into full practice, and many children dropped out of school long before the obligatory age or level of schooling had been reached.

4. IDB (1998:27). For the region as a whole, the secondary school gross enrollment rate was only 50.9 (UNESCO, 2000:116).

5. UNESCO (2000:118).

6. World Bank (1993:258–59). Comparable data are missing for Argentina, Bolivia, Chile, Colombia, Guatemala, Nicaragua, and Venezuela. Spending increased in Panama and Peru. By the mid-1990s, Latin America as a whole was spending more of its GNP on education than East and South Asian countries, but considerably less than was being spent in Europe and Central Asia, the Middle East and North Africa, Sub-Saharan Africa, and high-income countries (World Bank 1998:201).

7. Salaries were almost exclusively based on seniority, for example, and appointments and promotions were generally determined by patronage, not merit.

8. See Carnoy, Cosse, Cox, and Martínez (2001).

9. Indeed, many of these complaints gained in credibility through assessments of poverty and human welfare conditions in the region during the 1980s and 1990s (see, for example, IDB (1998); Stallings and Peres (2000). See also Braslavsky and Cosse (1996).

10. See Chalmers, Vilas, Hite, Martin, Piester, and Segarra (1997).

11. For a discussion of these views, see IDB (1996); Savedoff (1998).

12. First and second generation reforms are described in Naím (1995). On the contrast with education and other social sector reforms, see Nelson (1999a and 1999b).

13. Nelson (1999b:36).

14. Important theoretical contributions to this perspective are found in Alesina and Drazen (1991); Alesina and Perotti (1994); Bates (1981); Fernandez and Rodrik (1991); Geddes (1994); Rodrik (1994); Schamis (1999); Tommasi and Velasco (1996); and Weingast, Shepsle, and Johnson (1981). For empirical studies adopting this perspective, see individual chapters in Bates and Krueger (1993). For a critique, see Weyland (2002).

15. See especially Olson (1965).

16. See especially Puryear (1997); Corrales (1999); and Garcia-Huidobro S. (1999).

17. See, for example, CIDE-PREAL (1998:6). See Tendler (2002) for an insightful analysis of private sector perspectives on basic education in Northeast Brazil.

18. See, for example, Ortiz de Zevallos (1998:17).

19. See, for example, Martiniello (2000).

20. CIDE-PREAL (1998:4).

21. Institutionalist perspectives often define institutions as the "humanly devised constraints that shape human interaction" (North 1990: 3).

22. See, for examples, Lijphart and Waisman (1996); and Linz and Valenzuela (1994).

23. See, for examples, Brooks (2000); Corrales (1998); and Murillo (1998).

24. A large literature considers how institutions affect the fate of policy reforms. See especially Bates and Krueger (1993); Evans (1995); Haggard and Kaufman (1995); Nelson (1990); and Steinmo, Thelen, and Longstreth (1992).

25. For an example, see Wallis (1999).

26. For this argument, see Corrales (1999); Graham, Grindle, Lora, and Seddon (1999); and Grindle and Thomas (1991).

27. See González Rossetti (2001: chapter 2) for a discussion.

28. See, for example, Murillo and Ronconi (2003).

29. While these decisions have been seen as "veto points," they can also be understood as strategic moments when reforms can be moved forward (Nelson 1999a:1; González-Rossetti and Bossert 2000).

30. States in Brazil have considerable autonomy over education policy (see Draibe 2002). As a consequence, I selected a state as a more suitable site for investigation than the country as a whole.

31. Collier and Norden (1992).

32. The definition of basic education varies by country, but usually encompasses educational levels incorporated in nationally required years of education—usually eight to ten years. This generally means primary and some or all of secondary education. I focus most attention on efforts to improve the quality of primary education.

33. Trostle, Somerfeld, and Simon (1997).

34. For useful studies of the Chilean case, see Angell, Lowden, and Thorp (2001); Carlson (2000); and Gauri (1998).

CHAPTER TWO

1. *A Proposal for a Comprehensive Development Framework*, January 1999.
2. See, for example, Birdsall and Sabot (1996).
3. World Bank (2000:15).
4. For extensive analyses of the relationship between poverty, inequality, and education, see IDB (1998); Larrañaga (1997); Lustig and Deutsch (1998); and Reimers (2000a).
5. UNESCO (2000:17); World Bank (2000).
6. UNESCO (2000:115).
7. UNESCO (2000:114, 115).
8. See Reimers (2000a) for additional information on gender problems in Latin America's education systems. For a comparison of Latin America's education/gender problems with other regions of the world, see Conway and Bourque (1995).
9. UNESCO (2000:41, 60).
10. Data presented in Larrañaga (1997:331).
11. Schiefelbein and Tedesco (1995), cited in Reimers (1999b:16).
12. Wolff, Schiefelbein, and Schiefelbein (2000:319). The average Cuban student answered 85 percent of the questions correctly.
13. Except for Cuba, all median scores fell within one standard deviation of the regional median.
14. Mexico also participated, but the results were not made public.
15. UNESCO (2000:119). The figures given are estimates.
16. Departamento Nacional de Planeación, *Plan de apertura educativa: 1991–1994* (Bogota 1991:3), quoted in Hanson (1995:108).
17. Unless otherwise indicated, data in this paragraph are taken from Reimers (1999b:8–9).
18. Herrán and Van Uythem (2001:6).
19. PREAL (2001:10).
20. See Birdsall, Ross, and Sabot (1995); Birdsall and Londoño (1998); IDB (1996); Mingat (1998); and Savedoff (1998).
21. Navarro, Carnoy, and de Moura Castro (n.d.:18). See McMeekin (1998) for a review of statistical information and needs in Latin American education.
22. IDB (1996:293).
23. IDB (1996:307). In Chile, the management of teacher salaries was decentralized in the 1980s; in 1991, it was recentralized.
24. In Colombia, for example, local and regional politicians regularly hired and fired teachers at election time; teachers who were part of a national career system, however, enjoyed extensive security of tenure (Angell, Lowden, and Thorp 2001:177–79).
25. In the 1990s, in fact, the tenure of these ministers lengthened in a number of countries (Corrales 2003).
26. IDB (1996:304). For a discussion of union incentives to strike, see Murillo and Ronconi (2003).
27. Tiramonti (2000); and Loyo, de Ibarrola, and Blanco (1999).

28. IDB (1996:305).

29. On the issue of teacher salaries, see Urquiola, Jiménez, Talavera, and Hernany (2000); Liang (1999) and chapter 5.

30. Navarro, Carnoy, and de Moura Castro (n.d.:11–15).

31. Navarro, Carnoy, and de Moura Castro (n.d.:11); and Reimers (1999b:23).

32. For an extended discussion of the paucity of incentives for greater professionalism among Latin American teachers, see Navarro (2002).

33. Villegas-Reimers and Reimers (1996:478).

34. See Gershberg (1999a).

35. Interview, Mexico City, July 2, 2001.

36. *Gajardo (1999:9–10)*.

37. In addition to the Jomtien conference and numerous regional, academic, and NGO conferences, there was the World Summit for Children in 1990, the International Congress on Education for Human Rights and Democracy and the World Conference on Human Rights in 1993, a World Conference on Special Needs Education in 1994, a World Summit for Social Development in 1995, the Fifth International Conference on Adult Education in 1997, the First World Conference of Ministers Responsible for Youth and the Intergovernmental Conference on Cultural Policies for Development in 1998, as well as the World Conference on Higher Education; the Second International Congress on Technical and Vocational Education and the World Science Conference met in 1999 (UNESCO, 2000:75).

38. See, in particular, Burki, Perry, and Dillinger (1999); Gorostiaga (2000); Navarro, Carnoy, and de Moura Castro (n.d.); McGinn and Street (1986); Parry (1997); Winkler and Gershberg (2000); and World Bank (2000). Several small countries—Costa Rica, Panama, and Uruguay—debated decentralization but chose to maintain centralized systems for educational management.

39. de Moura Castro (1997:115).

40. Angell, Lowden, and Thorp (2001:165).

41. Arnove (1995:38).

42. Graham (1998:106).

43. See chapter 4.

44. Angell, Lowden, and Thorp (2001:177).

45. King, Ozler, and Rawlings (1999).

46. PREAL (2001:17).

47. For Chile, see Gauri (1998); for Mexico, see Gershberg (1999a) and chapter 3. See also Burki, Perry, and Dillinger (1999); and Winkler and Gershberg (2000).

48. See Vaillant (2002).

49. de Moura Castro (1997:114–15).

50. Among countries that sought to professionalize teaching and teacher training were Argentina, Colombia, Chile, the Dominican Republic, Costa Rica, Guatemala, Nicaragua, and Uruguay (PREAL 2001:11). In addition, in Bolivia, Chile, and Mexico, the number of school days per year and the number of classroom hours per day were increased (Martinic 2002:2–3).

51. See Kemmerer and Windham (1997); Savedoff (1998); and Navarro and de la Cruz (1998).

52. See Gauri (1998); and McMeekin (2000).

53. The first national testing system was put in place in 1982; it was replaced in 1988 by the Educational Quality Information and Measurement System (SIMCE). See Espínola and de Moura Castro (1999:8).

54. Navarro, Carnoy, and de Moura Castro (n.d.:32).

55. Gajardo (1999:27).

56. Student and teacher testing was a source of considerable contention, as teachers and their unions feared they would be used as an instrument of pressure and accountability against them.

57. These programs are well described in Winkler (1999:23) and Navarro and de la Cruz (1998).

58. Reimers (1999a), (2000b), and (2000c).

59. Winkler (1999); and Gauri (1998).

60. Reimers (2000a).

61. For analyses of conditions that stimulate neoliberal economic policy reforms, see Bates and Krueger (1993); Grindle and Thomas (1991); Haggard and Kaufman (1992); Nelson (1990); and Williamson (1994).

62. See, in particular, Grindle (1996); Grindle and Thomas (1991); Nelson (1990); and Williamson (1994).

63. Argentina (1991), Brazil (1993), Bolivia (1994), Chile (1993), Colombia (1994), Costa Rica (1995), Ecuador (1996), El Salvador (1991), Guatemala (1991), Honduras (1996), Mexico (1993), Nicaragua (1993), Panama (1997), Peru (1992), Uruguay (1995), and Venezuela (1989). The dates in parentheses indicate when a significant reform initiative was announced or approved. Several of these countries announced reforms but were not very successful in implementing them. For this analysis, they are treated as "reformers" because the issue of education reform got on the public agenda, even though they do not count in the list of countries that were able to make significant changes in their education systems during the 1990s. For each variable, the average, median, maximum, and minimum values were calculated, along with standard deviations. Ninety-five percent confidence levels were also calculated using the z-value and the t-value. Data were taken from World Bank, *World Tables,* for various years. Carolina Gutiérrez de Taliercio collected and analyzed the data, which is reported in Gutiérrez de Taliercio (2000).

64. The population mean of GDP growth rates was estimated to be between 0.89 percent and 4.36 percent four years prior to the reform; −0.02 percent and 5.08 percent three years prior to the reform; −0.16 percent and 4.04 percent two years prior to the reform; and 2.22 percent and 4.69 percent one year prior to the reform.

65. IMF (2001:29).

66. See Hunter and Brown (2000).

67. World Bank (2000:84).

68. Several of the hypotheses considered are discussed in Wallis (1999).

69. On the relationship between reforms of the state and the legislature, see Bresser Pereira (2003).

70. See Brown and Hunter (1999).

71. This is, for example, an important aspect of rational choice political economy and a fundamental assertion of pluralist political theory.

72. Reimers (2002); Schiefelbein and Schiefelbein (n.d.).

73. Rodríguez (1997:10); Corrales (1998:32).

74. Bruni Celli (2002).
75. Crespo (2000).
76. Bernbaum and Locher (1998).
77. Lowden (2002).
78. Corrales (1999:27–28).
79. See chapter 4.
80. Taliercio (1996); Doryan (1999).
81. See Filgueira and Moraes (1998).
82. Varley (1999).
83. On Nicaragua, see chapter 3; on Uruguay, see Filgueira and Moraes (1998); and Corrales (1998).
84. Filgueira and Moraes (1998:23).
85. Espínola and de Moura Castro (1999:41–49).
86. Ortiz de Zevallos (1998:8).
87. Taliercio (1996).
88. Ortiz de Zevallos (1998); Graham (1998); and Iguiñiz Echeverría (2000).
89. Angell, Lowden, and Thorp (2001); and Cominetti and Gropello (1998).
90. Grindle (2000a:52–64).
91. *Maestros populares* were appointed to schools in rebel-held areas and were identified with the opposition.
92. See chapter 3.
93. Murillo (1999a); Gorostiaga (2000); and Cominetti and Gropello (1998).
94. Paes de Barros and Mendonça (1998).
95. See chapter 3.
96. For Bolivia, see chapter 6; for Colombia, see Cominetti and Gropello (1998); and Hanson (1995).

CHAPTER THREE

1. See Hirschman (1981) on reform mongers; Harberger (1984) on heroes; and Srinivasan (1985), González-Rossetti and Bossert (2000), and Wallis (1999) on policy champions. See also Westlake (2000); Corrales (2003); and Weyland (2002).
2. On the content of the reform, see Cominetti and Gropello (1998); Gershberg (1999c); Pescador Osuna (1992); and Tatto (1999). In 1993, a general education law gave legal status to the agreement.
3. Murillo (1999b:39). At the time of the reform, the state-level education systems were providing services for 4.8 million preprimary, primary, and secondary students (Merino Juárez 1999:41).
4. The national government would continue to set basic salary and benefit terms for teachers; states could add additional resources and were given responsibility for managing any nonbasic terms of employment.
5. UNESCO (2000:145).
6. Laboratorio Latinoamericano de Evaluación de la Calidad de la Educación (1998:50–51).
7. Reimers (2000d:91).

8. Muñiz (2000); Schmelkes (2000).

9. CEPAL data, cited in Reimers (2000d:73).

10. Larmer (1989:4).

11. See Ornelas (1988:108–9).

12. On this system, see Duarte (1999:17); Martin (1993:153); and Murillo (1999b:37–41). In the late 1980s, dissident teachers alleged that the going rate for a teaching position was as much as $600 to $650. Teachers at the time were earning $150 a month (Larmer 1989:4; Rohter 1989:12).

13. See Arnaut (1998b:chapter 4).

14. Merino Juárez (1999:41). See also Murillo (1999b:38).

15. See Arnaut (1998b:245–55).

16. Fiske (1996:17–18).

17. By this time, the national ministry had become very large and complex. In 1982, it was "composed of 7 undersecretariats, 44 director-generalships, 304 managerships, 6 councils, an international general administration and budgeting committee, a controller's office, a general co-ordinator, 31 state delegations and nearly 60 co-ordinated institutions" (Ornelas 1988:107). To this could be added 800,000 employees and over 15 million students that were the direct responsibility of the national ministry. It distributed some 100 million textbooks and managed school siting and building around the country.

18. Cook (1996:268n.2).

19. Interview, July 2, 2001, Mexico City.

20. Arnaut (1996:148).

21. Personal communication, March 8, 2002, Cambridge, Massachusetts. Moreover: "The most reliable research also showed an enormously important fact: Women who finished primary school had fewer children (half as many) as those who did not finish. In a country with over 90 million inhabitants, one of the most effective and fairest means to slow demographic dynamics was by guaranteeing quality education for women" (Salinas de Gortari 2002:609).

22. Salinas de Gortari (2002:610). See also Loyo (1992:17).

23. Personal communication, March 8, 2002, Cambridge, Massachusetts.

24. The narrow and widely questioned victory even called into question the SNTE's ability to deliver the teachers' votes. It was likely that many voted for the PRD (Cook 1996:267).

25. See Grindle (1996:81–82).

26. Data in this paragraph taken from World Bank, *World Tables*.

27. Grindle (1996:81).

28. Salinas had been minister of planning and budgeting in the previous administration and was widely thought to be responsible for austerity measures that cut deeply into public sector salaries.

29. See Alvarez Béjar (1991:48–51); Cook (1996); and de la Garza (1991: 179–81).

30. Murillo (1999b:41); and Cook (1996:269–70).

31. *Crónica del Gobierno de Carlos Salinas de Gortari, Primer Año*, Mexico City: Fondo de Cultura Económica, 1994:132, quoted in Salinas de Gortari (2002:606).

32. Murillo (1999b:41); Rohter (1989:12); and Larmer (1989:4).

33. Cook (1996:269–70).
34. Salinas de Gortari (2002:607).
35. Cook (1996:269–70). The election was convened by the interior minister.
36. Cook (1996:271).
37. Interview, June 26, 2001, Mexico City. Bartlett had been one of the contenders for the PRI nomination in 1988.
38. Data in this paragraph are taken from World Bank, *World Tables*.
39. See Cornelius, Craig, and Fox (1994).
40. In December 1988, salaries were raised 10 percent, between May and July of 1989, a further 25 percent, in December, 10 percent, and between May and July of 1990, another 24 percent. In December 1990, another raise of 14 percent was granted, followed by a May–July 1991 increase of 16 percent, and a December increase of 13 percent. Although these increases just barely kept ahead of inflation, the teachers became relatively better off than most government workers (Cook 1996:280–81).
41. See Grindle (2000a:94–124) for a discussion of the Law for Popular Participation.
42. Data in this paragraph are taken from Secretaría Nacional de Educación, *Registro de docentes y personal administrativo*, 1994. In contrast to many countries, in which teaching is primarily a female profession, in Bolivia, 43 percent of all teachers were male.
43. UNDP (1998:164, citing the 1992 census).
44. Grindle (2000a).
45. Anaya (1995:4).
46. Contreras (1999b:491–92).
47. Grindle (2000a:112–16).
48. Victor Hugo Cárdenas, vice-president elect, who headed the incoming government's team on the transition commission established by the Jaime Paz government, recommended this approach. Moreover, the new minister of education had been a member of the design team and was a strong supporter of the MNR and the new president.
49. The other two were the law for capitalization of state-owned enterprises (privatization) and the law for popular participation.
50. Anaya (1995).
51. The governing pact was cemented through patronage appointments in government, rather than agreement on policy positions; this "policy for position" deal was central to the reformist accomplishments of the administration. See Gamarra (1994).
52. Mares Guia Neto (1994); Guedes, Lobo, Walker, and Amaral (1997); and Pinheiro (n.d.). On education reform in Brazil more generally, see Plank (1990a and 1990b).
53. Rocha (2001:6). Page numbers cited for this publication are from an English language version of the original. I am grateful to Mansueto Almeida of MIT for this translation.
54. Rocha (2001:7).
55. Draibe (2002:11). Teachers at the municipal level were particularly likely to be politically appointed by the mayors.

56. Some estimates place the total number of education workers in the state in 1990 at about 200,000. Of these, only some were teachers and of the teachers, probably only about 80,000 had regular teaching appointments. The others were appointed, usually by politicians, on an ad hoc basis. Interview by Madeleine Taylor, January 17, 2002, Belo Horizonte.

57. Interview by Madeleine Taylor, January 17, 2002, Belo Horizonte.

58. Rocha (2001:2).

59. The following account of the development of the reform draws primarily on Rocha (2001). In 1991, the new governor disbanded the PRS and joined the Partido Trabalhista Brasileiro.

60. In the 1980s, he had been municipal secretary in the state capital of Belo Horizonte while Tancredo Neves was governor (1982–1984). When Helio Garcia became governor for the first time in 1984, he asked Mares Guia Neto to become his minister of administrative reform and then the minister for science and technology.

61. Mares Guia Neto (1994:4), translation by the author. The minister had created Pitagoras, a network of private schools in the state. In the early days of this experience, Mares Guia Neto called in a business consultant to assess the roots of some of the problems he was experiencing. The consultant reported that he was trying to micromanage the schools. In consequence, Mares Guia Neto accorded the school directors much greater authority and believed that the success of this initiative owed much to this decision. His lesson, he reported later, was based on the idea that "you can't hold the bow lines of 60 ships all moving in different directions." If this was true for his business, it would certainly be true for the much larger public sector system, he argued. Interview by Madeleine Taylor, January 8, 2002, Belo Horizonte, Minas Gerais.

62. Rocha (2001:19).

63. Rocha (2001:19).

64. Rocha (2001:23).

65. Mares Guia Neto (1999:3).

66. Gershberg (1999b:756). The description of the program draws primarily on Gershberg (1999b). See also Fuller and Rivarola (1998); Nicaragua Reform Evaluation Team (1996); and King and Özler (1998).

67. This formula was based on the budget history of individual schools and then was adjusted for school attendance and per-pupil cost differentials between urban and rural schools. This was expected to be an incentive to keep children from dropping out of school; some critics argued that it encouraged teachers and school directors to inflate attendance records and to pass students to the next grade even when they were not ready academically for it—grade repetition being linked to dropout rates when students and their parents grew weary of slow progress and negative feedback. The parent-school councils were responsible for checking attendance records and teacher performance.

68. See Gaynor (1998).

69. Fuller and Rivarola (1998:2).

70. See, in particular, Carnoy and Samoff (1990:chapter 9).

71. Interview, January 12, 2001, Managua. See also Carnoy and Samoff (1990:335–52).

72. Interview, January 15, 2001, Managua.

73. See Arnove (1995:32–33). According to an article in the *Washington Post* in 1990, students "learned that 'G' is for guerrilla and 'C' is for Carlos Fonseca, founder of the Sandinista Front. They sang the Sandinista hymn and saluted the Sandinista red-and-black flag" (Hockstader, 1990:1). The Sandinista textbooks were popularly known as "Carlitos," after Carlos Fonseca.

74. See Carnoy and Samoff (1990:349–52).

75. Interview, January 17, 2001, Managua.

76. According to Arnove (1995:33), most of the Sandinista textbooks were shredded, but in the city of León, they were burned.

77. Hockstader (1990:1).

78. Arnove (1995:33).

79. Arnove (1995:41).

80. Arnove (1995:38).

81. Interview, January 15, 2001, Managua.

82. Arnove (1995:33–37).

83. Hockstader (1990:1).

84. United Press International, May 26, 1990.

85. Interview, January 11, 2001, San Marcos, Nicaragua.

86. Interview, January 11, 2001, San Marcos, Nicaragua.

87. Interview, January 11, 2001, San Marcos, Nicaragua.

88. See Gershberg (1999c).

89. See McConnell (1997:47–50).

90. Interview, January 11, 2001, San Marcos, Nicaragua.

91. Interview, January 11, 2001, San Marcos, Nicaragua.

92. Candidate Mahuad announced his bid for the presidency in a school and his first campaign commercial was about education. The Nicaragua, El Salvador, and Chilean education reforms had impressed him and influenced his positions on the issue.

93. Interview, May 3, 2000, Cambridge, Massachusetts. Mahuad had been mayor of Quito prior to being elected president.

94. In addition, following the model established by the Education for All meeting in Jomtien, Thailand, in 1990, Ecuador mandated a "basic cycle" of ten years of obligatory education (a year of preschool, six years of primary school, and three years of secondary school). Given a shortage of resources for expanding the preschool and secondary systems, however, this commitment led to no real changes in access to schooling.

95. Interview, March 31, 2000, Quito, Ecuador.

96. Isch (2000:4). Author's translation.

97. Data in this paragraph are taken from República del Ecuador (1990); and IDB (1999a).

98. The average level of schooling in rural areas was only 4.8 years, and in indigenous areas, 3.7 years, compared to 8.3 years in urban areas.

99. IDB (1999a).

100. Interview, April 4, 2000, Quito, Ecuador.

101. Interview, April 4, 2000, Quito, Ecuador.

102. As one annoyed minister complained: "One thing that never ceased to make me angry was how the ministry of finance would tell me that I hadn't disbursed all the money so therefore I could use a smaller budget. But they never released the money for me to spend!" Interview, March 28, 2000, Quito, Ecuador.

103. Information in the following paragraphs is based on interviews, ministry documents, and materials provided by international agencies, except as otherwise noted.

104. Interview, March 29, 2000, Quito, Ecuador.

105. Data in this paragraph taken from LAN (September, 29, 1998:450; and July 21, 1998:326).

106. Data in this paragraph taken from LAN (March 9, 1990:110; March 23, 1999:134; and March 30, 1999:152).

107. Jaramillo (1999).

108. Mares Guia Neto (1994:6–7).

CHAPTER FOUR

1. On the actions and impact of design teams more generally, see Centeno (1994); Conaghan and Malloy (1994); Domínguez (1997); González-Rossetti and Bossert (2000); Grindle (2000a); Schneider (1991); Valdés (1995); and Williamson (1994). See also Corrales (2003) on the conflict between technocracy and participation in reform initiatives.

2. Material in this section is based on interviews with Amalia Anaya, Manuel Contreras, Samuel Doria Medina, Gonzalo Sánchez de Lozada, Eric Sanjinés, Jorge Quiroga, officials of the World Bank and IDB, and leaders of the teachers unions, the Episcopal Commission on Education, and several NGOs concerned with education, carried out in La Paz, Bolivia, in 2000 and with Enrique Ipiña in 1998. In addition, see Anaya (1995); and Contreras (1995, 1999a, 1999b).

3. For a similar decision in Colombia, see Gaynor (1998:38).

4. Interview, February 16, 2000, La Paz, Bolivia. In a paper on the education reform, Anaya wrote of the ministry of education: "The Ministry of Education and Culture did not contain competent people because of conditions that it held in common with the public sector more generally: low salaries, job instability, the appointment of personnel on the basis of relationships of patronage and friendship, etc. . . . positions . . . were occupied by teachers, whether these were technical-pedagogic or others outside teaching expertise such as personnel administration, planning, information technology, or statistics. Of these positions, the most important were filled on the basis of recommendations made by the teachers union" (Anaya, 1995:7). Translation by the author.

5. At the end of 1990, the minister of education and high-level MIR officials asked the minister of planning to dismiss Anaya because, they argued, her activities were interfering with the work of the National Social Policy Council. She was critical of the heavy involvement of the Paz Zamora family and its allies in social policy, and she passed along information about the irregular activities of these people to the party.

6. Anaya (1995:12).

7. According to Anaya, the unions were opposed because they "knew there were many phantom teachers and those who were drawing double salaries; there was a lot of corruption." Interview, February 16, 2000, La Paz, Bolivia.

8. Substantial IDB funding for the reform was approved in December 1994. Bilateral support from the Swedish, Dutch, and German governments was also negotiated at that time.

9. Unions composed 48 percent of the delegates, and officials from the ministry of education another 20 percent, with additional representation of the Church (10 percent), the public universities (7 percent), and other important interests in the country.

10. Gamboa (1998:17).

11. The council was composed of the minister of education and two undersecretaries, one representative each from the teachers' union confederations (CONMERB and CTEUB), the Catholic Church, the Committee of Bolivian University Educators (CEUB), the National Private School Association (ANDE-COP), the Bolivian Workers Organization (COB), and the Single Union Confederation of Rural Workers of Bolivia (CSUTCB).

12. Anaya (1995:33–34).

13. Interview, February 16, 2000, La Paz, Bolivia.

14. Interview, February 15, 2000, La Paz, Bolivia.

15. Interview, February 22, 2000, La Paz, Bolivia.

16. Interview, February 22, 2000, La Paz, Bolivia. The Episcopal Commission was dismayed that the reform left out adult education, which it considered vital to improving the lives of the poorest Bolivians, as well as other forms of alternative education.

17. Indeed, most of the reforms carried out in Bolivia between 1985 and 2000 were designed by small groups of technocrats working in full or partial secrecy in La Paz (see Grindle 2003). Very little public discussion surrounded such efforts, and a series of political pacts entered into by successive governments generally eased legislation through congress with little debate or even discussion. The Sánchez de Lozada administration was particularly noted for its blitzkrieg approach to policy reform. "If you are going to do a reform, you have to do it quickly. There is no such thing as a gradual reform. If you choose to do it that way, the antibodies set in and destroy the reform" (interview, February 18, 2000, La Paz, Bolivia). While this strategy was relatively successful in promoting a wide range of reforms, it meant that opposition voices were forced to focus on policy implementation rather than contributing to the design of policy. Over time, the closed and technocratic nature of decision making of successive administrations built up a backlog of resentment among organized interests and lack of public awareness of the policies adopted. For the education reform, this process meant that the content and purpose of the reform were poorly understood.

18. Anaya (1995:32).

19. Interview, February 21, 2000, La Paz, Bolivia.

20. Interview, February 17, 2000, La Paz, Bolivia.

21. Interview, February 21, 2000, La Paz, Bolivia.

22. Much of the material in this section is based on Rocha (2001) and interviews carried out in Belo Horizonte by Madeleine Taylor. Among those inter-

viewed were Carlos Vasconcelos Rocha, Walfrido Mares Guia Neto, Ana Luiza Pinheiro, Zilá de Almeida, Edir Valadares, Iris Goulart, Claudio de Maura Castro, Magda Campbell, Joana Gontijo, Rosaura Magalhaes Pereira, Antonio Fuzzato, Helena Rolla, Otavio Elisio, and Neidson Rodrigues. Page numbers cited for the Rocha (2001) publication are from an English language version of the original. I am grateful to Mansueto Almeida of MIT for this translation.

23. Interview, January 9, 2002, Minas Gerais.

24. Pinheiro (n.d.:3).

25. Pinheiro (n.d.:3–5).

26. Rocha (2001:3).

27. Rocha (2001:3–4).

28. Rocha (2001:44–45).

29. Interviews, January 9 and 15, 2002, Belo Horizonte.

30. Rocha (2001:5).

31. Rocha (2001:5–6).

32. Interviews, January 8, 9, 14, 15, and 17, 2002, Belo Horizonte.

33. Mares Guia Neto (1999:4). While earlier education reformers had supported some of the same ideas, they were motivated primarily by an interest in gaining increased local participation in the schools. Under the new plan, the primary rationale for local engagement was to improve the management of the schools and to ensure that resources were used more efficiently. Moreover, the reform was expected to be an important way to develop a skilled labor force, to encourage the economic development of the state, and to improve its technological and economic integration with the rest of the world. This perspective encouraged the unions to denounce the reform as part of a neoliberal plan to reduce the role of the state in education and to subject education to market forces.

34. Rocha (2001:21–31).

35. Interview, January 8, 2002, Belo Horizonte.

36. Minas Gerais had a total of seventy-seven representatives in the state legislature; fifty-six of them were present for the education vote (Rocha 2001:31).

37. Interview, January 8, 2002, Belo Horizonte. He continued: "If a governor is committed, he will convince the legislature. But if the representatives see even the littlest opening, see that your support is limited, it's over. In this, Helio Garcia was impeccable."

38. Material in this section is based on interviews with Rosángela Adoum, Carlos Arco, Nathalie Celi, Carlos Larreategui, Jamil Mahuad, Benjamin Ortiz, Gabriel Pazmiño, Samia Peñaherrera, Roberto Salazar, Alfredo Vera Arato, officials of the teachers' union, journalists, and academics in Quito, Ecuador, during March and April 2000. In addition, see Crespo (2000); and IDB (1999a).

39. IDB (1999a:7)

40. Crespo (2000:10).

41. IDB (1999a:7–8).

42. Interview, March 28, 2000, Quito, Ecuador.

43. Interview, March 28, 2000, Quito, Ecuador.

44. Indeed, Belli was an inspiration to the design team. According to Peñaherrera: "I'd like to put him on an altar—he dared to do the necessary kind of

local level control reform that was needed." Interview, March 28, 2000, Quito, Ecuador.

45. "We gave the majority to the parents and the minority position to the teachers so that the parents could really control the teachers. This was very polemical; the teachers really resisted it. But we wanted to democratize the spaces of power in the local communities. We figured the communities would be our allies." Interview, March 28, 2000, Quito, Ecuador.

46. For this purpose, it would have $45 million of external credit and $5 million of government support that was to be disbursed over four years of program implementation.

47. Crespo (2000:11)

48. Interview, March 28, 2000, Quito, Ecuador.

49. Data in the rest of this paragraph are taken from IDB (1999b:2).

50. Interview, March 29, 2000, Quito, Ecuador.

51. See Rocha (1999).

52. Interview, March 29, 2000, Quito, Ecuador.

53. Interview, March 28, 2000, Quito, Ecuador.

54. The team was impressed by evidence demonstrating that mothers were more likely to use additional income to benefit children and the family more generally than would be the case if fathers received the money. Thus, they decided to make the scholarship payable to mothers with children between the ages of six and fifteen. Some 500,000 children were expected to benefit from the program over a two-year period.

55. The IDB and the World Bank would provide $90 million for the program, with additional funding for local community activities related to it, as well as for institutional strengthening activities. The total budget for the program was $110 million.

56. Interview, March 30, 2000, Quito, Ecuador.

57. Interview, March 28, 2000, Quito, Ecuador.

58. Interview, March 28, 2000, Quito, Ecuador.

59. Interview, March 28, 2000, Quito, Ecuador. Similar criticisms were voiced by a UNESCO official. "If parents have a legal obligation to send their children to school, how can you turn around and pay parents to do this. . . . And what happens when the program runs out in two years? Do the parents then realize that there's no reason to keep the children in school? What have you taught people about the value of education? And, if the quality of schooling is currently bad and not worth much in the labor market, it will still be the same in two years' time— what has been gained by keeping children in school? Part of the implicit message . . . is the idea that sending your kids to school is a good idea, it is worth it. But what if it isn't?" Interview, March 31, 2000, Quito, Ecuador.

60. Interview, March 28, 2000, Quito, Ecuador.

61. Interview, March 29, 2000, Quito, Ecuador.

62. Interview, March 28, 2000, Quito, Ecuador.

63. Reimers (2000d:87).

64. Interview, June 18, 1992, Mexico City, quoted in Grindle (1996:140).

65. See Grindle (1996:chapter 5); Centeno (1994).

66. Interview, June 18, 1992, Mexico City.

67. Some thirteen paragraphs of the 1992 agreement dealt with what needed to be revised and when the task needed to be accomplis

68. Salinas (2002:620, n. 20). One president told Salinas that prere dictator Porfirio Díaz appeared in more favorable light than he did.

69. DePalma (1993:9).

70. DePalma (1993:9).

71. Reid (1993:12).

72. DePalma (1993:9).

73. See, for examples, case studies in Williamson (1994).

74. This pattern was not unique to the case study countries. In Argentina, officials in the ministry of economy and the ministry of education collaborated on proposals for change. In Chile, the 1980s reform emerged from the thinking of a group of technocratic presidential advisers with a broad set of concerns about altering the provision of government services. Colombia's reform was the initiative of officials in the national planning agency, the ministry of finance, and the presidency.

75. On a similar strategy in Argentina, see Gorostiaga (2000:9). More generally, see Corrales (2003).

76. See, for example, three cases of democratic reformism and the relationship between design teams and political leaders in Grindle (2000a). See also Grindle (1996) on the vulnerability of technocratic teams.

77. See Corrales (2003).

78. Although the case of Nicaragua is not dealt with in this chapter, the role of international funders there was critical for the textbook program and the autonomous schools plan (see chapter 3).

CHAPTER FIVE

1. See, for a discussion of this point, Villegas-Reimers and Reimers (1996). See also Navarro (2002).

2. There were some exceptions to this general history of resistance to change. In Minas Gerais, education unions argued in favor of some reform initiatives. In the Dominican Republic, unions were part of a reformist coalition.

3. For an analysis of the relationship between labor mobilization and reform initiatives, see Collier and Collier (1991).

4. See Arnaut (1996:chapters 2 and 3).

5. Tiramonti (2000:4); Coppedge (1994:28).

6. Tiramonti (2000:4).

7. Klein (1992:chapters 7–8); Contreras (1999b).

8. Murillo (1999b:42).

9. Draibe (2002:11).

10. Tiramonti (2000:2).

11. Tiramonti (2000:3–4). In Venezuela, for example, state coffers expanded with oil revenues in the 1960s and 1970s and allowed for increased investment in education and encouraged further unionization of teachers.

12. CIDE-PREAL (1998:3–4).

13. Loyo, Ibarrola, and Blanco (1999:8).

14. Gauri (1998:15).

15. Bellei (1999:4–5).

16. Taliercio (1996); Trejos (1999:4).

17. Tiramonti (1999:7).

18. See Ornelas (1988).

19. Ornelas (1988:108–9).

20. Arnaut (1998a:13). After heading SNTE for more than a decade, Elba Ester Gordillo became head of the PRI after the presidential elections of 2000.

21. Tiramonti (2000:5).

22. Murillo (1999b:42–43).

23. Murillo (2001:143).

24. Costa Rica, Guatemala, and Nicaragua also had fragmented union structures. See Loyo, Ibarrola, and Blanco (1999:4)

25. Two of the main unions in Costa Rica are organized by level of teaching (primary and secondary education). See Broda (1999d).

26. Indeed, the number of teachers often grew even in periods of public sector budgetary austerity, suggesting the interest of the unions in the creation of jobs, even at the expense of salary increments. See IDB (1996:307).

27. Brazil is an exception to this practice. There, a tax equivalent to one day's pay is deducted from the salaries of all teachers and other professionals who work in the education sector. This payment is divided among unions, federations, and confederations. Loyo, Ibarrola, and Blanco (1999:6–7).

28. Loyo, Ibarrola, and Blanco (1999:5–6).

29. www.vheadline.com/9903/6018.htm, March 11, 1999.

30. Casanova (1998:13); Murillo (1999a).

31. Murillo (1999b) argues that this is a key factor in determining the capacity of unions to resist reform initiatives. See also Corrales (1998) on this issue.

32. Cook (1996); Tiramonti (2000:14).

33. Arnove (1995:41–42). Interview, January 8, 2001, Managua, Nicaragua.

34. Murillo (1999b:43).

35. Graham (1998:107).

36. Labor unions of all stripes were experiencing decreases in their power over government decision making and the ability to win concessions in confrontations with government during this period. This was largely due to widespread privatization of state-owned enterprises, economic reforms that replaced centralized decisions with those of market forces, constricted public sector budgets, legislation to "flexibilize" labor conditions, and, often, internal dissent within the unions.

37. See, for example, Anaya (1995); and Graham (1998).

38. See, for example, Cook (1996); and Street (1992).

39. Murillo (2001:144) cites a large number of such studies.

40. See Tiramonti (2000:7).

41. See UNESCO and OECD (2000:194).

42. See, for example, Vegas et al. (1999); and Piras and Savedoff (1998).

43. Psacharopoulos, Valenzuela, and Arends (1996).

44. Liang (1999). Data in this study are from twelve household surveys carried out in 1995 and 1996 by the Economic Commission for Latin America. The sam-

ples were national in ten countries, and urban only in Ecuador and Uruguay. Results were controlled for level of schooling, experience, and other labor market conditions.

45. Liang (1999:13).

46. Liang (1999:14).

47. Urquiola, Jiménez, Talavera, and Hernany (2000:60).

48. Piras and Savedoff (1998). The study uses 1993 household survey data from urban areas.

49. Piras and Savedoff (1998:8). A World Bank study of Bolivian teachers in the late 1990s, however, found that teachers with more education and experience were paid relatively well, while unqualified teachers—who made up a significant proportion of all teachers—were paid poorly (World Bank 1999b:93).

50. Another study, this one on teachers in Peru, found that 57 percent of male teachers and 33 percent of female teachers held second jobs. See Díaz and Saavedra (2000:37).

51. Bellei (1999:16–17).

52. Bellei (1999:16–17).

53. In state-supported private schools, they fell by 10 percent a year (Angell, Lowden, and Thorp, 2001:165).

54. Graham (1998:107).

55. Interview, February 15, 2000, La Paz, Bolivia.

56. Isch (2000:6), translation by the author.

57. Isch (2000:7).

58. Angell, Lowden, and Thorp (2001:282).

59. This was a conclusion of a study of teacher pay in Bolivia. See Urquiola, Jiménez, Talavera, and Hernany (2000:74).

60. In Argentina, strikes following the announcement of the decentralization of education to the provinces accounted for over a third of all strikes in 1991 (Murillo 1999b:44–45).

61. Angell, Lowden, and Thorp (2001:281–83); Gaynor (1998:38); Montenegro (n.d.).

62. Isch (2000:4), translation by the author.

63. Tendler (1997:7).

64. Ortiz de Zevallos (1998:17).

65. Consejo Nacional de la Educación (1999).

66. Interview, April 4, 2000, Quito, Ecuador.

67. In Colombia, a consultative process led to an alternative proposal from the teachers' union that was then used to negotiate a compromise agreement between the union and the reformers.

68. On this process in Argentina, see Gorostiaga (2000:9).

69. Interviews, January 8 and 15, 2001, Managua, Nicaragua.

70. Interview, April 4, 2000, Quito, Ecuador.

71. www.network.com.ar/docentes/marchas.htm, November 11, 1999, p. 1, translation by the author.

72. Ortiz de Zevallos (1998:9).

73. Tiramonti (2000:13).

74. Isch (2000:1), translation by the author.

75. www.netword.com.ar/docents/marchas/htm, November 11, 1999, p. 1, author's translation.

76. Gray-Molina, Pérez de Rada, and Yáñez (1998:31).

77. Interview, February 22, 2000, La Paz, Bolivia.

78. Quoted in Contreras (1999c:10).

79. Interview, February 22, 2000, La Paz, Bolivia.

80. Interview, February 22, 2000, La Paz, Bolivia.

81. Interview, February 22, 2000, La Paz, Bolivia.

82. Interview, February 22, 2000, La Paz, Bolivia.

83. Interview, February 22, 2000, La Paz, Bolivia.

84. Interview, January 12, 2000, Washington, D.C.

85. Interview, February 16, 2000, La Paz, Bolivia.

86. Interview, February 23, 2000, La Paz, Bolivia.

87. Urquiola, Jiménez, Talavera, and Hernany (2000:81).

88. Interview, February 15, 2000, La Paz, Bolivia.

89. Interview, February 17, 2000, La Paz, Bolivia.

90. Interview, February 23, 2000, La Paz, Bolivia. See also Contreras (1999c); and Gray-Molina, Pérez de Rada, and Yáñez (1998).

Chapter Six

1. Interview, July 4, 2001, Mexico City.

2. Interview, July 4, 2001, Mexico City.

3. Jesús Alvarez Gutiérrez, presentation at Harvard Graduate School of Education, April 23, 2003, Cambridge, Massachusetts.

4. Loyo (1992:20).

5. Interview, June 26, 2001, Lomas de Santa Fe, Mexico.

6. Gordillo (1992:13).

7. Gordillo (1992:13), translation by the author.

8. Cook (1996:279–80). After the presidential elections of 2000, in fact, Gordillo became head of the PRI.

9. Interview, June 26, 2001, Mexico City. At the time, Zedillo was considered a likely candidate for the presidency.

10. Interview, June 26, 2001, Lomas de Santa Fe, Mexico.

11. Interview, July 4, 2001, Mexico City.

12. Tatto (1999:278). Teachers could move on this ladder without having to leave teaching and move into an administrative role. The reform simultaneously offered an opportunity to good teachers to remain in teaching roles and also added many new positions at higher salaries without creating more administrators. By 1999, 193,000 teachers were incorporated into the new system (SEP 2000:156).

13. Interview, June 27, 2001, Lomas Anáhuac, Mexico.

14. Interview, June 27, 2001, Mexico City.

15. Salinas de Gortari (2002:615–16).

16. Salinas de Gortari (2002:617).

17. Murillo (1999b:44).

18. The union, convinced that the ministry was imposing this new set of standards for training, promotion, and remuneration, was initially very suspicious of

the *carerra magisterial.* Its leaders believed that this new system strengthened the ministry's position over the advancement of teachers and was part of governmental efforts to reduce costs and weaken the union. See Tatto (1999:272–74); and Street (1998:11).

19. For a discussion of the contents of the National Agreement for the Modernization of Basic Education, see Pescador Osuna (1992).

20. Interviews, January 7, 10, 14, 15, and 17, 2002, Belo Horizonte.

21. Interview, January 10, 2002, Belo Horizonte.

22. According to union officials, once inflation was controlled in the 1990s, the union was less likely to strike over the issue of salary adjustments. Interviews, January, 7, 10, 14, 15, and 17, 2002, Belo Horizonte.

23. Rocha (2001:16).

24. A similar situation existed in Venezuela, where a plethora of unions, each identified with a political party, represented teachers. Jockeying among these parties, along with changes in electoral outcomes, meant that teachers' positions were very unstable. Teachers, then, sought an end to the clientelist system of hiring and promoting teachers. Along with the Minas Gerais case, this suggests that when unions were not solely in control of the clientelist system, they opposed it. See Bruni Celli (2002:5–6).

25. Interviews, January 10, 14, 2002, Belo Horizonte.

26. Interview, January 17, 2002, Belo Horizonte.

27. Rocha (2001:22).

28. Interview, January 8, 2002, Belo Horizonte.

29. Rocha (2001:22).

30. Rocha (2001:22–34).

31. Interview, January 8, 2002, Belo Horizonte.

32. Rocha (2001:17).

33. Rocha (2001:17–18) claims that while the board was supportive, some of its members were not in agreement with the direct election idea.

34. Interview, January 17, 2002, Belo Horizonte.

35. Interview, January 17, 2002, Belo Horizonte.

36. Rocha (2001:33).

37. See Contreras (1999a). The rural teachers' union (CONMERB) had supported the idea of bilingual education and was somewhat less intransigent than the union representing urban teachers.

38. Talavera Simoni (1999:191–92).

39. Gamboa (1998: 39).

40. Anaya (1999).

41. In the discussion, both the minister of education and the minister of labor objected to confronting the unions. In the end, the minister of education agreed to the plan "with very ill grace," recalled Anaya. Interview, February 16, 2000, La Paz, Bolivia.

42. Events described in the following paragraphs are taken from three daily newspapers, *La Prensa, Presencia,* and *La Razón.* I am grateful to the Centro Boliviano de Investigación y Acción Educativas (CEBIAE) for providing access to their newspaper archives.

43. *La Prensa,* June 20, 1999.

44. The vice president characterized the struggle as an encounter between David and Goliath. "Goliath is the teachers' union and David is the two million children who aren't getting a good education. How can this equation be changed?" Altering public perceptions was one way to do it. As he recalls: "I saw a newpaper picture of a child dressed in his school uniform, with the caption 'I want to go to school.' I immediately ordered [my assistants] to get that picture; we made a poster of it. This was the kind of strategy we had, to show the parents that their children were David, being kept from their rights to education by the teachers' Goliath." And, according to Vice-Minister Anaya: "We were trying to get across the point that strikes should not be the daily sport of teachers." Interviews, February 16 and 21, 2000, La Paz, Bolivia.

45. Part of the reluctance of teachers to strike as frequently as in the past was linked to the government's policy of not paying for strike days. According to one teacher, for example: "Look, in the past we went out on strike and they didn't dock our pay, but now the discounting is terrible and I think many teachers don't go out on strike because of this." Quoted in Urquiola, Jiménez, Talavera, and Hernany (2000:93), translation by the author.

46. Financial Times Information, September 18, 2000, October 6, 2000; Agence France Presse, September 20, 2000; Inter Press Service, September 25, 2000; Associated Press, October 7, 2000.

47. Agence France Presse, May 1, 2001.

48. BBC, June 14, 2001; June 21, 2001.

49. Interview, January 15, 2001, Managua.

50. Molinski (1990).

51. UPI, May 28, 1991.

52. Interview, January 8, 2001, Managua.

53. There is considerable disagreement between the union and the government about whether Sandinista teachers were tracked down and fired or whether they simply took up the government's buyout option in the face of certain public sector downsizing.

54. Interview, January 8, 2001, Managua.

55. BBC, January 18, 1994.

56. Interview, January 8, 2001, Managua.

57. Arnove (1995:41–42).

58. Interview, January 15, 2001, Managua.

59. Comisión Nacional de Educación (2000). *Plan Nacional de Educación,* 2001–2015, December 11, 2000.

60. Interview, January 8, 2001, Managua.

61. Interview, January 8, 2001, Managua.

CHAPTER SEVEN

1. Equally important, it was assumed that the reforms being implemented were ones that would lead to improved educational performance. This faith was not necessarily backed up with clear evidence that the reforms could produce the desired impact. As with the wide variety of educational reforms put in place in the

1990s in the United States, it would be some time before it would become clear which among them were effective in raising school performance. In Latin America, assessing outcomes was particularly difficult, given the incipient nature of many national testing and evaluation systems.

2. Interview, January 9, 2001, Managua.

3. After the Mahuad administration was overthrown in 2000, the Network of Friends program was taken over by the new government. By that year, thirty-six networks existed, each encompassing between ten and twenty schools. Together with its urban counterpart program, about 10 percent of children were enrolled in networked schools. See Gershberg (2000).

4. Rocha (2001:14).

5. Rocha (2001:32). Those selected in 1991 were to be in office for two years. Those selected through the same process in 1993 and 1996 were to remain in office for three years. School directors could serve for two consecutive terms.

6. Secretaría de Educación Pública (2000b:261–62).

7. Secretaría de Educación Pública (2000b:261–62).

8. Much of the central government's remaining responsibilities were accounted for by basic education in the federal district, which was not decentralized in the 1992 agreement.

9. Ornelas (n.d.:12).

10. Ministerio de Educación, Cultura, y Deportes (n.d., n.p).

11. Instituto Nacional de Estadística (2001), www.ine.gov.bo/cgi-bin/iwdie.exe/TIPO.

12. Mares Guia Neto (1999:4).

13. According to the head of the parent-teacher organization: "You can't even buy a cabbage (for school lunches) if it's not in the budget!" Interview, January 9, 2002, Belo Horizonte.

14. Reforms of the 1980s had introduced the idea of elections, but this reform was not widely implemented and fell into disuse except in a few communities. Some 56 percent of the directors in 1990 were selected on the basis of patronage.

15. Interview, January 8, 2002, Belo Horizonte.

16. Interview, January 10, 2002, Minas Gerais; Rocha (2001:32).

17. Rocha (2001:32–33). The supreme court made its preliminary ruling in 1991, but due to a failure to communicate the decision in the appropriate manner, the first and second selection processes went ahead as scheduled in 1991 and 1993. In 1996, the court decision became final.

18. Rocha (2001:32).

19. Rocha (2001:33).

20. Pinheiro (n.d.:3); UNESCO/OREALC (n.d.:8).

21. UNESCO/OREALC (n.d.:9).

22. Cabrero Mendoza, Flamand Gómez, Santizo Rodall, and Vega Godínez (1997:330).

23. Ornelas (n.d.:2–3).

24. Through this agreement, the national government was obligated to provide the resources equal to or greater than they had invested in each state prior to the agreement.

25. Ornelas (n.d.:1).

26. Merino Juárez (1999:51).

27. Cabrero Mendoza, Flamand Gómez, Santizo Rodall, and Vega Godínez (1997:348).

28. Cabrero Mendoza, Flamand Gómez, Santizo Rodall, and Vega Godínez (1997:348), translation by the author.

29. Jesús Alvarez Gutiérrez, presentation at the Harvard Graduate School of Education, April 24, 2003, Cambridge, Massachusetts.

30. Merino Juárez (1999:51). Despite this division of overall responsibility, the national government determined curricula, the school calendar, and the contents of textbooks.

31. Alvarez Gutiérrez (2000:3).

32. Secretaría de Educación Pública (2000b:261–62). In addition to the six states that had no preexisting system, five states opted for a direct transfer to the state-level secretariat of education. Eleven states moved to fuse the two systems through law. And nine states opted to create decentralized institutes to administer the former national school system, keeping them separate from the state systems. Of these nine, five maintained two leadership structures for managing the systems separately.

33. Ornelas (n.d.:13).

34. Ornelas (n.d.:14).

35. Fierro Evans and Tapia García (1999:177–80).

36. Fierro Evans and Tapia García (1999:235–36).

37. Fierro Evans and Tapia García (1999:236).

38. Mejía Ayala (1999:263).

39. Mejía Ayala (1999:297), author's translation.

40. Mejía Ayala (1999:298).

41. Loera Varela and Sandoval Salinas (1999:438–39).

42. Possibly as a result of this difficult situation, Chihuahua fell from being number fifteen in terms of the number of students finishing primary school before 1992 to number twenty-two after decentralization. Loera Varela and Sandoval Salinas (1999:455).

43. Ruiz Cervantes (1999:513).

44. Ruiz Cervantes (1999:522–28).

45. Cabrero Mendoza, Flamand Gómez, Santizo Rodall, and Vega Godínez (1997:347).

46. Cabrero Mendoza, Flamand Gómez, Santizo Rodall, and Vega Godínez (1997:347). According to one study, the average years of schooling increased from 6.8 years in 1990 to 8.4 in 1998, school attendance increased from 83 percent in 1992 to 95 percent in 1997, and the number of children finishing primary school increased from 86 percent of those beginning school in 1987 to 93 percent of those beginning in 1991 (Zorrilla Fierro, 1999:386–87). See also Alvarez Gutiérrez (2000).

47. Secretaría de Educación Pública (2000a:760).

48. An education council brought together officials, academics, union leadership, and teachers to discuss plans for reform, and gradually officials within the education institute became convinced of the importance of change. An education plan created local commissions of teachers and supervisors that became experts in

some aspect of schooling and developed innovations around this expertise. The state-level institution in charge of education instituted a regionalized administrative system as a way of decentralizing decision making. English language training and computers were introduced into the classrooms. Zorrilla Fierro (1999: 346–47).

49. SEP (2000a:765). See also Alvarez Gutiérrez (2000).

50. See also Rhoten (2000).

51. Interview, July 2, 2001, Mexico City. The power of the PRI in national politics as well as the central government's dominance over education policy also meant that there was concern that schools might become sites for partisan competition. The PRI and the opposition parties were equally uncertain about who would benefit from this situation—the power of the dominant party was feared by the opposition, but it in turn was concerned with the ability of the opposition to enter the classroom. "In terms of promoting participation, there is some fear that if the school is opened up to participation, it will become a political space, and particularly a space for opposition—the PAN and the PRD above all. So there is real concern to keep the school as free of this as possible." Interview, July 4, 2001, Mexico City.

52. Interview, July 4, 2001, Mexico City.

53. Interview, July 2, 2001, Mexico City.

54. Interview, June 26, 2001, Lomas de Santa Fe, Mexico.

55. A similar situation existed in Chile, where parent councils were created, but the continued centralization of control over most important education decisions meant that there was little reason for them to meet or to mobilize a significant range of community input for local schooling. Equally important, the voucher system in Chile meant that many children attended schools outside of their local communities, making it difficult for parents to communicate and find common interests (Graham 1998:64).

56. Interview, July 2, 2001, Mexico City.

57. Zuckerman (2001).

58. Gershberg (1999b:15).

59. See especially Fuller and Rivarola (1998); and King, Özler, and Rawlings (1999).

60. Gershberg (1999b:16).

61. Interview, January 9, 2001, Managua.

62. Equipo de Evaluación de la Reforma en Nicaragua (1998). Among the 226 schools were 46 rural school "clusters" that generally shared a director and administrative staff.

63. The sample included 157 school directors and 45 directors of rural cluster schools, 173 members of the school councils, 427 teachers, 3,071 students, 3,536 parents, a total of 7,909 individuals. See Equipo de Evaluación de la Reforma en Nicaragua (1998).

64. Equipo de Evaluación de la Reforma en Nicaragua (1998:29–37). The eighteen schools included eight that were primary schools (six that were autonomous— three urban and three rural plus two centralized schools).

65. Equipo de Evaluación de la Reforma en Nicaragua (1998:40–42).

66. Gershberg (1999b:17–18).

67. Gershberg (1999b:18).
68. Gershberg (1999b:18).
69. Interview, January 8, 2001, Managua.
70. Fuller and Rivarola (1998:37).
71. Fuller and Rivarola (1998:12).
72. Equipo de Evaluación de la Reforma en Nicaragua (1998:43).
73. Interview, January 9, 2001, Managua.
74. Equipo de Evaluación de la Reforma en Nicaragua (1998:40).
75. Gershberg (1999b:20).
76. Equipo de Evaluación de la Reforma en Nicaragua (1998:42, 55).
77. Fuller and Rivarola (1998:58–59).
78. Equipo de Evaluación de la Reforma en Nicaragua (1998:42).
79. Equipo de Evaluación de la Reforma en Nicaragua (1998:44).
80. Equipo de Evaluación de la Reforma en Nicaragua (1998:41).
81. See also Gershberg (1999b:25–26).
82. Gershberg (1999b:16). Fuller and Rivarola (1998:59–60) report that teachers at times believed they would be fired if they did not sign the petition to become autonomous.
83. Gershberg (1999b:18).
84. See Contreras (1998).
85. Ministerio de Educación, Cultura, y Deportes (n.d.:4–5).
86. In 1999, the average of term time transfers of teachers was reduced from an average of fifty-four thousand to seven thousand. IDB, World Bank, et al. (1999:1)
87. Ministerio de Educación, Cultura, y Deportes (n.d.:4–5).
88. IDB, World Bank, et al. (1999:2).
89. Ministerio de Educación, Cultura, y Deportes (n.d.:5).
90. IDB, World Bank, et al. (1999:1–2).
91. IDB, World Bank, et al. (1999:3–4).
92. World Bank (1999b:101–2).
93. IDB, World Bank, et al. (1999:1–2).
94. IDB, World Bank, et al. (1999:3).
95. Ministerio de Educación, Cultura, y Deportes (n.d.:7).
96. Interview, February 17, 2000, La Paz.
97. Urquiola, Jiménez, Talavera and Hernany (2000:53, 150).
98. Interview, February 15, 2000, La Paz.
99. Interview, February 18, 2000, La Paz.
100. Interview, February 18, 2000, La Paz.
101. Urquiola, Jiménez, Talavera and Hernany (2000:53, 145).
102. National educational councils, which were frequently set up after reforms were approved to help keep education on national political agendas and to build and sustain public and elite interest in the reforms, were another possible source of new voices for education in Latin America. Experience in the 1990s, however, did not result in very positive assessments of these councils. In Argentina, for example, the Federal Council for Culture and Education was weak because it lacked its own resources and did not have a formal role in policy decision making (Cominetti and Gropello 1998:47). In Colombia and Chile, councils formed to support reform did not become significant protagonists in educational decision making.

In Mexico, a national council never managed to meet in anything more than pro forma fashion. Its top-down creation, as well as the continued monopoly of information and decision making by the national ministry, provided little incentive for members to engage in genuine discussions of education needs in the country. In Nicaragua, a national council was created in the 1980s and survived through the 1990s but "on paper only" (interview, January 8, 2001, Managua). In contrast, similar councils in El Salvador and Uruguay had more input into education planning and were important in maintaining education on national agendas (Corrales 1999:27–28).

103. See Villegas-Reimers and Reimers (1996).

104. Uribe (1999:10).

105. For an interesting example of community participation in education in Brazil, see Dellagnelo (1998:8).

106. See Gaynor (1998:39).

107. As with other aspects of the new education policies, participation tended to vary by locale. This same pattern was evident beyond the case studies. In one reform-oriented state in Colombia, for example, school councils were effective in bringing together large numbers of parents, engaging them in educational planning and implementation, and improving the responsiveness of teachers and school directors to reform objectives. In other states, however, such councils were never given impetus by mayors, who used their newfound authority over the education system to expand the number of teaching positions filled for partisan ends (Angell, Lowden, and Thorp 2000:179). In Peru, the effectiveness of parent associations also varied by locale, but their role was generally limited to providing resources for school maintenance, supplies, and festivals (Graham 1998:108). While reformers in El Salvador and Nicaragua also found that parental involvement varied, they were in general much more active in encouraging local-level participation in school management than was the case in most other countries (Navarro, Carnoy, and de Moura Castro n.d.: 19; IDB 1996; Burki, Perry, and Dillinger 1999:57; Gershberg 1999a).

Chapter Eight

1. PREAL (2001:20–21).

2. This was the case, for example, in Peru (see Graham 1998:32; and Ortiz de Zevallos 1998: 19–20). Even reforms that are adopted can become subverted by the positive political benefits that can be achieved through investments in educational infrastructure rather than directly improving quality. This was the outcome in many municipalities after decentralization initiatives in Colombia. See Angell, Lowden, and Thorp (2001).

3. Corrales (2003:20).

4. Fuller and Rivarola (1998:3).

5. PREAL (2001:5). See also *The Economist* (May 11–17, 2002:34–35).

6. See McMeekin (1998).

7. See, for example, the dissenting views in the PREAL report card (PREAL 2001:26). In addition, see Carlson (2000); and Reimers (2000a).

8. See Williams and Somers (1999).

9. A study based on achievement tests from the third and fourth grades in thirteen Latin American countries found that factors such as school culture and the attitudes and practices of teachers were important in explaining differences in levels of achievement. Among other factors, parental involvement in the classroom was also important, as was the degree of autonomy that school directors had. See UNESCO/OECD (2000:105).

10. For a discussion of why business elites might not be interested in education reform, see Tendler (2002).

11. On this point more generally, see Trostle, Somerfeld, and Simon (1997).

12. On the issue of teacher engagement and incentives, see Navarro (2002).

13. See, for example, IDB (n.d.:40–43).

14. Juan Carlos Navarro, remarks at a workshop on education reform, Woodrow Wilson Center for Scholars, Washington, D.C., April 4–5, 2002.

15. By the end of the decade of the 1990s, in fact, preschooling and secondary schooling were receiving more attention from policy makers, and important new initiatives were being discussed to professionalize the teaching corps.

BIBLIOGRAPHY

Alesina, Alberto, and Allan Drazen. 1991. "Why Are Stabilizations Delayed?" *American Economic Review* 81, no. 5 (December).

Alesina, Alberto, and R. Perotti. 1994. "The Political Economy of Budget Deficits." *NBER Working Paper*, no. 4637.

Alvarez Béjar, Alejandro. 1991. "Economic Crisis and the Labor Movement in Mexico." In Kevin J. Middlebrook, ed., *Unions, Workers, and the State in Mexico*. La Jolla: University of California at San Diego, Center for U.S.-Mexican Studies.

Alvarez Gutiérrez, Jesús. 2000. "La descentralización de la educación en Aguascalientes: Hacia un nuevo federalismo educativo." Unpublished manuscript, Mexico (no other information).

Anaya, Amalia. 1999. "Presentation to the President, January 22." Personal notes provided to the author.

———. 1995. "Proceso de formulación de la reforma educativa." Prepared for Maestrías para el Desarrollo, Catholic University of Bolivia, January 1995, La Paz.

Angell, Alan, Pamela Lowden, and Rosemary Thorp. 2001. *Decentralizing Development: The Political Economy of Institutional Change in Colombia and Chile.* Oxford: Oxford University Press.

Arnaut, Alberto. 1998a. "La federalización educativa y el Sindicato Nacional de Trabajadores de la Educación de México." FLACSO/PREAL Boletín Nro. 1, Buenos Aires: Proyecto Sindicalismo Docente y Reforma Educativa en América Latina (October).

———. 1998b. *La federalización educativa en México.* Mexico City: El Colegio de México, Centro de Investigación y Docencia Económicas.

———. 1996. *Historia de una profesión: Los maestros de educación primaria en México, 1887–1994.* Mexico City: El Colegio de México, Centro de Investigación y Docencia Económicas.

Arnove, Robert F. 1995. "Education as Contested Terrain in Nicaragua." *Comparative Education Review* 59, no. 1.

Bates, Robert. 1981. *Markets and States in Tropical Africa.* Berkeley: University of California Press.

Bates, Robert, and Anne O. Krueger, eds. 1993. *Political and Economic Interactions in Economic Policy Reform.* Cambridge, Mass.: Blackwell Publishers.

Bellei, C. 1999. "El talón de aquiles de la reforma: Análisis sociológico de la política de los '90 hacia los docentes en Chile." Unpublished paper, PREAL/CIDE, Santiago, Chile.

Bernbaum, Marcia, and Uli Locher. 1998. "EDUCA: Business Leaders Promote Basic Education and Educational Reform in the Dominican Republic." Report prepared for USAID/Dominican Republic.

Birdsall, Nancy, and Juan Luis Londoño. 1998. "No Tradeoff: Efficient Growth via More Equal Human Capital Accumulation." In Nancy Birdsall, Carol Graham, and Richard H. Sabot, eds., *Beyond Tradeoffs: Market Reform and Equitable Growth in Latin America*. Washington, D.C.: Inter-American Development Bank and Brookings Institution.

Birdsall, Nancy, David Ross, and Richard Sabot. 1995. "Inequality and Growth Reconsidered: Lessons from East Asia." *World Bank Economic Review* 9, no. 3.

Birdsall, Nancy, and Richard H. Sabot, eds. 1996. *Opportunity Foregone: Education in Brazil*. Baltimore, Md.: Johns Hopkins University Press for Inter-American Development Bank.

Braslavsky, Cecilia, and Gustavo Cosse. 1996. Las actuales reformas educativas en América Latina: Cuatro actors, tres lógicas y ocho tensiones. Santiago, Chile: PREAL.

Bresser Pereira, Luiz Carlos. 2003. "Reflections of a Reformer: Amending the Constitution in Democratic Brazil." In Ben Ross Schneider and Blanca Heredia, eds. *The Political Economy of Administrative Reform: State Building in Developing Countries*. Ann Arbor: University of Michigan Press.

Broda, Andrea. 1999a. "Teacher Unions in Venezuela." Unpublished manuscript, Kennedy School of Government, Harvard University.

———. 1999b. "Teacher Unions in Chile." Unpublished manuscript, Kennedy School of Government, Harvard University.

———. 1999c. "Teacher Unions in Mexico." Unpublished manuscript, Kennedy School of Government, Harvard University.

———. 1999d. "Teacher Unions in Costa Rica." Unpublished manuscript, Kennedy School of Government, Harvard University.

———. 1999e. "Teacher Unions in Argentina." Unpublished manuscript, Kennedy School of Government, Harvard University.

———. 1999f. "Teacher Unions in Colombia." Unpublished manuscript, Kennedy School of Government, Harvard University.

Brooks, Sarah. 2000. "Social Protection and the Market: A Political Economy of Pension Reform in Latin American and the World." Paper prepared for the 2000 meeting of the Latin American Studies Association, Miami, March 16–18.

Brown, David S., and Wendy Hunter. 1999. "Democracy and Social Spending in Latin America, 1980–1992." *American Political Science Review* 93, no. 4.

Bruni Celli, Josefina. 2002. "The Politics of Education Reform in the 90's: The Case of Venezuela." Paper prepared for a conference on "The Politics of Education Reform in Latin America," Woodrow Wilson Center for Scholars, Washington, D.C., April 4–5.

Burki, Shahid Javed, Guillermo Perry, and William Dillinger. 1999. *Beyond the Center: Decentralizing the State*. Washington, D.C.: The World Bank, Latin American and Caribbean Studies.

Cabrero Mendoza, Enrique, Laura Flamand Gómez, Claudia Santizo Rodall, and Alejandro Vega Godínez. 1997. "Claroscuros del nuevo federalismo mexicano: Estrategias en la descentralización federal y capacidades en la gestión local." *Gestión y Política Pública* 6, no. 2.

Carlson, Beverley A. 2000. "Achieving Educational Quality: What Schools Teach Us. Learning from Chile's P900 Primary Schools." Santiago, Chile: CEPAL.

Carnoy, Martin, Gustavo Cosse, Cristián Cox, and Enrique Martínez. 2001. "The Lessons of Education Reform in the Southern Cone." Unpublished manuscript. Washington, D.C.: Inter-American Development Bank.

Carnoy, Martin, and Joel Samoff. 1990. *Education and Social Transition in the Third World*. Princeton, N.J.: Princeton University Press.

Casanova, Ramón. 1998. "El sindicalismo educativo hoy día: Exploraciones desde la perspectiva venezolana." FLACSO/PREAL Boletín Nro. 2, Buenos Aires: Proyecto Sindicalismo Docente y Reforma Educativa en América Latina (December).

Centeno, Miguel Angel. 1994. *Democracy within Reason: Technocratic Revolution in Mexico*. University Park: Pennsylvania State University Press.

Chalmers, Douglas A., Carlos M. Vilas, Katherine Hite, Scott B. Martin, Kerianne Piester, and Monique Segarra, eds. 1997. *The New Politics of Inequality in Latin America: Rethinking Participation and Representation*. Oxford: Oxford University Press.

CIDE-PREAL (Centro de Investigación y Desarrollo de la Educación and Programa de Promoción de la Reforma Educativa en América Latina y el Caribe). 1998. "Obstáculos políticos, negociaciones y grupos de interés en las reformas educativos en América Latina: Términos de referencia del grupo de trabajo." Unpublished manuscript (no information about location).

Collier, David, and Deborah L. Norden. 1992. "Strategic Choice Models of Political Change in Latin America." *Comparative Politics* (January).

Collier, Ruth Berins, and David Collier. 1991. *Shaping the Political Arena*. Princeton, N.J.: Princeton University Press.

Cominetti, Rossella, and Emanuela de Gropello. 1998. "Descentralización de la educación y la salud: Un análisis comparativo." In Emanuela de Gropello and Rossella Cominetti, eds., *La descentralización de la educación y la salud: Un análisis comparativo de la experiencia latinoamericana*. Santiago, Chile: Comisión Económica para América Latina y el Caribe.

Comisión Nacional de Educación. 2000. *Plan Nacional de Educación, 2001–2015*. Managua, December 11.

Conaghan, Katherine M., and James M. Malloy. 1994. *Unsettling Statecraft: Democracy and Neoliberalism in the Central Andes*. Pittsburgh, Pa.: University of Pittsburgh Press.

Consejo Nacional de Educación. 1999. "Estrategia nacional de educación." Managua, Nicaragua.

Contreras, Manuel. 1999a. "A la luz de la Reforma Educativa: El conflicto entre maestros/as y gobierno." FLACSO/PREAL Boletín Nro. 4/5, Buenos Aires: Proyecto Sindicalismo Docente y Reforma Educativa en America Latina (October).

———. 1999b. "Reformas y desafíos de la educación." In Fernando Campero Prudencio, ed. *Bolivia en el Siglo XX*. La Paz: Harvard Club de Bolivia.

———. 1999c. "El conflicto entre los maestros/as y el gobierno a la luz de la reforma educativa." *Conflictos* 2, no. 2/3. La Paz: CERES.

———. 1998. "Formulación, implementación y avance de la reforma educativa en Bolivia." *Ciencia y Cultura*, no. 3 (July), Journal of the Catholic University of Bolivia, La Paz.

Contreras, Manuel. 1995. "Proceso de formulación de la Reforma Educativa: Bolivia." Unpublished manuscript. La Paz: Catholic University of Bolivia, Maestrías para el Desarrollo.

Conway, Jill Kerr, and Susan C. Bourque, eds. 1995. *The Politics of Women's Education: Perspectives from Asia, Africa, and Latin America*. Ann Arbor: University of Michigan Press.

Cook, Maria Lorena. 1996. *Organizing Dissent: Unions, the State, and the Democratic Teachers' Movement in Mexico*. University Park: Pennsylvania State University Press.

Coppedge, Michael. 1994. *Strong Parties and Lame Ducks: Presidential Partyarchy and Factionalism in Venezuela*. Stanford, Calif.: Stanford University Press.

Cornelius, Wayne A., Ann L. Craig, and Jonathan Fox, eds. 1994. *Transforming State-Society Relations in Mexico: The National Solidarity Strategy*. La Jolla: University of California, San Diego, Center for U.S.-Mexican Studies.

Corrales, Javier. 2003. "The Conflict between Technocracy and Participation in Education Reform in Latin America." Paper presented at the Twenty-fourth International Congress of the Latin American Studies Association, Dallas, Tex., March 27–29.

————. 1999. "The Politics of Education Reform: Bolstering the Supply and Demand; Overcoming Institutional Blocks." Washington, D.C.: World Bank, Education Reform and Management Series, 2, no. 1.

————. 1998. "Party-Accommodating Transitions to the Market: Executive-Ruling Party Relations and Economic Reforms in Latin America." Unpublished Paper. Amherst, Mass.: Amherst College, Department of Political Science.

Crespo, Carlos. 2000. "Escenario, conflictos y proceso de cambio educativo en el caso del Ecuador." Paper prepared for a conference sponsored by CIDE and PREAL, Reformas educativas y política en América Latina, Santiago, Chile, January 17–19.

CTEUB (Confederación de Trabajadores de la Educación Urbana de Bolivia). 1991. "Construyendo una educación contestataria." La Paz: CTEUB.

Dellagnelo, Lúcia. 1998. "Brazil: Community Participation: What Do Communities Get Out of It?" *DRCLAS News*. Cambridge: Harvard University (spring).

de la Garza, Enrique. 1991. "Independent Trade Unionism in Mexico: Past Developments and Future Perspectives." In Kevin J. Middlebrook, ed., *Unions, Workers, and the State in Mexico*. La Jolla: University of California at San Diego, Center for U.S.-Mexican Studies.

de Moura Castro, Claudio. 1997. "Latin America: The Battle between Borrowing and Creating." *Prospects* 27, no. 1 (March).

de Moura Castro, Claudio, and Aimee Verdisco. 2002. "Performance vs. Innovation: Education in Asia and Latin America." In Claudio de Moura Castro and Aimee Verdisco, eds., *Making Education Work: Latin American Ideas and Asian Results*. Washington, D.C.: Inter-American Development Bank.

DePalma, Anthony. 1993. "New Battles Flare Over Mexico's Past." *New York Times*, August 29, p. 9.

Díaz, Hugo, and Jaime Saavedra. 2000. "La carrera de maestro: Factores institucionales, incentivos económicos y desempeño." Working Paper R-410. Washington, D.C.: Inter-American Development Bank (August).

Domínguez, Jorge. 1997. *Technopols: Freeing Politics and Markets in the 1980s.* University Park: Pennsylvania State University Press.

Doryan, Eduardo. 1999. "Managing the Politics of Reform in Costa Rica." Presentation at the World Bank, Education Reform and Management Thematic Group, September 22, 1999.

Draibe, Sônia M. 2002. "The Politics of Educational Policy Reform in Brazil." Paper presented at a workshop on "The Politics of Education Sector Reforms in Latin America," Washington, D.C., Woodrow Wilson Center, April 4–5.

Duarte, Jesús. 1999. "Política y educación: Las tentaciones particularistas en la educación latinoamericana." Paper prepared for a conference on education reform in Latin America, Santiago, Chile: CIDE and PREAL (January).

Equipo de Evaluación de la Reforma en Nicaragua. 1998. "Segundo vistazo a la reforma 1995–1997." Managua (August).

Espínola, Viola, 1997. "Decentralización del sistema educativo en Chile: Impacto en la gestión de las escuelas." Washington, D.C.: Human Development Group, Latin America and Caribbean, Report No. 10 (May).

Espínola, Viola, and Claudio de Moura Castro. 2002. "Economic Principles in Education Management in Chile." In Claudio de Moura Castro and Aimee Verdisco, eds., *Making Education Work: Latin American Ideas and Asian Results.* Washington D.C. Inter-American Development Bank.

Evans, Peter. 1995. *Embedded Autonomy: States and Industrial Transformation.* Princeton, N.J.: Princeton University Press.

Fernandez, Raquel, and Dani Rodrik. 1991. "Resistance to Reform: Status Quo Bias in the Presence of Individual-Specific Uncertainty." *American Economic Review* 81, no. 5 (December).

Fierro Evans, María Cecilia, and Guillermo Tapia García. 1999. "Decentralización educativa e innovación: Una mirada desde Guanajuato." In María del Carmen Pardo, ed., *Federalización e innovación educativa en México.* Mexico: El Colegio de Mexico.

Filgueira, Fernando, and Juan Andrés Moraes, with Carlos Filgueira, José Fernández, and Constanza Moreira. 1998. "Political Environments, Sector Specific Configurations and Strategic Devices: Understanding Institutional Reform in Uruguay." Unpublished manuscript. Montevideo: Centro de Informaciones y Estudios del Uruguay.

Fiske, Edward B. 1996. *Decentralization of Education: Politics and Consensus.* Washington, D.C.: World Bank.

Fuller, Bruce, and Magdalena Rivarola. 1998. "Nicaragua's Experiment to Decentralize Schools: Views of Parents, Teachers, and Directors." Washington, D.C.: World Bank, Working Paper Series on Impact Evaluation of Education Reforms, No. 5.

Gajardo, Marcela. 1999. "Reformas educativas en América Latina: Balance de una década." Santiago, Chile: PREAL.

Gamarra, Eduardo. 1994. "Crafting Political Support for Stabilization: Political Pacts and the New Economic Policy in Bolivia." In William C. Smith, Carlos H. Acuña, and Eduardo A. Gamarra, eds., *Democracy, Markets, and Structural Reform in Latin America.* New Brunswick, N.J.: Transaction Publishers.

Gamboa, Franco. 1998. *Contra viento y marea: Tras las huellas de la reforma educativa en Bolivia*. La Paz: Centro de Documentación e Información.

García-Huidobro S., Juan Eduardo. 1999. "Conflictos y alianzas en las reformas educativos: Siete tesis basadas en la experiencia chilena." Overheads prepared for a conference on education reform in Latin America, Santiago, Chile: CIDE and PREAL (January).

Gauri, Varun. 1998. *School Choice in Chile: Two Decades of Education Reform*. Pittsburgh, Pa.: University of Pittsburgh Press.

Gaynor, Cathy. 1998. *Decentralization of Education: Teacher Management*. Washington, D.C.: World Bank.

Geddes, Barbara. 1994. *Politician's Dilemma: Building State Capacity in Latin America*. Berkeley: University of California Press.

Gershberg, Alec Ian. 2002. "Empowering Parents while Making Them Pay: Autonomous Schools and Education Reform Processes in Nicaragua." Paper prepared for a workshop on "The Politics of Education and Health Sector Reforms," Woodrow Wilson Center, Washington, D.C. (April).

———. 2000. "Education and Health Decentralization in Ecuador: Practice, Plans, and Prospects." Unpublished paper. New York: New School University.

———. 1999a. "Fostering Effective Parental Participation in Education: Lessons from a Comparison of Reform Processes in Nicaragua and Mexico." *World Development* 27, no. 4.

———. 1999b. "Decentralization, Citizen Participation, and Role of the State: The Autonomous Schools Program in Nicaragua." *Latin American Perspectives* 26, no 4 (July).

———. 1999c. "Education 'Decentralization' Processes in Mexico and Nicaragua: Legislative versus Ministry-Led Reform Strategies." *Comparative Education* 35, no. 1.

González-Rossetti, Alejandra. 2001. *The Political Dimension of Health Reform: The Case of Mexico and Colombia*. Ph.D. dissertation, Department of Public Health Policy, London School of Hygiene and Tropical Medicine.

González-Rossetti, Alejandra, and Thomas J. Bossert. 2000. "Enhancing the Political Feasibility of Health Reform: A Comparative Analysis of Chile, Colombia, and Mexico." Cambridge: Harvard School of Public Health.

Gordillo, Elba Esther. 1992. "El SNTE ante la modernización de la educación básica." *El Cotidiano* Year 8 (November–December).

Gorostiaga, Jorge M. 2000. "Educational Decentralization in Argentina and Brazil: Contexts and Rationales of the Policies of the 1990s." Paper prepared for the 2000 Meeting of the Latin American Studies Association, Miami, March 16–18.

Graham, Carol. 1998. *Private Markets for Public Goods: Raising the Stakes in Economic Reform*. Washington, D.C: Brookings Institution.

Graham, Carol, Merilee Grindle, Eduardo Lora, and Jessica Seddon. 1999. "Improving the Odds: Political Strategies for Institutional Reform in Latin America." Washington, D.C.: Inter-American Development Bank.

Gray-Molina, George, Ernesto Pérez de Rada, and Ernesto Yáñez. 1998. "La economía política de reformas institucionales en Bolivia." Unpublished manuscript, La Paz: Fundación Diálogo.

Grindle, Merilee S. 2003. "Shadowing the Past? Policy Reform in Bolivia, 1985–2002." In Merilee S. Grindle and Pilar Domingo, eds., *Proclaiming Revolution: Bolivia in Comparative Perspective*. (Cambridge, Mass.: David Rockefeller Center for Latin American Studies and Harvard University Press).

———. 2000a. *Audacious Reforms: Institutional Invention and Democracy in Latin America*. Baltimore, Md.: Johns Hopkins University Press.

———. 2000b. "The Social Agenda and the Politics of Reform in Latin America." In Joseph S. Tulchin and Allison M. Garland, eds., *Social Development in Latin America*. Boulder, Colo.: Lynne Rienner.

———. 1996. *Challenging the State: Crisis and Innovation in Latin America and Africa*. Cambridge: Cambridge University Press.

Grindle, Merilee S., and John W. Thomas. 1991. *Public Choices and Policy Change: The Political Economy of Reform in Developing Countries*. Baltimore, Md.: Johns Hopkins University Press.

Guedes, Andrea, Thereza Lobo, Robert Walker, and Ana Lucia Amaral. 1997. "Gestíon descentralizada de la educación en el estado de Minas Gerais, Brasil." Report No. 11, Latin America and Caribbean Region, World Bank. Washington, D.C.: World Bank.

Gutiérrez de Taliercio, Carolina. 2000. "Preconditions for Reform in Latin America." Data analysis prepared for Professor Merilee Grindle. Cambridge: Kennedy School of Government, Harvard University.

Haggard, Stephan, and Robert R. Kaufman. 1992. *The Politics of Economic Adjustment*. Princeton, N.J.: Princeton University Press.

Hanson, E. Mark. 1995. "Democratization and Decentralization in Colombian Education." *Comparative Education Review* 39, no. 1.

Harberger, Arnold C. 1984. "Economic Policy and Economic Growth." In Arnold C. Harberger, ed., *World Economic Growth*. San Francisco: Institute for Contemporary Studies.

Hardy, Clarisa. 2002. "Una nueva generación de reformas sociales en América Latina." Funación Chile, Collección Ideas, Year 3, no. 17 (March).

Herrrán, Carlos A., and Bart Van Uythem. 2001. "Why Do Youngsters Drop Out of School in Argentina and What Can Be Done Against It?" Washington, D.C.: Inter-American Development Bank, Operations Department 1 (September).

Hirschman, Albert O. 1981. "Policymaking and Policy Analysis in Latin America—A Return Journey." In Albert O. Hirschman, *Essays in Trespassing: Economics to Politics and Beyond*. Cambridge: Cambridge University Press.

Hockstader, Lee. 1990. "Battle Looming over Nicaragua's Schools; Government Wants to Purge Education of Sandinista Influence." *Washington Post*, July 30, p. 1.

Hunter, Wendy, and David S. Brown. 2000. "World Bank Directives, Domestic Interests, and the Politics of Human Capital Investment in Latin America." *Comparative Political Studies* 33, no. 1 (February).

Iguiñiz Echeverría, Manuel. 2000. "La educación peruana al final de la década." Paper prepared for a conference on education reform in Latin America, Santiago, Chile: CIDE and PREAL (January).

IDB (Inter-American Development Bank). 1999a. "Ecuador: Programa de Redes Escolares Autonomas Rurales, (EC-0125), Propuesta de Prestamo." Washington, D.C.: Inter-American Development Bank.

IDB (Inter-American Development Bank). 1999b. "Ecuador: Programa de Protección Social (EC-0190). Perfil II." Washington, D.C.: Inter-American Development Bank.

———. 1998. *Facing Up to Inequality in Latin America*. Washington, D.C.: Inter-American Development Bank.

———. 1996. *Cómo organizar con éxito los servicios sociales*. Part Three of *Progreso económico y social en América Latina, 1996*. Washington, D.C.: Inter-American Development Bank.

———. n.d. *Reforma de la educación primaria y secundaria en América Latina y el Caribe*. Washington, D.C.: Inter-American Development Bank, Department of Sustainable Development.

IDB (Inter-American Development Bank) and World Bank. 1999. *Misión conjunta de evaluación anual del programa de reforma educativa, Press Release*. La Paz: IDB and World Bank.

ILO (International Labour Organization). 1996. "The Impact of Structural Adjustment on the Employment and Training of Teachers." Paper prepared for a joint meeting on the Impact of Structural Adjustment on Educational Personnel, Geneva.

IMF (International Monetary Fund). 2001. "Structural Conditionality in IMF-Supported Programs." www.imf.org/exernal/np/pdr/cond/2001/eng/struct/index.htm.

Instituto Nacional de Estadística (2001). www.ine.gov.bo/cgi-bin/iwdie.exe/TIPO.

International Association for the Evaluation of Educational Achievement. 1996a. Mathematics Achievement in the Middle School Years: IEA's Third International Mathematics and Science Study. Boston: TIMSS International Study Center, Boston College.

———. 1996b. *Science Achievement in the Middle School Years: IEA's Third International Mathematics and Science Study*. Boston: TIMSS International Study Center, Boston College.

Isch L., Edgar. 2000. "El sindicalismo docente en el Ecuador: Una historia de avances y retos cada vez más amplios." Unpublished paper, Unión Nacional de Educadores, Quito (November).

Jaramillo, Fidel. 1999. "El colapso económico de Ecuador." (December) (no additional information).

Kemmerer, Frances N., and Douglas M. Windham. 1997. *Incentives Analysis and Individual Decision Making in the Planning of Education*. Paris: UNESCO.

King, Elizabeth M., and Berk Özler. 1998. "What's Decentralization Got to Do with Learning? The Case of Nicaragua's School Autonomy Reform." Paper prepared for the Annual Meeting of the American Educational Research Association, San Diego, Calif., April 13–17.

King, Elizabeth M., Berk Özler, and Laura B. Rawlings. 1999. "Nicaragua's School Autonomy Reform: Fact or Fiction?" Washington D.C.: World Bank,

Working Paper Series on Impact Evaluation of Education Reforms, no. 19.

Klein, Herbert S., 1992. *Bolivia: The Evolution of a Multi-Ethnic Society.* 2d ed. New York: Oxford University Press.

Laboratorio Latinoamericano de Evaluación de la Calidad de la Educación. 1998. *Primer estudio internacional comparativo.* Santiago, Chile: UNESCO.

LAN (Latin American Newsletters). Various years. *Latin American Weekly Report.*

Latinobarómetro. 1998. *Opinión Pública Latinoamericana.*

———. 1995. *Opinión Pública Latinoamericana.*

Larmer, Brook. 1989. "Mexico Teacher Strike Tests Salinas," *Christian Science Monitor,* April 21:4.

Larrañaga, Osvaldo. 1997. "Educación y superación de la pobreza en América Latina." In José Vicente Zevallos, ed., *Estrategias para reducir la pobreza en América Latina y el Caribe.* Quito, Ecuador: United Nations Development Programme.

Liang, Xiaoyan. 1999. "Teacher Pay in Twelve Latin American Countries: How Does Teacher Pay Compare to Other Professions, What Determines Teacher Pay, and Who Are the Teachers?" Washington, D.C.: World Bank, Human Development Department, LCSHD Paper Series No. 49.

Lijphart, Arendt, and C. Waisman, eds. 1996. *Institutional Design in New Democracies: Eastern Europe and Latin America.* Boulder, Colo.: Westview.

Linz, Juan, and Arturo Valenzuela, eds. 1994. *The Failure of Presidential Democracy.* Baltimore, Md.: Johns Hopkins University Press.

Loera Varela, Armando, and Fernando Sandoval Salinas. 1999. "La innovación educativa en el proceso de descentralización en el estado de Chihuahua." In María del Carmen Pardo, ed., *Federalización e innovación educativa en México.* Mexico: El Colegio de Mexico.

Lowden, Pamela. 2002. "Education Reform in Colombia: The Elusive Quest for Effectiveness." Paper prepared for a conference on education reforms in Latin America, Woodrow Wilson Center for Scholars, Washington, D.C.: April 4–5.

Loyo, Aurora. 1992. "Actores y tiempos politicos en la modernización educativa." *El Cotidiano,* Mexico City, Vol. 8 (November–December).

Loyo, Aurora, Maria de Ibarrola, and Antonio Blanco. 1999. "Estructura de sindicalismo docente en América Latina." Santiago, Chile: PREAL.

Lustig, Nora, and Ruthanne Deutsch. 1998. *The Inter-American Development Bank and Poverty Reduction.* Washington, D.C.: Inter-American Development Bank.

Mares Guia Neto, Walfrido. 1999. "Education Reform in Minas Gerais, Brazil." Paper prepared for a workshop on "Education Experiences from Japan, Asia, and Latin America," Okinawa, Japan, June 23–26.

———. 1994. "La política educacional de Minas Gerais, 1991–1994." Unpublished paper (no additional information) (January).

Martin, Chris. 1993. " 'UPE' on the Cheap: Educational Modernization at School Level in Mexico." *Oxford Studies in Comparative Education* 3, no. 2.

Martinic, Sergio. 2002. "El tiempo y el aprendizaje en América Latina." *Formas y Reformas de la Educación,* Year 4, no. 11. Santiago, Chile: PREAL.

Martiniello, Mariá. 2000. "Participación de los padres en la educación: Hacia una taxonomía para América Latina." In Juan Carlos Navarro, Katherine Taylor,

Andrés Bernasconi, and Lewis Tyler, eds., *Perspectivas sobre la reforma educativa: América Central en el contexto de políticas de educación en las Américas*. Washington, D.C.: U.S. Agency for International Development, Inter-American Development Bank, and Harvard Institute for International Development.

McConnell, Shelley. 1997. "Institutional Development." In Thomas W. Walker, ed., *Nicaragua without Illusions: Regime Transition and Structural Adjustment in the 1990s*. Wilmington, Del.: Scholarly Resources.

McGinn, Noel, and Susan Street. 1986. "Educational Decentralization: Weak State or Strong State?" *Comparative Education Review* 30, no. 4.

McMeekin, Robert W. 2000. "Implementing School-Based Merit Awards: Chile's Experience." Washington, D.C.: World Bank, Technical Notes, Education Reform and Management Publication Series 3, no. 1 (June).

———. 1998. *Education Statistics in Latin America and the Caribbean*. Washington, D.C.: Inter-American Development Bank, Sustainable Development Department, Education Unit.

Mejía Ayala, José Antonio. 1999. "Federalismo e innovación educativa en México: El caso de Neuvo León." In María del Carmen Pardo, ed., *Federalización e innovación educativa en México*. Mexico: El Colegio de Mexico.

Merino Juárez, Gustavo. 1999. "Decentralization of Education and Institutional Change: A Look at Mexico." *DRCLAS News*. Cambridge: Harvard University (spring).

Mingat, Alain. 1998. "The Strategy Used by High-Performing Asian Economies in Education: Some Lessons for Developing Countries." *World Development* 26, no. 4 (April).

Ministerio de Educación, Cultura, y Deportes. n.d. "Reforma educativa." La Paz, Ministerio de Educación, Cultura, y Deportes.

Mizala, Alejandra, Pablo González, Pilar Romaguera, and Andrea Guzmán. 2000. "Los maestros en Chile: Carreras e incentivos." Working Paper R-403. Washington, D.C.: Inter-American Development Bank (July).

Molinski, Michael. 1990. "Sandinistas Call for Strikes, Protests, Civil Disobedience." UPI Release (September 25).

Montenegro, Armando. n.d. "An Incomplete Educational Reform: The Case of Colombia." Unpublished paper (no other information).

Muñiz M, Patricia E. 2000. "The Schooling Situation of Children in Highly Underprivileged Rural Localities in Mexico." In Fernando Reimers, ed., *Unequal Schools, Unequal Chances: The Challenges to Equal Opportunity in the Americas*. Cambridge: Harvard University Press.

Murillo, María Victoria. 2001. "Una aproximación al estudio del sindicalismo magisterial en América Latina." *Estudios Sociológicos* 19, no. 55.

———. 1999a. "Sindicalismo docente y reforma educativa en América Latina: Estado de arte." Department of Political Science, Yale University (May).

———. 1999b. "Recovering Political Dynamics: Teachers' Unions and the Decentralization of Education in Argentina and Mexico." *Journal of Interamerican Studies and World Affairs* 41, no. 1.

———. 1998. "From Populism to Neoliberalism: Labor Unions and Market Reforms in Latin America." Paper prepared for the Twenty-first Congress of the Latin American Studies Association, Chicago, Ill., September 24–26.

———. 2003. "The Politicization of Public Sector Labor Relations: Argentine Teachers' Strikes in a Decentralized Education System." Unpublished paper.

Murillo, Maria Victoria, and Lucas Ronconi. 2003. "The Politicization of Public Sector Labor Relations: Argentine Teachers' Strikes in a Decentralized Education System." Unpublished paper, Department of Political Science, Yale University.

Naím, Moisés. 1995. "Latin America's Journey to the Market: From Macroeconomic Shock to Institutional Therapy." Occasional Paper No. 62, International Center for Economic Growth, San Francisco: ICS Press.

Navarro, Juan Carlos. 2002. *Quiénes son los maestros? Carreras e incentives docents en América Latina*. Washington, D.C.: Inter-American Development Bank.

Navarro, Juan Carlos, and Rafael de la Cruz. 1998. "Federal, State and Nonprofit Schools in Venezuela." In William D. Savedoff, ed., *Organization Matters: Agency Problems in Health and Education in Latin America*. Washington, D.C.: Inter-American Development Bank.

Navarro, Juan Carlos, Martin Carnoy, and and Claudio de Moura Castro. 2000. "La reforma educativa en América Latina: Temas, componentes e instrumentos." In Juan Carlos Navarro, Katherine Taylor, Andrés Bernasconi, and Lewis Tyler, eds., *Perspectivas sobre la reforma educativa: América Central en el contexto de políticas de educación en las Américas*. Washington, D.C.: U.S. Agency for International Development, Inter-American Development Bank, and Harvard Institute for International Development.

Navarro, Juan Carlos, Martin Carnoy, and Claudio de Moura Castro. n.d. "Education Reform in Latin America and the Caribbean." Washington, D.C.: Inter-American Development Bank, Background Education Strategy Paper No. 1.

Nelson, Joan. 1999a. "Propositions on the Politics of Social Sector Reforms." Prepared for a Workshop on the Politics of Social Sector Reform. Washington, D.C.: Overseas Development Council, June 14.

———. 1999b. *Reforming Health and Education: The World Bank, the IDB, and Complex Institutional Change*. Washington, D.C.: Overseas Development Council.

Nelson, Joan, ed. 1990. *Economic Crisis and Policy Choice: The Politics of Adjustment in the Third World*. Princeton, N.J.: Princeton University Press.

Nicaragua Reform Evaluation Team. 1996. "Nicaragua's School Autonomy Reform: A First Look." Washington, D.C.: World Bank: Working Paper Series on Impact Evaluation of Education Reforms, No. 1.

North, Douglass. 1990. *Institutions, Institutional Change and Economic Performance*. Cambridge: Cambridge University Press.

OECD (Organisation for Economic Co-operation and Development) and UNESCO (United Nations Educational, Scientific, and Cutural Organization). 2001. *Teachers for Tomorrow's Schools: Analysis of the World Education Indicators*. Paris: OECD and UNESCO.

Olson, Jr., Mancur. 1965. *The Logic of Collective Action: Public Goods and the Theory of Groups*. New York: Schocken Books.

Ornelas, Carlos. 1988. "The Decentralization of Education in Mexico," *Prospects* 18, no. 1.

Ornelas, Carlos. n.d.. "The Politics of Educational Decentralization in Mexico." Unpublished paper, Autonomous Metropolitan University of Mexico, Mexico City.

Ortiz de Zevallos, Gabriel, 1998. "La economía política de reformas institucionales en el Perú: Los casos de educación, salud y pensiones." Unpublished manuscript, Lima: Instituto Apoyo.

Paes de Barros, Ricardo, and Rosane Mendonça. 1998. "The Impact of Three Institutional Innovations in Brazilian Education." In William D. Savedoff, ed., *Organization Matters: Agency Problems in Health and Education in Latin America*. Washington, D.C.: Inter-American Development Bank.

Parry, Taryn Rounds. 1997. "Achieving Balance in Decentralization: A Case Study of Education Decentralization in Chile." *World Development* 25, no. 2.

Pescador Osuna, José Angel. 1992. "Acuerdo Nacional para la Modernización de la Educación Básica: Una visión integral." *El Cotidiano* Year 8 (Mexico City).

Pinheiro Machado, Ana Luiza. n.d. "El rol de los gestores educativos en el contexto de la descentralización hacia la escuela." Unpublished paper.

————. n.d. "La política educacional de Minas Gerais, Brasil (no additional information).

Piras, Claudia, and William Savedoff. 1998. "How Much Do Teachers Earn?" Washington, D.C: Office of the Chief Economist, Inter-American Development Bank.

Plank, David. 1990a. "Public Purpose and Private Interest in Brazilian Education." *New Education* 12, no. 2.

————. 1990b. "The Politics of Basic Education Reform in Brazil," *Comparative Education Review* 34, no. 4.

PREAL (Programa de Promoción de la Reorma Educativa en América Latina y el Caribe). 2001. *Lagging Behind: A Report Card on Education in Latin America*. Washington, D.C.: PREAL (November).

Psacharopoulos, George, J. Valenzuela, and M. Arends. 1996. "Teacher Salaries in Latin America: A Review." *Economics of Education Review* 15, no. 4.

Puryear, Jeffrey. 1997. *La educación en América Latina: Problemas y desafíos*. Santiago, Chile: PREAL.

Reid, Michael. 1993. "Mexico Rewrites its History," *The Guardian*, August 21, p. 12.

Reimers, Fernando. 2002. "Something to Hide? The Politics of Educational Evaluation in Latin America." Working Papers on Latin America: The David Rockefeller Center for Latin American Studies, Harvard University, No. 01–02–1. Cambridge.

————. 2000a. *Unequal Schools, Unequal Chances: The Challenges to Equal Opportunity in the Americas*. Cambridge: Harvard University Press.

————. 2000b. "Compensatory Policies and Programs in Latin America: What Remains to Be Learned." Paper prepared for a conference on Poverty and Education in the Americas, Harvsard University, May 3–4.

————. 2000c. "La igualdad de oportunidades educativas como prioridad de políticas en América Latina." In Juan Carlos Navarro, Katherine Taylor, Andrés Bernasconi, and Lewis Tyler, eds., *Perspectivas sobre la reforma educativa: América Central en el contexto de políticas de de educación el las Américas*. Washington, D.C.: U.S. Agency for International Development, Inter-American Development Bank, and Harvard Institute for International Development.

———. 2000d. "Educational Opportunity and Policy in Latin America." In Fernando Reimers, ed., *Unequal Schools, Unequal Chances: The Challenges to Equal Opportunity in the Americas.* Cambridge: Harvard University Press.

———. 1999a. "El estudio de las oportunidades educativas de los pobres en América Latina," *Revista Latinoamericana de estudios educativos* (Mexico) 29, no. 1.

———. 1999b. "Education, Poverty, and Inequality in Latin America." Unpublished paper, Cambridge: Harvard Graduate School of Education.

República del Ecuador. 1990. "Programa Redes Amigas." Quito: Ministerio de Educación y Cultura.

Rhoten, Diana. 2000. "From Policy Ideals and Intentions to Policy Interpretations and Actions: The Case of Education Decentralization in Argentina, Chile and Uruguay." Paper prepared for the 2000 meeting of the Latin American Studies Association, Miami, March 16–18.

Rocha, Carlos Alberto de Vasconcelos da. 2001. "The Political-Administrative Decentraliztaion of Public Education in Minas Gerais: A Case of Institutional Change." English translation of parts of a Ph.D. thesis, Department of Political Science, State University of Campinas, Brazil.

Rocha, Sonia. 1999. "Minimum Income Programs: How Do They Apply to Brazilian Metropolitan Nuclei?" Washington, D.C.: Report prepared for the World Bank (March).

Rodríguez, Alejandro Esteban. 1997. "Concertación y política educativa en Argentina (1984–1996)." Santiago: University of Chile, Masters in Management and Public Policy, Case Study 24.

Rodrik, Dani. 1994. "The Rush to Free Trade: Why So Late? Why Now? Will It Last?" In Stephan Haggard and Steven Webb, eds. *Voting for Reform: Democracy, Political Liberalization, and Economic Adjustment.* New York: Oxford University Press.

Rohter, Larry. 1989. "Mexican Labor Chiefs Feel the Heat." *New York Times,* February 27, p. 2.

Ruiz Cervantes, Francisco José. 1999. "El proceso de federalización educativa en Oaxaca." In María del Carmen Pardo, ed., *Federalización e innovación educativa en México.* Mexico: El Colegio de México.

Salinas de Gortari, Carlos. 2002. *Mexico: The Policy and Politics of Modernization.* Barcelona: Plaza y Janés.

Savedoff, William D., ed. 1998. *Organization Matters: Agency Problems in Health and Education in Latin America.* Washington, D.C.: Inter-American Development Bank.

Schamis, Hector E. 1999. "Distributional Coalitions and the Politics of Economic Reform in Latin America," *World Politics* 51, no. 2.

Schiefelbein, Ernesto, and Juan Carlos Tedesco. 1995. *Una nueva oportunidad: El rol de la educación en el desarrollo de América Latina.* Buenos Aires: Santillana.

Schiefelbein Ernesto, and Paulina Schiefelbein. n.d. "Three Decentralization Strategies in Two Decades: Chile 1981–2000." Unpublished paper, Santo Tomás University, Santiago, Chile.

Schmelkes, Sylvia. 2000. "Education and Indian Peoples in Mexico: An Example of Policy Failure." In Fernando Reimers, ed., *Unequal Schools, Unequal Chances: The Challenges to Equal Opportunity in the Americas.* Cambridge: Harvard University Press.

Schneider, Ben Ross. 1991. *Politics within the State: Elite Bureaucrats and Industrial Policy in Authoritarian Brazil.* Pittsburgh, Pa.: University of Pittsburgh Press.

Secretaría de Educación Pública (SEP) (Mexico). 2000a. *Memoria del quehacer educativo, 1999–2000.* Mexico City: Secretaría de Educación Pública, 2 volumes.

———. 2000b. *Informe de labores, 1999–2000.* Mexico City: Secretaría de Educación Pública.

———. 2000c. Perfil de la educación en México. Mexico City: Secretaría de Educación Pública.

Srinivasan, T. N. 1985. "Neoclassical Political Economy: The State and Economic Development." *Politics and Society* 17, no. 2.

Stallings, Barbara, and Wilson Peres. 2000. *Growth, Employment and Equity: The Impact of the Economic Reforms in Latin America and the Caribbean.* Washington, D.C.: Brookings Institution and the Economic Commission on Latin America and the Caribbean.

Steinmo, Sven, Kathleen Thelen, and Frank Longstreth. 1992. *Structuring Politics: Historical Institutionalism in Comparative Analysis.* Cambridge: Cambridge University Press.

Street, Susan. 1998. "El sindicalismo docente en México: Fuerza institucional o sujeto social?" FLACSO/PREAL Boletín Nro. 2, Buenos Aires: Proyecto Sindicalismo Docente y Reforma Educativa en América Latina. (December).

———. 1992. *Maestros en movimiento: Transformaciones en la burocracia estatal* (1978–1982). Mexico: La Casa Chata.

Talavera Simoni, Maria Luisa. 1999. *Otras voces, otros maestros.* La Paz: Programa de Investigacion Estrategica en Bolivia.

Taliercio, Robert. 1996. "Costa Rica's Minister of Education Faces a Dilemma." Cambridge: Kennedy School of Government Case Program, Harvard University.

Tatto, Maria Teresa. 1999. "Education Reform and State Power in Mexico: The Paradoxes of Decentralization." *Comparative Education Review* 43, no. 3.

Tendler, Judith. 2002. "The Fear of Education." Paper prepared for a Conference on "Inequality and the State in Latin America and the Caribbean. Washington, D.C.: World Bank (fall 2003).

———. 1997. *Good Government in the Tropics.* Baltimore, Md.: Johns Hopkins University Press.

Tiramonti, Guillermina. 2000. "Sindicalismo docente y reforma educativa en la América Latina de los 90." Santiago, Chile: PREAL.

Tommasi, Mariano, and Andres Velasco. 1996. "Where Are We in the Political Economy of Reform?" *Journal of Policy Reform* 1, no. 2.

Trejos, Maria Eugenia. 1999. "Pendiente negativa en el sindicalismo docente en Costa Rica." FLACSO/PREAL Boletín Nro. 4/5, Buenos Aires: Proyecto Sindicalismo Docente y Reforma Educativa en América Latina (October).

Trostle, James A., Johannes U. Somerfeld, and Jonathon L. Simon. 1997. "Strengthening Human Resource Capacity in Developing Countries: Who Are the Actors? What Are Their Actions?" In Merilee S. Grindle, ed., *Getting Good Government: Capacity Building in the Public Sectors of Developing Countries.* Cambridge: Harvard University Press.

UNDP (United Nations Development Programme). 1998. *Desarrollo humano en Bolivia, 1998.* La Paz: UNDP.

UNESCO (United Nations Educational, Scientific, and Cultural Organization). 2000. *World Education Report, 2000. The Right to Education: Towards Education for All throughout Life.* Paris: UNESCO.

————. 1998. *World Education Report, 1998: Teachers and Teaching in a Changing World.* Paris: UNESCO.

UNESCO and OECD (Organization for Economic Cooperation and Development). 2000. *Investing in Education: Analysis of the 1999 World Education Indicators.* Paris: UNESCO.

UNESCO and OREALC (Oficina Regional de Educación para América Latina y el Caribe). n.d. "El viraje en la política educativa en el estado brasileño de Minas Gerais: Calidad y democratización de la educación" (no additional information).

Uribe, Claudia. 1999. "Colombia: Teacher and School Incentives," *DRCLAS News.* Cambridge: Harvard University (spring).

Urquiola, Miguel, Wilson Jiménez, María Luisa Talavera, and Werner Hernany. 2000. *Los maestros en Bolivia: Impacto, incentivos y desempeño.* La Paz: Universidad Católica de Bolivia.

Valdéz, Juan Gabriel. 1995. *Pinochet's Economists: The Chicago School in Chile.* Cambridge: Cambridge University Press.

Vaillant, Denise. 2002. "Formación de formadores. Estado de práctica." Santiago, Chile: PREAL.

Varley, Pamela. 1999. "Tackling Poor Performance, Extreme Inequality and Public Complaisance: Brazil's Education Minister Forges a New Role for the Ministry." Cambridge: Kennedy School of Government Case Program, Harvard University.

Vegas, E., Lant Pritchett, and W. Experton. 1999. "Attracting and Retaining Qualified Teachers in Argentina: Impact of the Level and Structure of Compensation." World Bank, Latin America and the Caribbean, LCSHD Series No. 38S. (April).

Villegas-Reimers, Eleanora, and Fernando Reimers. 1996. "Where Are 60 Million Teachers? The Missing Voice in Education Reforms around the World." *Prospects* 26, no. 3 (September).

Wallis, Joe. 1999. "Understanding the Role of Leadership in Economic Policy Reform," *World Development* 27, no. 1.

Weingast, Barry, Kenneth Shepsle, and C. Johnsen. 1981. "The Political Economy of Benefits and Costs: A Neoclassical Approach to Redistributive Politics," *Journal of Political Economy* 89.

Westlake, Martin, ed. 2000. *Leaders of Transition.* New York: St. Martin's Press.

Weyland, Kurt. 2002. "Limitations of Rational Choice Institutionalism for the Study of Latin American Politics." *Studies in Comparative International Development* 37, no. 1 (spring).

Williamson, John, ed. 1994. *The Political Economy of Policy Reform*. Washington, D.C.: Institute for International Economics.

Willms, Douglas J., and Marie-Andrée Somers. 1999. *Schooling Outcomes in Latin America, 1999: A Report for UNESCO*. New Brunswick: University of New Brunswick.

Winkler, Donald. 1999. "Educating the Poor in Latin America and the Caribbean: Examples of Compensatory Education." Unpublished paper, Washington, D.C.: Human and Social Development Group, Latin America and the Caribbean Region, World Bank.

Winkler, Donald R., and Alec Ian Gershberg. 2000. "Los efectos de la descentralización del sistema educacional sobre la calidad de la educación en América Latina." Santiago, Chile: PREAL.

Wolfensohn, James. 1999. *A Proposal for a Comprehensive Development Framework*. Washington, D.C.: World Bank.

Wolff, Larence, Ernesto Schiefelbein, and Paulina Schiefelbein. 2000. "El costo-efectividad de las políticas de educación primaria en América Central, Panamá y República Dominicana: Un estudio basado en la opinión de expertos." In Juan Carlos Navarro, Kathering Taylor, Andrés Bernasconi, and Lewis Tyler, eds., *Perspectivas sobre la reforma educativa*. Washington, D.C.: U.S. Agency for International Development, Inter-American Development Bank, and Harvard Institute for International Development.

World Bank. 2001. *World Development Report, 2000/2001*. Washington, D.C.: World Bank.

———. 2000. "Educational Change in Latin America and the Caribbean." Washington, D.C.: World Bank.

———. 1999a. *Education Sector Strategy*. Washington, D.C.: World Bank Group: The Human Development Network.

———. 1999b. *Bolivia: Public Expenditure Review*. Washington, D.C.: World Bank.

———. 1998. *World Development Report, 1998*. New York: Oxford University Press.

———. 1993. *World Development Report, 1993*. New York: Oxford University Press.

———. Various years. *World Tables*.

Zorrilla Fierro, Margarita María. 1999. "Federalismo e innovación educativa en Aguascalientes, 1992–1998: De un modelo armado a un modelo para armar." In María del Carmen Pardo, ed., *Federalización e innovación educativa en México*. Mexico: El Colegio de México.

Zuckerman, Leo. 2001. "Quién gobierna en México?" *El Universal*, December 19.

INDEX

A *t* following a page reference indicates a table; *fig* indicates a figure.

AAMG (Associação de Professores Publicos de Minas Gerais) [Brazil], 73

ADEOMG (Associação dos Directores das Escolas Oficiais de Minas Gerais) [Brazil], 75, 149, 151, 173

Adoum, Rosángela, 82–83, 86–87, 104–5, 107–8, 109, 110, 111

Almeida, Zila de, 103

Alvarez, Jamil, 107

AMIE (Associação Mineira de Inspetores Escolares) [Brazil], 148

AMISP (Associação Mineira de Supervisores Pedagogicas) [Brazil], 148

Anaya, Amalia, 69, 93, 95, 96–97, 98, 99, 100, 117, 118, 138, 152

ANDEN (Asociación Nacional de Educadores Nicaragüenses) [Nicaragua], 79, 81, 90, 155–56, 158, 182, 183

APPMG (Associação de Professores Publicos de Minas Gerais) [Minas Gerais], 148

Argentina: education reform initiatives in, 9*t*; efficiency of primary education in, 32*t*; National Pedagogical Congress of, 54; percentage of illiterates in, 30*t*; primary education levels/enrollment in, 31*t*; private school enrollment in, 36*t*; public expenditures on education in, 35*t*; standardized testing introduced in, 43; student language/mathematics achievement in, 33*t*

Banzer, Hugo, 100, 138, 153

Bartlett, Manuel, 66

Belli, Humberto, 55, 76, 79, 80, 81, 82, 89–90, 106, 155, 156, 179

Bolivia: education map created by reformers in, 41; education reform initiatives in, 9*t*; efficiency of primary education in, 32*t*; NPE (New Economic Policy) of, 68; percentage of illiterates in, 30*t*; political preparation for education reform in, 45; primary education levels/enrollment in, 31*t*; private school enrollment in, 36*t*; public expenditures on education in, 35*t*; student language/mathematics achievement in, 33*t*; World Bank study of teachers in, 223n.49

Bolivian education reform: bilingual education as part of, 100; comparing implementation strategies to other cases, 167–71, 169*t*; comparing leadership to other case studies, 88*t*–92; comparing teachers' union and reformers conflict to other cases, 160–64; comparison of politics of policy design and, 114–18; constraints of leadership sponsoring of, 66–71; decentralization as part of, 66; designing reform in, 95–100, 218n.17; economic improvements as part of, 67–68; *escuela única* approach included in, 67; government-teachers' unions conflict affecting, 68, 71; implementation/sustainment of, 171–74, 183–86; institutional sources of power in, 200, 202; international financial institutions involvement in, 95–96, 99; language of instruction issue in, 67; most important aspects of, 24*t*; opposition by teachers' union, 68, 71, 97, 100; strategic choices made by reformers during, 204; teachers' union and reformers conflict during, 151–55

Bolsa-Escola program (Ecuador), 109

Brazil: *bolsa escola* program of, 44; education reform initiatives in, 9*t*; estimates of grade repetition in, 37*t*; percentage of illiterates in, 30*t*; primary education levels/enrollment in, 31*t*; private school enrollment in, 36*t*; public expenditures on education in, 35*t*; school-based management reforms in, 42; standardized testing introduced in, 43; student language/mathematics achievement in, 33*t*. *See also* Minas Gerais education reform

Callardo de Cano, Cecilia, 56

Cárdenas, Victor Hugo, 70, 97, 98

Catholic Church: Bolivian reformer/teachers' union conflict negotiated by, 155; ed-